Praise for

A dark, complex story, powerfully vivid, thanks to Bailey's narrative flair.

Sydney Morning Herald

Bailey enthrals us . . . A blend of Steinbeck, Hemingway and Maugham. With a dash of Hansard . . . A fascinating and important book.

Australian

John Bailey possesses that special talent that makes a true story read like a rollicking tale of fiction, and his book, *The White Divers of Broome*, has quite rightly been compared to Simon Winchester's *The Surgeon of Crowthorne*. It's a riveting read that evokes an exotic and dangerous frontier Australia.

West Australian

The author, in telling the white divers' story, paints a picture of a time and place that still carries a certain shimmering lustre.

Canberra Times

Bailey has constructed a stirring narrative . . . he invests the past with new life . . . to animate early Broome and its seaways, with all their colour, eccentricity and brutality. He demonstrates anew how little we still know of a history which many misconstrue as bland, safe and comfortable. We are well served by books of this calibre which struggle to tell it like it was, not the way we might like it to have been.

Courier-Mail

Also by John Bailey

The White Divers of Broome
The Lost German Slave Girl
Mr Stuart's Track

THE WHITE DIVERS OF
BROOME

The true story of a fatal experiment

JOHN BAILEY

PAN
Pan Macmillan Australia

First published 2001 in Macmillan by Pan Macmillan Australia Pty Limited
This edition published 2002 in Pan by Pan Macmillan Australia Pty Limited
1 Market Street, Sydney

Reprinted 2002, 2003 (twice), 2004, 2006

National Library of Australia
Cataloguing-in-Publication data:

Bailey, John, 1944 Dec. 15–.
The white divers of Broome.

ISBN 0 330 36338 7 (pbk.).

1. Pearl divers – Western Australia – Broome. 2. Pearl industry and trade –
Western Australia – Broome. 3. Western Australia – History – 1901–1914. I. Title.

639.412099414

Typeset in 12pt Adobe Garamond by Post Pre-Press Group
Printed in Australia by McPhersons Printing Group
Cover design by Jeremy @ Bland Design
Text design by Gayna Murphy
Maps by Colin Wynter Seton

Contents

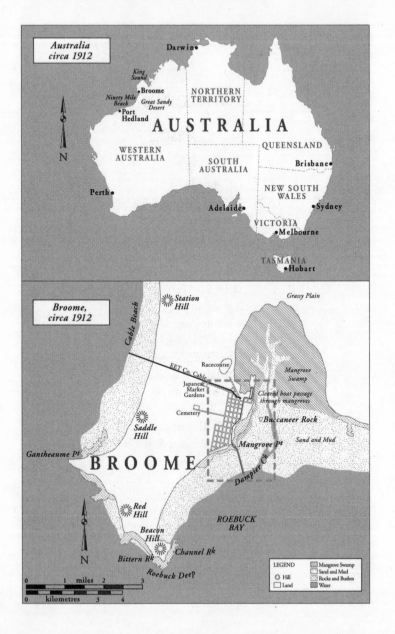

Australia
circa 1912

Darwin

King
Sound

Broome
Ninety Mile
Beach
Port
Hedland

Great Sandy
Desert

NORTHERN
TERRITORY

AUSTRALIA

QUEENSLAND

WESTERN
AUSTRALIA

SOUTH
AUSTRALIA

Brisbane

Perth

Adelaide

NEW SOUTH
WALES

Sydney

VICTORIA
Melbourne

TASMANIA
Hobart

N

Broome,
circa 1912

Station
Hill

Grassy Plain

Cable Beach

EET Co. Cable

Racecourse

Japanese
Market
Gardens

Cemetery

Saddle
Hill

Gantheaume Pt

BROOME

Mangrove
Swamp

Cleared boat passage
through mangroves

Buccaneer Rock

Sand and Mud

Mangrove Pt

Dampier Ck

Red
Hill

Beacon
Hill

Bittern Rk

Channel Rk

Roebuck Deep

ROEBUCK
BAY

N

0   1   miles   2   3

0   kilometres   3   4

LEGEND
⚙ Hill
☐ Land

Mangrove Swamp
Sand and Mud
Rocks and Bushes
Water

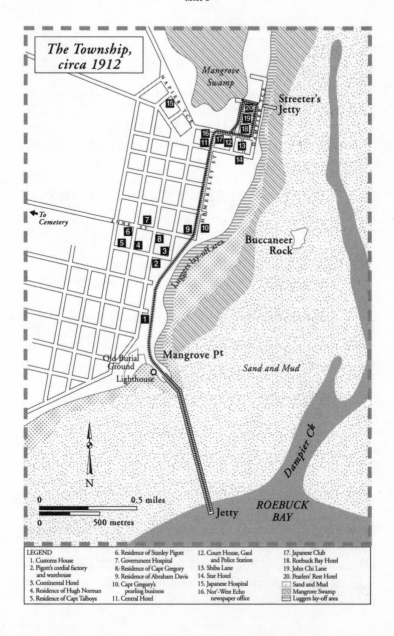

The Township, circa 1912

NAPIER TCE

Mangrove Swamp

Streeter's Jetty

20
19
18

16
11 · 17 · 12
13
14

← To Cemetery

7
6
5 · 4 · 8 · 3
2

9
10

HAMERSLEY ST

Luggers lay-off area

Buccaneer Rock

1

Old Burial Ground
Lighthouse

Mangrove Pt

Sand and Mud

Dampier Ck

N

0   0.5 miles
0   500 metres

Jetty

ROEBUCK BAY

LEGEND
1. Customs House
2. Pigott's cordial factory
   and warehouse
3. Continental Hotel
4. Residence of Hugh Norman
5. Residence of Capt Talboys

6. Residence of Stanley Pigott
7. Government Hospital
8. Residence of Capt Gregory
9. Residence of Abraham Davis
10. Capt Gregory's
    pearling business
11. Central Hotel

12. Court House, Gaol
    and Police Station
13. Shiba Lane
14. Star Hotel
15. Japanese Hospital
16. Nor'-West Echo
    newspaper office

17. Japanese Club
18. Roebuck Bay Hotel
19. John Chi Lane
20. Pearlers' Rest Hotel

⬚ Sand and Mud
⬚ Mangrove Swamp
⬚ Luggers lay-off area

vii

A NOTE ABOUT TERMINOLOGY

Kanzo Makame, the diver, sturdy and small Japanee,
Seeker of pearls and of pearl-shell down in the depths of the
sea,
Trudges o'er the bed of ocean, searching industriously.

Over the pearl-grounds, the lugger drifted – a little white
speck:
Joe Nagasaki, the 'tender', holding the life-line on deck,
Talked through the rope to the diver, knew when to drift or to
check.

'The Pearl Diver' by A.B. 'Banjo' Patterson

TODAY A TOURIST SEEKING places of historical interest in
Broome is directed towards Chinatown at the tip of the peninsula
jutting into Roebuck Bay. It was not known as Chinatown during its
heyday, and quite rightly so, because few Chinese people lived there.
The locals called it Japtown and in official publications it was
referred to as the Asiatic Quarter. Depending on the context, I use
both terms.

Tourist maps take you, in the middle of Chinatown, to Sheba Lane. Visitors wonder how it got such an exotic name (did the Queen of Sheba ever visit?). The answer is that it was named after Mr K. Shiba, the proprietor of the Bay View Restaurant, and corrupted from there. John Chi Lane in the Asiatic Quarter was named after a noodle shop he operated along that dusty alleyway. In October 1910 a motion was presented to Broome council proposing that the names of both John Chi and Shiba lanes be changed to something more appropriately British. The council agreed and offered a 'most valuable prize' to ladies and gentlemen suggesting suitable alternatives. Thankfully, nothing came of it.

Because this book is concerned with events in Broome prior to World War I (at a time when the modest Mr Shiba was still possessed of the title to his lane) and in tribute to its endurance despite a municipal attempt at assassination, Shiba, and not Sheba, survives in this book. For similar reasons, I call that hot, desolate stretch of sand, off which a fortune in mother-of-pearl was harvested, Ninety Mile Beach and not Eighty Mile Beach – presumably someone remeasured it in the 1930s. And while on the topic of miles, I have used them – along with chains and feet and inches, which I like the sound of – rather than converting to metric. I also refer to tons and hundredweights (cwts) and pounds (lbs). And I think it is silly to convert pounds, shillings and pence (or £ s d in short form) to dollars and cents because the ravages of inflation have made the result quite misleading. A pound, which became two dollars in 1966 when Australia adopted the decimal system, was worth a great deal during the times of which I write. A workman earning £5 a week would have considered himself most fortunate indeed. And to give some idea of depths, I mention that a fathom is 6 feet, or about 2 metres.

Presently there is a resort hotel at Cable Beach, so named because that is where the cable messages beached after being dotted and dashed from Europe. Prior to World War I, although the location was often called Cable Beach, the place where the hotel now is was called Cosy Corner, and on Sunday afternoons a horse cab taking picnickers there would leave promptly at three-thirty from the Central Hotel – return fare five shillings.

In naming the many different nationalities of those who came to dive in the waters off Broome, I have followed the custom of the times rather than anticipating the creation of nations such as the Philippines, Indonesia, Sri Lanka, and Vietnam. Hence you will read of Manilamen, Javanese, Koepangers, Cingalese, Dyaks and Saigons. The term 'Malay' was commonly used by the pearlers to describe men from anywhere in South East Asia – for example in the memoirs of Henry Taunton, published in 1903, one reads that 'the pearler who depended on Malay labour had to sail his vessel over to Timor'.[1] In the local press, and even in official publications, the original inhabitants, the Aboriginal people, were referred to, usually in disparaging terms, as Binghis, niggers, blacks or natives – and rarely as Aborigines and never as the Indigenous people. My purpose is to tell it as it was, so generally I have retained the language of the source, although I understand its use in today's context is often offensive to readers. It was also the manner of the times for Australians, including those who had been born in Australia, to call themselves Britishers, or even English, and to speak of England as home, referring to a place they had never seen. It would be another generation before the tribalism of the Empire ceased to have a hold on the imaginings of the average Australian.

It appears that officialdom was not too fussy how the names of the twelve men brought out from England for the white experiment were spelt. For example, Beasily is sometimes spelt Beesley and Brearly, Sanders is also spelt as Saunders, Hanson as Hansen, Reid as Read, Noury as Nourey and Nowry, and Hockliss as Heckliss and Heckless. I have used the first-mentioned of the above versions on the basis that this is what they called themselves (although even this was not consistent), unless I am quoting directly from documents. To assist the reader in identifying the English divers and tender, and those who employed them, a list appears below. I also recognise there are now several generations who think entirely in metres and kilograms, so at the end of this note appears a conversion table between the imperial and metric systems.

Occasionally I have used specialist, slang or archaic terms associated with the industry of pearl-shelling. The meaning of most is obvious, but to assist the reader I list the more obscure.

The duties of the tender to a diver are described in chapter 14 but it is sufficient at this stage to explain that his task was to watch over the safety of the diver while he was underwater and ensure that the air supply was pure and constant.

The white men who owned the luggers were called shellers, pearlers, or master pearlers. I use these terms interchangeably.

A shell-opener was the person who opened the shell in the search for pearls.

A snide pearl was one from a dubious source, usually stolen.

Diving apparatus, consisting of a rubberised canvas suit, a domed helmet, leaden boots and yards of rubber pipe, was given various names by the pearlers: dress suit, full-dress suit, diving suit (but not hard hat, an Americanism from the 1950s). The helmet was screwed into the corselet which in turn was attached to the suit. Gloves were not usually worn.

The English divers and tenders

William Webber (diver) and William Reid (tender) were engaged by Moss & Richardson. The principals of the firm were George Moss and Hugh Richardson.

Frederick Beasily, Ernest Freight (divers) and Harry Hanson (tender) were engaged by Robison & Norman. The principal of the firm was Hugh (Pa) Norman.

Stephen Elphick, Fred Harvey (divers) and Charles Andrews (tender) were engaged by Stanley Pigott.

John Noury, James Rolland and Stanley Sanders (divers) were engaged by Sydney Pigott. Reginald Hockliss (diver) arrived in Broome later than the others, and was engaged by Sydney Pigott.

Conversion table: imperial to metric

Length (approximate only)
1 inch = 2.54 centimetres
1 foot = 12 inches = 0.305 metres
1 yard = 3 feet = 0.914 metres
1 chain = 66 feet = 20.12 metres
1 mile = 1.609 kilometres

Weight (approximate only)
1 pound = 16 ounces = 0.454 kilograms
1 stone = 14 pounds = 6.35 kilograms
1 hundredweight = 50.80 kilograms
1 ton = 20 hundredweight = 1016 kilograms

INTRODUCTION

All . . . history, as one of our wits remarked, is no more than accepted fiction.

Voltaire

THE STORY OF DIVING for pearl-shell has become part of the Australian legend. It is a legend of men toiling aboard luggers sailing through tropical seas. Its tales are those of cyclones ripping through the fleet, the opening of shells the size of dinner plates to find pearls worth a king's ransom, and of divers struck down with paralysis from the bends. Its images, viewed through the sepia of old photographs, are of divers in bloated canvas suits wearing helmets of copper (helmets which now sell at Christie's auctions in London for thousands of pounds), and of Aboriginal men and women staring dolefully into the camera lens. Its themes are of adventures, disasters and quick fortunes.

Pearling was all of that. But it was much more. There is another story of deep racism, of violence, of the subjugation of the original inhabitants, and a privileged group which became rich from the labours of others. It chronicles the history of the Japanese community which established itself in Broome in the 1890s and set up shops, a hospital and a social and welfare club which began to challenge the authority of the master pearlers. It is a story which acknowledges the contribution of the Aboriginal people who, during the first twenty years of the industry, collected thousands of tons of shell for their white masters.

Broome during the first decade of the twentieth century was a port of pearling luggers. It was established in the northwest of Australia, on one of the most isolated coastlines in the world, surrounded by the Indian Ocean to the west and a desert to the east. Within a decade of its declaration in 1883 Broome had became a town of enormous wealth derived entirely from the pearl-shell. Each year over two and a half thousand indentured workers from Asia were assembled there to work on pearling grounds stretching a thousand miles from Shark Bay to King Sound. The white population was less than 700 and there was a firm system of social and legal controls to provide security for the ruling whites.

Then in 1911 the town's prosperity, indeed its very existence, came under threat – not from market forces but from the Australian Parliament. The settlement of what was essentially an Asiatic community was viewed with distaste by the government. A coloured workforce on Australian soil offended the ideals of the White Australia Policy. In 1911 the Minister of External Affairs announced that from January 1913 only white divers would be allowed to collect shell. The master pearlers were appalled. They claimed they could never afford white wages. They doubted they would be able to recruit white men prepared to put up with the discomfort of working for months on end in the cramped conditions of a lugger, or risk working in an occupation where one in ten die each year.

To prove that the industry was suitable for whites, twelve ex-navy men experienced in deep-sea diving were brought out from England in

1912, in a venture that became known as the White Experiment. This book tells the story of this undertaking and its tragic outcomes. Woven around it is the story of the fate of the Aboriginal people, the fortunes made by the master pearlers, the increasing power of the Japanese, and the ultimate decline of the industry during World War I.

The white experiment exposed in a stark way issues relating to the Australian identity and racial attitudes towards Asia – issues which continue to confront the nation today.

And finally this story is true. I have created some scenes, particularly those relating to the experience of diving for pearl-shell, but they are based on research and primary sources.

If my wife Anne (who has been a patient inspiration) tries to tell you I enjoyed writing this book, don't believe her. It has been a drawn-out wrestle with the devil. I give my thanks to Tom Gilliatt, Bernadette Foley, Jo Jarrah, Anne Mullin, Margo Sare and Geraldine Moore for their helpful and constructive advice.

John Bailey
Ocean Shores

PROLOGUE

THE MAN, STILL WRAPPED in the blanket from the *Eurus*, lay on a table at the Japanese hospital. The doctor unfolded the blanket and tried to tug it from under the man's buttocks, but so heavy was his trunk, the doctor couldn't pull it clear. He called to a nun to help and together they lifted the man while she grabbed the blanket and slid it free. It smelt of stale fish and human perspiration, and Dr Suzuki watched as the nun threw it across the table into a corner of the room. Silently and in unison, they turned back to the body. They could see pain twisted into the man's face – his eyes were knotted shut, his lips were glued with dried spittle and his fists were clenched tight. The nun forced the man's arms across his chest in a pose of rest, pushed a strand of hair off his forehead and traced a cross there. She glanced up at Dr Suzuki. He nodded. They moved closer and began to undress the man. The nun loosened his belt and tugged at his trousers while Dr Suzuki pushed down on his shoulders to stop him sliding down the tin-covered table. His underwear was blotched yellow and greasy-moist to touch. His cotton shirt was crumpled.

The doctor hesitated for a moment, imagining the man struggling for life in the heat of the cabin as the lugger made its way back to Broome.

Dr Suzuki adjusted the concave mirrors behind the acetylene jets so that the light was thrown directly onto the body. It was the first time he had performed a postmortem on a Caucasian and he was taken aback by the huge expanse of pink, hairless flesh. The man's stomach was like a small hillock, the bellybutton stretching into a thin smile. His legs seemed ridiculously thin to support such weight. His penis was red, an odd colour to Dr Suzuki, and finger thin, and his testicles seemed to have shrivelled in death and retreated into the sandy-coloured hair gathered around his crotch. The nun ran a finger across the man's brow attempting to smooth the pain away and as she did so, a tear leaked out of the corner of his eye and trickled down his cheek. She pulled a handkerchief from her pocket and wiped his face. She tucked the handkerchief back out of sight, within the black folds of her habit. The acetylene jets spluttered for a moment, then resumed a gentle hiss.

The nun handed the doctor a scalpel. Dr Suzuki positioned himself at the man's pelvis and placed his hand there to steady himself for a long incision down the thigh. The scalpel cut easily through the skin, but then the doctor paused. He had noticed a semicircular bruise just near the man's left collarbone. The doctor reached for his notebook and pencil and wrote a description of the bruise. He must ask Reid if the man had taken a fall in the days before his death. Or perhaps it was caused by the corselet of the helmet. He had seen that in a Koepanger the previous month. In that case the man – no, a boy really – had been squeezed to death by the weight of the water at 20 fathoms and a circle of puckered flesh had formed across his shoulders and back where the helmet had clamped down on his body.

Dr Suzuki studied the man's face; a fine-featured, direct face with a neat moustache. He pushed the man's lips apart. They were purple in colour. His teeth were clenched shut. The doctor noticed a plug of dried blood in the man's ear hole. He walked around to the other side of the body and saw that the other ear was clear. He returned to stand next to the nun, carefully wrote down his observations and handed his notebook back to her. He picked up the scalpel again.

It seemed strange to Dr Suzuki that a disease which could strike the body so catastrophically – paralysing limbs, destroying the brain and causing death – should, to all intents and purposes, leave no trace of its progression. How could it work that way, tearing a body apart and then dissolving itself into nothing? Dr Suzuki had written to his old professor at the Tokyo Medical School and asked him to send all the literature he could find on the subject. Long articles from English and American medical journals arrived at the hospital. Dr Suzuki laboriously translated them with the aid of an Anglo-Japanese dictionary.

On the pearling grounds it was known as the bends. In the scientific literature it was called caisson disease. A caisson was a cavern beyond an airlock, protected by iron doors, built at the bottom of an underwater construction site where men worked under multiples of normal air pressure. Projects requiring deep foundations seemed to demand a heavy toll of workmen. An American, Dr Jaminet, had studied caisson disease during the building of the St Louis Bridge, where 119 workers out of 352 had suffered from the disease; 50 men were paralysed and fourteen had died. During construction of the Brooklyn Bridge in New York, Dr Andrew Smith recorded 110 cases of caisson disease and three deaths. The Hudson tunnel: three deaths a month. Across the Atlantic at the Toulon dry dock: 43 cases of caisson disease and two deaths. The Blackwall tunnel: 50 cases and four deaths. The Douchy mines: 63 cases. The Felesti Bridge: 55 cases and five deaths. In 1900 the fleet surgeon of the British Navy reported similar deaths and paralysis for those engaged in deep-sea diving.

It was clear that exposure to high air pressure could kill. But how? Theories abounded: arteries flattened under pressure and could not supply blood to vital organs, lateral forces on the spinal cord caused it to malfunction, intestinal gases expanding on decompression acted like a huge cupping glass, inducing veins to haemorrhage.

But then English and French experimenters at the turn of the century pointed to excesses of nitrogen as the likely culprit. Dr Suzuki read articles by professors at the College of Surgeons in London, who explained that under pressure the body tissue became saturated with nitrogen, then, as the pressure was lifted, nitrogen was released into the bloodstream, like bubbles in a bottle of soda water when the stopper is removed. The nitrogen bubbled into veins, blocking them off, causing embolism, paralysis and death; cartilage between joints was pushed apart and the spinal cord became distorted. Dr Suzuki read reports of experiments with Admiralty divers conducted in England. The analysis of the blood and urine of the men after they had been subjected to several atmospheres of air pressure showed high levels of nitrogen. It was suggested that if the divers came up from the deep in stages, the gases would dissipate harmlessly.

Dr Suzuki wondered if other factors were in play. Why, he asked himself, were some divers able to dive month after month, year after year, with perfect immunity, even though they ignored all safe ascending times, yet other men, some young and otherwise fit-looking, were brought in dead after just a few weeks? Why were there more fatalities at the end of the season than at the beginning? It was said by the crews that thin men with long necks didn't get the bends while men with large chests and short necks were likely to die. It was said that white men were especially susceptible to the bends. Could this be so?

Dr Suzuki read of Professor Haldane's work establishing that fatty tissue absorbed five times as much nitrogen as other tissue and was the slowest to desaturate. After conducting experiments on overweight rats and fat dormice, researchers writing in the Cambridge University *Journal of Hygiene* advised that 'plump men should be excluded from high pressure caissons or in diving to more than about 10 fathoms'.[1] Dr Suzuki read of theories that if a man was of a nervous or excitable disposition and breathed quickly, the danger was greater. He read of the work of Dr Graham Blick at the government hospital in Broome, who recommended massage and electrical stimulation of paralysed limbs. Dr Suzuki decided to perform as many autopsies as possible to identify which part of the body failed, and then classify characteristics that predisposed some men to caisson disease. Lives could be saved because men susceptible to the disease could be weeded out from the start.

The man on Dr Suzuki's autopsy table was in his mid thirties. He was fit looking and had broad shoulders. Dr Suzuki cut through layers of flesh around the man's left leg – the place, according to the crew, that the man had held as he screamed in pain. There, within the tissue surrounding his knee, was congealed blood – a sign of the air bubbles tearing the joint apart. Then he followed a vein from the knee back up the thigh. He found nothing unusual. Dr Suzuki cut into the man's right knee. There was no sign of trauma. The doctor paused to make a note of this. Why was it only the left knee that seemed to be injured? He must ask Reid if the man had ever injured his left leg, something that may have made it more susceptible.

The nun brought Dr Suzuki a cup of tea and a biscuit, so he sat on a stool to rest. He looked at his watch. It was past midnight and only the two of them were in the hospital. He felt tired, but realised he must continue. He decided to look into the man's backbone. The man's body had become stiff and was hard to move. The nun came to assist and when they had him on his side, they wedged a block of wood under his stomach to hold him steady. Dr Suzuki hunched over the body, exposed the backbone and carefully prised apart several vertebrae. He found a strong, grey-coloured spinal cord, healthy and seemingly capable of conveying messages vital to life. He carefully examined each knot on the man's backbone. When he next looked at his watch, an hour had passed. The nun sat asleep on a stool, her head resting on her chest. He let her be – he knew she had been up since dawn, working in the wards – and wearily he turned the man onto his back.

He picked up his scalpel and glanced around to see that the nun was now at his side, holding the man's shoulder as he cut through the chest wall to access the heart. He lifted the heart free and suddenly felt a spark of excitement. He went over to the washbasin and cleaned his hands of blood. He picked up his notebook and pencil, stood next to the body and carefully drew a sketch of what was now exposed. The veins on the surface of the heart were beaded with air. He pushed at the heart with his finger. It was like a bladder. He pushed it harder and it gurgled loudly, frothing brown like the scum on brewing beer.

Dr Suzuki withdrew into the darkness and sat on a stool writing up his notes. Was it small bubbles drawn by the heart into the innermost chamber which had caused the man's death? Those tiny bubbles may have built up enough pressure to upset the rhythm of the heart. It was possible. So vulnerable are we.

He lit a cigarette. The nun brought him another hot drink. He sighed and looked back at the body spotlighted on the table. Both legs were pared to the bone. Bloody lumps of flesh hung loose. The chest cavity was exposed where he had taken out the heart. The heart itself sat on the man's chest, dribbling blood onto the table.

Dr Suzuki finished his cigarette, drank the last of the tea and returned to the body to sew it together. Behind him the nun wrapped up the dead man's clothes in the blanket and took them away. She would boil them up the next day and send them to the Aboriginal mission at Beagle Bay.

1 Whitewashing the Ocean

The industry has hitherto enjoyed a certain amount of immunity from the rigorous 'White Australia' laws of the Commonwealth, but in 1911 the Federal Authorities decided that the industry must conform to the alien restriction laws. Bowing to the inevitable, the pearlers are now engaged in the training of Europeans to serve as divers and tenders on the fleets, so that the industry may be prepared for the whitewashing in 1913.

Immigration and Tourist Department, *The Handbook of Western Australia*, Perth, 1912 (issued under the authority of the Hon. the Colonial Secretary), p. 208

ON 31 JANUARY 1912, eight deep-sea divers and three tenders arrived at the Port of Fremantle, Western Australia, after a six-week voyage from England. They lined up as neat as bowling pins along the rail of the SS *Waimana* as she approached the broad sweep of the Swan River and proceeded into the inner harbour – eleven men in dark suits with stiff collars, some wearing derbys and some in straw boaters. It was one of those sparkling, sun-filled mornings which come with monotonous regularity to the west coast of Australia. The air was already hot and the men's clothing, woven for the English climate, was causing discomfort, but no one moved below deck. The long sea journey was over and they were ready to embark on a great adventure and determined to catch an early glimpse of the new land.

Before the men left England they had been warned by James Davis – a representative of Siebe, Gorman & Co., the great manufacturer of diving equipment, and the brother of the general manager of the firm – that there would be journalists waiting to interview them when they docked. Perhaps, added Davis, it would be best if he guided them through that experience – after all, the journalists would write down everything they said and telegraph heaven knows what to the papers in the eastern states in time for breakfast the next day. Sure enough, as a tug pulled alongside the *Waimana,* they could see several men standing on the deck waving notebooks at them. And there was James Davis himself, dressed in a cream linen suit with a carnation on the lapel. Davis had taken an earlier steamer out to Australia and had alerted the press to the men's arrival. If the white experiment was to be a success, Davis was there to make sure it was a success for Siebe, Gorman as well. Davis exuded the careless assurance of someone who had wealth and power. He waved his cane in welcome to the men leaning over the rail and then, using that courtesy to advantage, returned his stick to a position in front of the feet of the journalists, thus establishing his claim to be the first to clamber aboard.

As soon as the tugboat came alongside, James Davis climbed up the ladder. He seemed to have remembered each of the men's names. He shook their hands, the ends of his neatly clipped moustache rising in a broad smile. Then, holding his boater in one hand and his cane in the other, he ushered them along the passageway and into the saloon bar. Not to buy them a drink, but to make a speech to the press who hurried in after them.

After positioning the eleven Englishmen in a semicircle, he

presented them to the assembled journalists. The men shuffled forward and smiled. Davis told everyone what a momentous occasion it was. The arrival of these diving men had been foreshadowed for months and what they were about to achieve had been debated in the federal and state parliaments of Australia for years. These were the men to show the world the superiority of the Britisher over the Asiatic. No other self-governing nation in the British Empire would tolerate for a moment a situation in which one of its main primary industries was monopolised by a race of Asiatics with no care or concern for the good husbandry of the natural resources of the sea. Well, these were the men to put a stop to it. Let the Japs, the Malays and the Koepangers be warned. Their reign was about to end.

Davis waited until the scribble of the pencils had caught up, then introduced the eight divers in turn: William Webber, Stephen Elphick, Ernest Freight, Fred Harvey, John Noury, James Rolland, Stanley Sanders and Frederick Beasily. All were top divers, all navy trained and experts in what they did, he told the reporters. Some had brought their own tenders, trained in the operation of the latest diving equipment, including the engine-driven compressor which had not previously been used on the pearling grounds of the northwest. He asked the three tenders, Charles Andrews, Harry Hanson and William Reid, to step forward. They were all skilled mechanics, he told the reporters.

By the time the *Waimana* was ready to dock, the gentlemen of the press had several pages of notes in their possession and a small sheet of paper explaining what a proficient and public spirited company Siebe, Gorman was.

Davis' drawcard had been William Webber and the press were keen to talk to him. Webber was something of a celebrity in England at a time when deep-sea divers were the derring-do workmen of the age. They competed in the popular press with aviators and submariners for stories of astounding feats of bravery and scientific achievement. Webber was easy to turn into a hero – he was a handsome, well-built young man with an open face and a ready smile. He was the son of a

Welsh gamekeeper and had signed on for service with the navy at the age of sixteen. He commenced training aboard HMS *Cambridge* in 1898, and readily demonstrated that he had what it took to be a good diver – the ability to remain calm and in control of one's wits when plunged into fathoms of water dressed in the rudimentary outfit of the time. He soon became one of the Admiralty's top operatives and dived extensively in the Mediterranean off Gibraltar. In 1903, at the age of 24, he left the navy to work for Siebe, Gorman in diving ventures all over the United Kingdom.

In 1910, amidst a flurry of publicity, he signed on with the Pieces of Eight Syndicate to work on the salvage of the Spanish treasure ship *Florencia*, blown up in 1588 in Tobermory Bay, Scotland, by the highland chief Donald Glas Maclean. The legend of the Maclean family was that Donald, who was held captive, had blown himself up along with 500 Spaniards aboard. Webber brought up cannons, some swords and muskets, and a handful of gold coins, but no treasure – which is hardly surprising since research years later established that despite the heartfelt belief of Clan Maclean, the *Florencia* had returned safely to Spain and the vessel sunk in Tobermory Bay was probably the *San Juan Batista* of Sicily.

An article about the arrival of the English divers in Australia appeared in the Melbourne *Argus* on 2 February 1912. Webber was described as the foreman of the group and he was quoted as saying that he had no doubts whatever that the white man could perform the work equally as well as the Asiatic. He also said that the diving areas in the northwest of Australia were shallow compared to the depths he was used to. He said he 'had only recently finished a 27 fathoms job off the north coast of Scotland, and previously he had worked in 30 fathoms of water off the coast of Lisbon'.[1] These comments suggest that Webber had no idea what he was getting into. His description of himself as the foreman was curious. While he was on the pearling grounds, he was not likely to be in charge of anyone. The men were engaged by four different master pearlers, and were to be sent out on separate luggers for months at a time, to collect shell along a coast of hundreds of miles. If they returned to port at the same time, it would be merely fortuitous and it was more than possible they would not see each other during the entire year. Moreover, Webber might have believed that he and the others were to dive in shallow waters, but that was not the plan their employers had for them.

The men's destination was Broome, a town in the Kimberleys, on the edge of the pindan scrub. It was over a thousand miles north of Perth and to reach it required a journey of eight days by coastal steamer. With the sea on one side and desert on the other, Broome was truly one of the most isolated places in the world. Inland, it was surrounded by a rugged area half the size of Europe with a sparse population in scattered settlements. It was a place of extremes of heat and monsoonal rain.

Six months earlier, in his home in York Road, Battersea, William Webber had discussed with his wife the uncertainty of twelve months on the other side of the world. While she reminded him of his responsibilities to her and their child, he wondered if he could make a fortune in such an outlandish place. He took up an atlas, opened it out on the kitchen table and located Broome, a mere spot on the map, a bump on the West Australian coastline poking into the expanse of the Indian Ocean. He ran his finger up and down the coast and read the exotic names of headlands and bays – Gantheaume Point, Cape Boileau, Cape Baskerville, Lagrange Bay, Cape Jaubert, Desault Bay. Apart from Broome, there seemed to be no towns or settlements. Inland he saw a blank space called the Great Sandy Desert. There the cartographer had allowed rivers to dissipate into vague dotted lines leading nowhere, and had noted of tracks: 'location uncertain', and of lakes: 'seasonal'.

But it was a boom town, he was told. Fortunes could be made from pearls worth thousands of pounds. He was given a four-page contract with the leading pearling house of Moss & Richardson saying he was entitled to a commission of $2\frac{1}{2}$ per cent on all the pearls he collected. This was in addition to a wage.

Undeniably, Broome was flourishing in 1912. Cables from the New York and London auctions told of eager buyers pushing the price of mother-of-pearl up towards £210 a ton. In the hotels of Broome, men drank Moet from beer mugs and smoked Dutch cigars. They gave barmaids misshapen pearls for tips and cream-coloured ones for an evening of sleep between breasts.

Robison & Norman, general merchants of Dampier Crescent in the town's centre, advertised the best and finest from around the world: Heidsieck's Monopole champagne, Kupper's pilsener, Albschloss lager and Munro's whiskies. Tokumaru Bros imported Asahi sake and lagers, Hirano champagne and Citron aerated waters for the Japanese seamen. The Malays drank potato-juice gin brought in from Singapore at a low seven shillings and sixpence a bottle. Fresh vegetables were shipped in from Melbourne by steamer, tropical fruits from Singapore, oranges from Italy, and tinned cheese and canned peas from Mortons of London. Only the previous year Mr Mau had unloaded a 4-ton ice-making machine from the wharf and now delivered blocks daily to homes for a reasonable 30 shillings a month. The Pigott brothers ran a soft drinks plant next to their packing shed on Hammersley Street, and a Japanese company bottled soya sauce from a factory in the Asiatic Quarter.

A telephone system was spreading its tentacles out from the post office, and although the wires were regularly blown away by cyclones, people were quickly out on ladders festooning them back again from tree to tree. Several banks competed for business. All sorts of commercial gentlemen found it worth their while to catch the steamer up from Perth: piano tuners and dentists, real estate agents clutching folders of desirable properties in Cottesloe and South Melbourne, furniture salesmen from Sandovers, and milliners with the latest from Paris. There were six hotels built of shiny new iron, a dozen sly grog shops and gambling joints, and several brothels. Opium was brought in from Singapore, hidden in hands of bananas, in pickle jars and in terracotta pots. There were four bakeries, three dairies, a sailmaker, three tailors, two billiard saloons, a blacksmith and an undertaker, as well as a newspaper, two hospitals, a gaol, two lawyers, a resident magistrate and a bishop. All this for a town that had only existed officially since 1883, with a permanent population of about a thousand, and with another two and a half thousand indentured workers from almost every region of the Far East working on the luggers.

2 In Bare Pelt

*The thirst for shells, for pearls for success, brutalises . . . no day
is respected, no dark man's life is valued . . . but the utmost of
diving must be sucked out of them, killing them or not.*

Inquirer, 1875[1]

THERE WAS A TIME when mother-of-pearl could be picked up
from the beach. Women gathering crabs and shellfish found it in
deep rock pools exposed at low tide. They found it in reed beds along
tidal creeks. Children jumped naked into the sea from cliffs, turned
in a somersault and breaststroked through clear waters to a bottom
littered with huge sea oysters, their mouths agape to feed on the wash
of the tide. The women took the shells back to camp and when they
were opened, the smooth surface inside shimmered with light. Men
carved the shells into spearheads or made them into tools. The
women fashioned them into ornaments which they hung around
their necks with braids made from their own hair. The shells were so
large that when children held them in front of their faces, all that

could be seen were the colours of the rainbow. The men of the tribe traded the shells with the desert people to the south for ground-edge hatchets and stone knives. The chewy muscle holding the shell together was cooked over an open fire. And every now and then, perhaps once or twice a season, they would find, tucked inside the folds of oyster flesh, a smooth, hard object the size of a small pebble, tinted with the deep mellow lustre of the moon.

They were the Jukun people. They were the Warwa people; they were the Ngumbarl, the Yawuru, the Jabirrjabirr, the Nyul Nyul, the Karadjari and the Bardi. It had been their land for thousands of years. They were hunters and gatherers without domestic animals – apart from the dingo – without crops, fixed dwellings or encampments. They stored little, they lived in the present, secure in the knowledge that the land would feed and the seas would provide. They saw themselves as integral to the land – it was a place of spirits, guarded by ancestors, with stories and rituals associated with every piece of it. It was owned by no one and, within the natural boundaries of the tribe, owned by everyone. It was a way of life about to be shattered forever by the arrival of strangers.

THE LITERATE buccaneer William Dampier sailed down the west coast of Australia in 1688, and while his vessel the *Cygnet* was beached in King Sound for repairs, he made several excursions into the interior. On his return to England, Dampier published an account of his travels and his colourful imaginings prejudiced European views of the west coast and its Indigenous people for generations.

> The inhabitants of this country are the miserablest people in the world. The Hodmadods of Mouomatapa [the Hottentots], though a nasty people, yet for wealth are gentlemen to these;

who have no houses and skin garments, sheep, poultry, and fruits of the earth, ostrich eggs & etc, as the Hodmadods have: and setting aside their human shape, they differ but little from brutes. They are tall, straight-bodied, and thin, with small long limbs. They have great heads, round foreheads, and great brows. Their eyelids are always half-closed, to keep the flies out of their eyes, they being so troublesome here, that no fanning will keep them from coming to one's face . . . so that from their infancy being thus annoyed with these insects, they do never open their eyes as other people: and therefore they cannot see far, unless they hold up their heads, as if they were looking at somewhat over them.

They have great bottle noses, pretty full lips, and wide mouths. The two foreteeth of their upper jaw are wanting in all of them, men and women, old and young . . . Their hair is black, short and curled, like that of the negroes . . .

They have no houses, but lie in the open air, without any covering; the earth being their bed, and the heavens their canopy . . . Their only food is a small sort of fish, which they get by making weirs of stones across little coves or branches of the sea, every tide bringing in the small fish . . . In other places at low water they seek for cockles, mussels, and periwinkles . . . There is neither herb, root, pulse nor any sort of grain for them to eat, that we saw, nor any sort of bird or beast that they can catch, having no instruments wherewithal to do so.[2]

The French explorer Commodore Nicholas Baudin sailed along the coast of the northwest in 1803, and nothing he reported altered the views spread abroad by Dampier. He was followed in 1818 by Captain Freycinet. One of those with him, Monsieur Arago, wrote: 'The coast from the moment we saw it exhibited nothing but a picture of desolation; no rivulet consoled the eye, no tree attracted it; no mountain gave variety to the landscape, no dwelling enlivened it. Everywhere reigned sterility and death.'[3]

Further voyages of exploration by Lieutenant Philip King and later by lieutenants Stokes and Grey did little to improve perceptions of this region, so when the colony of Western Australia was founded in 1829, it is no surprise that the far north coast was largely ignored. In fact it wasn't until 1837 that the government bothered to survey the coast further.

But then men who were more used to the Australian landscape – and who were not seeking a replica of Europe's green pastures – began to explore the area. In 1861 Mr F.T. Gregory led a party inland from Nickol Bay. When he returned he enthused about what he had seen, describing fertile and well-grassed flats adjacent to flowing rivers – all good grazing country. Claims that these plains were capable of supporting thousands of head of cattle and sheep were spread by enthusiastic entrepreneurs such as Walter Padbury, who set up pastoral companies feeding upon the eagerness of men seeking, as their own, properties the size of English counties. The truth relating to the fertility of the region lay somewhere between the views of Gregory and Dampier, depending on the disposition and motive of the observer and whether one walked though grasslands at the end of the wet season, or baked plains at the end of the dry.

By the early 1860s, the first of the settlers, optimistically preferring Gregory to Dampier, were moving in. Surveyors in Perth drew squares of 100,000 acres on maps and the government offered settlers free pasturage for twelve months and then rent-free leaseholds for three years. A land grab was on, and a clash with the original occupiers was inevitable.

In 1864 a police inspector named Panter stepped ashore on Roebuck Bay, near the future township of Broome. He had taken leave of absence from the force and had joined a party of settlers backed by a pastoral company, largely composed of Melbourne investors, looking for suitable land to seize. Panter, accompanied by two other settlers, set off to explore the area behind Lagrange. It was a fateful decision which was to lead to the death of all three and the battle of

Roebuck Bay, which would set the bloody pattern for future relations between the Aboriginal people and the white invaders.

When Panter's party failed to return, one of the settlers, a head-strong youth of 21 years named Maitland Brown, took it on himself to organise a search party. From the outset Brown assumed that Panter and the others had been murdered and he was leading a punitive expedition. After days of fruitless searching for a trace of the three men in spinifex country inland from Roebuck Bay, Brown became convinced he was being led astray by his Aboriginal guides. His mood hardened. He came across a tribal group which he decided to secure with leather thongs because he concluded that 'from their confident free and easy gaze [they had] seen white people before, and having all the look of murderers about them'.[4] Two were subsequently shot in the back and killed while attempting to escape. On horseback Brown galloped down another man, slung a rope around his neck and hauled him across the spinifex. It was a system of investigation that led to many false confessions and many needless miles. An Aboriginal leader, Karimba, after being chained and having his cheek split open by Brown's fist and cracked on the head with a gun-barrel, agreed to take Brown to a place where several bodies lay in a creek bed – there the party was shown the bones of three Aborigines who had been killed by white miners. Undeterred, and after more false starts and another six days of searching, Brown came upon the bodies of Panter and his companions laid out in their camp site. Evidently they had been clubbed to death as they slept and then speared. Brown felt fully justified in the blood-letting that followed. He came across a group of men, women and children, and killed about twenty. In later memoirs Brown, in an attempt to turn a massacre into a battle, was full of acclaim for the resolution of the people he killed.

> The natives stood their ground with the savage, though not cool, pluck of an Englishman, and not one of the number wounded uttered a sound expressive of either fear or pain, and even after they found they had no chance with us and decided

to retreat to the mangroves, they disdained to throw down their arms, picking up everyone that came in their way, and resisting savagely to the last . . .

It was evident that this was the first lesson taught the natives in this district, of the superiority of civilised men and weapons . . . [5]

In standing their ground, the Aborigines were following a traditional approach to warfare – by a show of numbers, an aggressive display and the throwing of spears, an opposing tribe, sensing defeat, has the option of retreating without bloodshed. To Brown and his men on horseback, with guns at 30 yards, they were the easiest of targets.

Men from Brown's party stripped the flesh from the three-month old corpses of the murdered white men and, after wrapping the bones in linen, rode to the coast to take a boat to Perth. Brown took with him two Aborigines whom he judged to be the murderers, bound in chains. There was no trial, however, because according to Brown the prisoners jumped overboard – one escaped, the other drowned. But Perth had the remains of three pioneers for a big funeral and Brown was hailed as a hero. A memorial recording his deeds was erected by public subscription, a grateful government appointed him to the magistracy and Mount Maitland was named after him.

The settlement of the northwest was not discouraged by the death of Inspector Panter and his two companions – Maitland Brown had shown that the natives were no match for a rifle, and clearly white sentiment would support a firm hand being taken against any Blacks contesting the right of the newcomers to fence off tribal lands. The colonists continued to arrive, unloading stores and livestock on bays and beaches along the coast.

The lands they claimed were bedevilled by flooding monsoons and long harsh droughts. So uncertain was the rainfall and so poor the pastures that the settlers required vast acreages to turn just a modest profit, and even then no amount of terrain was of value without permanent water. The first task of a prudent farmer was to fence in scarce waterholes and then subdue any wild Blacks likely to threaten his stock. Dogs kept Aborigines at bay, and those who crossed the white man's fences or came near his livestock were shot at from a distance. These new settlers were often born and bred in the colony, and appeared to have a contempt for the Aboriginal people that was absent in their parents who had first settled the lands along the Swan River.

For the next 50 years there was spasmodic and disorganised resistance from Aboriginal warriors, especially in outlying districts, but they soon learnt of the pastoralists' zeal for excessive and random revenge. Within a decade, the Aborigines in the settled areas were a broken people. Bronchitis, smallpox, rheumatic fever and tuberculosis found a population without resistance. Measles rippled through their communities carrying off the children, and the common cold was well able to slay the young and the elderly. A smallpox epidemic swept through the northwest during the winter of 1866 causing hundreds of Aboriginal deaths. According to one pioneering family, 'Bodies could be found in the mangroves and throughout the country for many months. The wailing and howling of the Aborigines around Roebourne at night was eerie.'[6] To some tribal elders, it seemed as if the very smell of the white man was killing their people.[7]

But it was something more. A sickness of the soul poisoned the community. Aboriginal spirituality was embedded in the place and its associations – to the trees, the soaks, the rock holes, the caverns, the boulders and the hills. These were places where their ancestors had roamed. They were places explained by intricate stories of the Dreamtime, embracing serpents, kangaroos, birds and fish. With the coming of the white man, the Indigenous people's connection to their place was dislocated. Their society collapsed and their way of life was destroyed. Communities were excluded from sites sacred to their ancestors, sites they now had to ask permission to visit, or could only enter as servants carrying picnic baskets for women in flowing dresses and men in straw boaters. They were pushed into camps on the pastoralists' land, where the master could keep an eye on them.

They were kept alive with a bag of flour and asked to perform corroborees for visitors from the cities.

Children born on the station were regarded as the property of the master. He had the right to turn the boys into stockmen and the girls into housemaids. He could bestow children as servants on neighbouring farms or apprentice them to skippers of pearling luggers. Discipline on the stations was harsh. Station owners complained that their workers had a timeless approach to tasks and an inclination to go walkabout for reasons incomprehensible to Europeans. The Blacks may have taken instantly to white men's food and tobacco, but that did not mean they were much interested in the white man's ways and his fervour for incessant work.

As the pioneers struggled to make a living in a region of isolation, heat and dust, they remained largely unaware that along the coast lay a fortune in pearl-shell. However from about 1864, enterprising pastoralists around Nickol Bay (several hundred miles to the south of the present site of Broome) began to use the Aborigines on their properties to collect shell for them along the foreshore of the bay. Credit for the first payable collection of shell is normally given to a young stockman named Tays. In 1867 he borrowed a cart and a pair of horses from a nearby cattle station and drove some Aboriginal people down to the beach. The rise and fall of the tides in Nickol Bay are so large that Tay's workforce was able to search a vast seabed. Shells were found in their hundreds on the exposed reefs and tidal flats, and within hours a large mound had been built on the sand. During the next few weeks more than 12 tons of shell were collected. Anxious to cash in his treasure, the jubilant Tays loaded 6 tons of it onto the schooner *Emma* and set sail for Perth. The ship was wrecked en route, taking Tays and his shell to the bottom. While mourning his death, others began to reflect on what 12 tons of shell would have brought at the London auctions, and within six months of Tay's drowning, the search for shell had begun in earnest.

It soon became apparent that shore collection required a lot of labour, and no one was better placed to access it than the new owners of the land. Pastoralists considered the Aborigines camped on their stations as theirs, so they took them to the coast in drays and set them to picking up shell. The men tended to regard this work as beneath them, so it was the women and children who moved across the beach to follow the retreat of the sea on each ebb tide. After a few weeks of beachcombing, the women and children were sent back to their camps with trinkets, or flour and tobacco, and the farmers remained to count the fortune in shell mounted alongside their beach camps. To the farmers it was easier than herding sheep – and much more profitable: shell was selling for £90 to £100 a ton in Perth, and a ton could be collected by a team of Aborigines in several days. This was at a time when a labourer could be hired for £100 a year.

That is how it was at the start, with Aboriginal women and children in an exploitative but benign barter of trade goods in exchange for shell collection. Then as news spread of the fortunes to be made, a rush of speculators headed north – a motley bunch of ex-convicts, miners uprooted when the seam ran out, young men sick of being clerks, and whisky adventurers out to make or restore a fortune. Within a few years much of the mother-of-pearl had been stripped from the beaches, bays and inlets along hundreds of miles of coast. The Aborigines were now being ordered to wade into the sea and search for shell by the touch of their feet. As they were being buffeted by breakers in deepening waters, it became clear that mother-of-pearl was not a mere coastal creature. The deeper the women and children went, the more shell they found, and a longboat taken beyond the waves was likely to bring up even more. So began the era of skin diving, which ran from the late 1860s to the mid 1880s. It was to prove one of the most brutal and bloody businesses in Australia's history.

Some of the early shellers brought in South Sea Islanders to dive for shell. They were a sea people, used to skin diving, with the added advantage of being trapped thousands of miles from home. Others turned to Asia. Edwin Streeter and his partner Thomas Haynes carried divers from the small island of Solor (near Timor) to dive for them. Streeter reported that many of his divers died from scurvy and beri beri, which is not surprising considering the rice-based diet provided. In his book *Pearls and Pearling Life*, published in 1886, Streeter wrote of his bewilderment when sixteen out of 61 of his divers died in the space of a month. Streeter also described 'fits' – possibly the bends – but he concluded that the vast majority of these cases were feigned. He also described the hazards of repeated dives to the bottom of the sea:

> Six weeks of steady diving went on, and after 'their ears were broken,' the Sooloo men did fairly well. If a man ceases to dive for a few months, he experiences great pain in his ears on again commencing, and this is slightly alleviated by oil and laudanum [tincture of opium]. After persevering from four to six days, something suddenly appears to give way in the ears when under water, and then all pain disappears; the man can at once proceed to greater depths, and will suffer no inconvenience for the rest of the season. There is no discharge of blood, neither is the sense of hearing impaired.[8]

But it quickly became apparent that there was no need to go to the distant Pacific or the islands to the north – superb divers were to be found among the local people. Even Aborigines brought in from the interior who had never seen a sheet of water bigger than a billabong could be turned into divers. Photographs of tribal groups in the 1880s show lanky men with ribcages projecting through muscle and graceful women with long legs and small breasts. They all dived naked 'or in bare pelt' as it was called by the men in charge of the boats.[9] Their eyes were keen and they could dive to 6 or 7 fathoms on a chest full of air. Women were preferred by the shellers. They were more tractable than the men and, so it was said, could hold their breath longer and had keener eyesight. And the younger the better – to train and to get used to the ways of their white masters on the boats at night.

By 1868 swarms of small boats were sailing the coast crewed by men looking to entice Aborigines with trinkets or threaten them with violence to dive for shell. The typical operation involved a mother ship, usually a lugger or a schooner, with half a dozen dinghies or longboats in tow. Up to 40 Aborigines were crammed aboard the mother ship. They slept on the deck, on the hatch or in the dinghies, while the white men slept in the cabin or, in humid weather, on the roof away from the swarms of cockroaches and sandflies that plagued the boats. The food consisted of rice, maize, flour and spices, and lots of fish, dugong and turtle.

At daybreak the dinghies were launched, each with eight Aboriginal divers aboard and in charge, a white man, standing on the thwart, sculling across the water. Favourite places to dive were over shallow reefs and into narrow channels between the islands and the land. On a calm day the water could be so clear that when the oars were lifted, it felt as if the dinghy was floating in air over a floor of rocks, sand and weed.

On the first plunge of the day, the divers leapt into the water together to frighten away the sharks. They jumped high, went in feet first, turned in a somersault and, with a few scissor kicks, sped to the floor below. If the tide was running the white man aboard had to watch that none of the divers was left behind. In murky water he watched for the line of each diver's bubbles; in heavy surf he had to count them as they surfaced after each dive. The divers brought up the shells, threw them aboard, climbed aboard themselves for a few moments of rest, then jumped off again. Between sunrise and sunset this was repeated hundreds of times, and the dinghy could easily drift miles from the mother ship. If the grounds had not been overrun by another boat, a diver might find a shell once in every eight dives. No lunch was allowed and there was no variation in the food offered for the evening meal and breakfast. At nightfall the Aboriginal divers, exhausted by the day's exertions, lay down on the deck and usually slept without disturbance till dawn.

An adventurer Henry Taunton wrote about his time on the boats in the 1880s. He explained that the natives dived in feet first because constantly plunging head first brought on severe headaches. He added:

> So painful is diving in anything over three fathoms to new hands . . . that the only way of making sure that they do reach the bottom is to insist on their bringing up pieces of weed, coral, or sponge. Sometimes it is necessary to order two of the old hands to take hold of the recalcitrant's wrists and swim with him to the bottom.[10]

Taunton imposed the regime of a martinet on his boats:

> As may well be imagined, when three or four white men had to control and compel some thirty or forty natives to carry on work which they detested, a very strict discipline had to be maintained. It was the rule that no talking was allowed amongst the divers in the dinghy, nor were they even permitted to address the white man, unless, maybe, to answer a question as to the nature of the bottom, whether 'nanoo' (sand) or 'bannin' (shelly bottom), etc., or unless some urgent necessity arose. Sometimes, indeed, I have pushed off from the vessel's side of a morning and have not heard a word spoken until we returned on board at night.[11]

Skin divers who, gasping for breath, hung onto the side of the dingy for too long had their fingers hit with an oar to set them off again. The Bishop of Perth, Matthew Gibney, complained that he had seen Aborigines returning from diving with crushed hands and reported that women in the later stages of pregnancy were being forced to dive. Anyone challenging authority was flogged and chained. Cases were reported of divers who fell ill being let loose on a beach miles from their home in case they infected the others. When deaths occurred, the bodies were silently slipped over the side at night or dug into the sand just above the high-water mark. Sometimes there was no body at all and the divers would watch in horror as one of their number, surrounded by a circle of crimson water, was pulled down by a shark. Streeter claimed that although sharks were numerous, the loss of life was only from half to one per cent in a season.

By the late 1870s over-exploitation had led to a sustained decline in the amount of shell being taken in the seas around Nickol Bay. At the same time it became apparent to the shellers that the pearling grounds to the north were limitless and the shell found there was a larger, more valuable species. Crew sailing north found that the coastline was composed of sandy beaches with few harbours safe from the periodic cyclones that roared through from the northeast. An exception was the mangrove-fringed Roebuck Bay, the site of the future township of Broome, where the pearlers could pull their boats ashore up the winding Dampier Creek. The newcomers found that it was a place of heat, humidity and mosquitoes of exceptional ferocity.

The Indigenous people of Roebuck Bay were not known as being warlike; they fished along the mudflats and creeks of the bay and avoided the more aggressive tribes to the north and inland. As boxes and kegs and trunks were unloaded onto the beach, they took shelter in the bush and cautiously watched the activity, for they had heard that the presence of white men usually ended grievously for the black man. Contact between Aborigines and whites along the northwest coast seemed to fall into a pattern of initial friendly contact, mutual curiosity, then a rapid deterioration of relations, leading to the complete subjugation of the original inhabitants by force of arms. Events at Roebuck Bay followed that dismal course. Within months, arguments over the whites taking black women and the Blacks' theft of white property had caused relationships to sour, and although Dampier Creek may have been a relatively safe haven from the sea, it was no longer from the land. The white men, moored in boats, soon learnt to keep guard and, if the Aborigines started to congregate, to move their vessels out to sea and shoot randomly at shadows they could see moving between the trees.

All along the coast as the bloody reputation of the pearling boats spread, there developed a distinct reluctance by the Aboriginal people to take on shell diving. In 1875, the Dutch authorities in Batavia, alarmed at the number of deaths among villagers taken to the Australian shelling fields, imposed stringent conditions on recruitment, including one that the sheller forfeited a bond of 200 florins if the diver was not returned within thirteen months. These restrictions effectively cut off the source of labour from the East Indies. Faced with a shortage of Indigenous people or Islanders prepared to work on the boats, the shellers, with varying degrees of sophistication, turned to blackbirding. In some cases payments would be made to the elders of an Aboriginal community to hand over young men and women for work as divers on the boats. In other cases Aborigines were persuaded to work off a familiar beach for a few days, only to find that once they were on board, the boat turned out to sea and sailed many miles down the coast.

Increasingly more forceful methods of obtaining labour were required, and the men of the pioneering families looked forward with anticipation to the commencement of the pearling season when the hunt for bush Aborigines began. As a correspondent for a Perth newspaper, Mr R. Thatcher, wrote: 'Then comes the most important part . . . the picking up of niggers . . . for pearling after all would never pay white labour.'[12] Men rode out with rifles, stock whips and shackles on dawn raids of black camps. While one held a rifle at the ready, another would dismount and attach neck chains around the throats of the healthy-looking for the long walk overland to the coast. Anyone who protested was beaten into submission.

Professional blackbirders began to ply their trade. They offered to kidnap and supply Aborigines for £5 each – or have them shot for two shillings and sixpence. White men with chains and rifles took Aborigines to nearby islands where their resistance was weakened by starvation pending a sale to shellers looking for crews. Women were held on island barracoons as prostitutes for visiting crews. Bishop Gibney described the heart-rending wail he heard from a group of

Aborigines mourning the loss of young men who had been forcibly detained on a pearling boat and who had drowned making an attempt to escape from their captors. They had never seen the sea before and believed they could swim a distance of 6 miles to the shore. Reports abounded of rapes and murders, and drunken fights on board the boats over Aboriginal women. Graziers complained that female servants and stockmen they had raised and educated were being abducted. One wrote to the Governor that an Aboriginal worker of his was fired at by blackbirders and the man's wife raped. The protesting Aborigine was peppered with buckshot as his wife was dragged away. The grazier also complained that a young girl was taken: 'I went down for her myself the following day but found her such a little thing she could not travel home with me; I don't believe she is seven years old, she said she was not well and I do not wonder at it.'[13]

So frequent were the claims of brutality on the boats that legislation was passed in an attempt to rein in the more flagrant abuses. Legislation in 1871 and 1873 prohibited the use of women and children at sea, and the employment of Aboriginal men required a written agreement countersigned by a justice of the peace or a police constable. The agreement had to stipulate that the worker concerned would be returned home after the engagement. Not surprisingly, the passing of laws in a city a thousand miles away did little to control practices along a vast coastline. The abuses continued and few were prosecuted, so further laws were passed: the labour agreement now had to be in the form of a schedule to the Act and the official it was presented to had to make sure the Aborigine understood it. Further, a JP could order the release of an Aborigine from the agreement if the Act was being breached.

These laws were impossible to enforce on the hundreds of boats operating along the desolate western shoreline. In 1880 the Governor made further regulations specifying adequate food rations and prohibiting the employment of youths under the age of puberty diving beyond 6 fathoms, or at all on a Sunday. An eight-hour day was prescribed and there had to be a break of an hour at midday. Shellers protested about these new conditions, so in 1881 a watered-down set of regulations was promulgated, including the provision that Aborigines were now allowed to dive to 7 fathoms and a lunch break was no longer required. None of this law-making went so far as to specify that the Aborigines had to be paid for their work and indeed they were not. A gift of alcohol, tobacco, perhaps an axe, or a bag of flour was deemed sufficient by most pearlers for several months work.

About this time, in 1883, Broome was created – by a notice in the *Western Australian Government Gazette*. A visitor to Broome in that year would have seen nothing more than the camps of shellers seeking temporary anchorage. The Governor, Sir Frederick Napier Broome, wrote to the Colonial Secretary complaining that he hadn't been asked if he would like to have the town named after him. He protested that the town 'is likely to remain a mere dummy townsite, inhabited by the tenants of three graves ... My present idea is to have the name cancelled.'[14] He was informed that it was too late – maps had been prepared. Wistfully he wrote to the Surveyor General saying that he hoped some day the town which bore his name may have an inhabitant.

He had no cause for concern. Broome was not to be a dummy townsite. The seas surrounding it proved to lie over the richest shelling grounds in the world. Undreamt-of wealth began to be hauled from them. Within a few years of its establishment Broome had hotels, shops and houses, and a population of several thousand.

By the mid 1880s, as the shallow waters became depleted of shell, the boats were forced to move further out to sea and the shore became a line in the distance. Harsh measures were required to force divers into deeper and deeper waters. After several days of diving to depths of 6 to 8 fathoms, the Aboriginal divers would rise to the surface with blood dribbling from their ears or pouring from their noses. While lying at night on the decks they moaned with shooting pains in their limbs and paralysis of their arms.

As the shellers stood in the dinghies supervising their divers, they could see even more shell, tantalisingly beyond reach, in 8 or 9 fathoms. The obvious answer lay in use of diving apparatus. There had been attempts to use intricate pumps, rubberised canvas suits, copper-domed helmet and spools of rubber pipe. But the expense could hardly be justified when until now there was plenty of shell in shallow water and naked Aboriginal divers could do the job just as well.

The first divers in copper helmets and dress suits were white men who, after reading the Siebe, Gorman manual of instruction, dropped into the waters of Roebuck Bay. They found plenty of shell but their enthusiasm for working all day in fathoms of water did not last. It was, as they soon realised, arduous and dangerous work. The pearlers found that the Aborigines could not be induced to plunge over the side in a canvas suit with a helmet bolted down over their heads. Another source of labour would have to be found. For that the pearlers turned to Asia. Malays, Koepangers and Manilamen were recruited initially, but then pearlers in the Torres Strait began to use Japanese seamen, and those in Western Australia followed their lead.

The 1880s later became known as the Fat Years. Everywhere there was shell just waiting to be picked up by men in canvas suits – strewn across the seabed, in bays, surrounding coral islands and in deep sounds, anywhere the spat (as the larval oysters are called) could find a purchase on something and be fed by the tides. There were few cases of paralysis because there was no need to dive deep. All the pearl-shell anyone wanted could be found in 10 to 12 fathoms, all along Ninety Mile Beach.

However, skin diving was not abandoned overnight, and right into the 1890s some shellers regarded men in rubberised suits as a mere novelty. There was still plenty of shell in reach of skin-divers if you knew where to look and could force the Aborigines to dive deep enough. There were other advantages, too. When the rush of water at spring tide made the use of diving apparatus impossible, skin-divers could still take to the water. A dinghy could float across sand bars and follow twisting channels too dangerous for luggers to follow.

Aboriginal divers could venture into rock- and coral-strewn areas where the risk to the full-dress diver of getting his lifeline entangled on the rocks was too great. So proficient were the skin-divers that if a new pearling ground was discovered, dress-divers complained that a schooner with half a dozen dinghies full of skin-divers would clear an area like a plague of locusts.

But over time the superiority of the suited diver in deeper water became obvious, and the shellers who adopted the new technique began collecting vast amounts of shell. After two decades of unpaid exploitation, Aborigines in bare pelt were no longer required. They had made hundreds of white men rich and gained nothing for themselves. A few Aborigines remained as deckhands and some became shell openers, but even these positions were in jeopardy. In the new century the Japanese had begun to demand of the master pearlers that the entire crew be Japanese.

The old-style shellers claimed that all the fun went out of the game when the diving suit came in. Before then anyone could be a sheller. You didn't need special equipment and there was none of the frustration of dealing with the argumentative Japanese or the temperamental Malays. There had been no red tape involved as there was now with workers having to be brought in from overseas. It had been a good life. A ton of shell would bring £150 – all for the outlay of a boat, several dinghies, a few rifles and half a dozen hard-drinking men to maintain discipline over the Blacks.

3 Boodungarry

I have seen Policeman Wilson 'marry' plenty of gins.

Boodungarry, Aboriginal prisoner, aged about fourteen[1]

BY THE 1880s, THE treatment of the Aboriginal population in Western Australia had become a public scandal. Journals in Australia and Britain carried articles claiming that the punishment handed out to the Aborigines in the north was worse than it had been in the slave states of America. Stories appeared of runaways being locked up each night in 'a kind of second Calcutta black hole', random killings, the taking of infants and the use of a whip, or a crack across the head with a stirrup iron, as a common form of castigation.

A persistent critic of the pastoralists, Anglican clergyman J.B. Gribble published a tract entitled *Dark Deeds in a Sunny Land*, and his accusations of atrocities were widely published in the eastern states and in England. He held public meetings in Melbourne where the details he revealed were so horrific that women and children were denied entry. Finally the Western Australian Government, after much delay, established a Royal Commission on the Condition of the Natives, headed by Dr Walter E. Roth, surgeon, anthropologist and Protector of Natives in Queensland.

Roth took much of his evidence in the northwest of the state. He examined policemen, gaolers, priests, missionaries, shellers, magistrates, a light-keeper and, somewhat surprisingly, Aboriginal prisoners. He completed his report in December 1905.[2] It was more trenchantly critical of the police, the magistracy and the pearling and pastoral industries than those in government who had ordered the commission could ever have contemplated. Roth revealed a system of neglect by the Protector of Natives, habitual police violence, prostitution of Aboriginal women by the pearling crews, and the exploitation of Aboriginal children on the luggers. He pointed out that although the employment of Aborigines was supposed to be under the supervision of the Chief Protector, this officer had no legal status, no authority and a staff of just one clerk/accountant.

As far as Roth could see, legislation for the apprenticeship of young Aborigines provided, in effect, for the legalised stealing of children to work for station holders and on the pearling luggers. Indentures of apprenticeship were supposed to be approved by the resident magistrate; many were not, but even if they were, this offered no protection at all. Parents were never consulted. The Chief Protector said he considered six to be a suitable age at which to commence an apprenticeship. At the discretion of the magistrate, the indenture ran through until the apprentice turned eighteen or 21. The child received no guarantee of training during this period, and absconders were pursued by the police, chained and returned to the punishment of the master. Roth noted that there was 'nothing to prevent the greatest scoundrel unhung, European or Asiatic, putting under contract any blacks he pleases'.

Dr Graham Blick, the acting resident magistrate in Broome in 1904, gave evidence to the Roth Commission that when he took over, there were no proper records of indentures and most had not been filled in correctly. He did not know if the indentures were still in force, and it was not part of his duties to check up on what had happened to the apprentices once the indentures were signed. The law was that children were not supposed to work on pearling luggers, but the law also allowed children to sign on as apprentice seamen. Dr Blick was asked whether the children on the boats received wages. 'There is no mention of it. I should not think they would. It is almost certain that they do not.' Adults did not fare much better. Blick told the commissioner that 'clothing, food, medical attention and tobacco is about all that is paid. The majority get a shilling every now and again, but there are no specific wages.'

As Aboriginal society broke down, it seemed that the only thing the crews of the luggers wanted from the Aboriginal camps was their women. One of Roth's witnesses was Constable Bertram Fletcher, stationed at Lagrange Bay. Fletcher told of nightly incursions of the crews from the luggers into the camps seeking to barter tobacco and alcohol in exchange for women. He said that venereal disease was rife in the Aboriginal community and recently eighteen women had died of it, some only sixteen years old. Aboriginal men walked 100 miles from the inland to trade their women for rice, flour, clothes, tobacco and pipes. The women did not go onto the boats willingly, but were forced by their men. Constable Fletcher explained that as a preventive measure, he would muster the Aborigines in one or two places along the creek, and whenever he saw crewmen coming ashore, he would go down to the camps and put the women in chains for the night.

The gaols across the north were full of Aborigines, and Roth found that 90 per cent of these inmates were imprisoned for livestock killing. He described police behaviour towards Aborigines as 'a most brutal and outrageous condition of affairs'. Police gave evidence that the pastoralists expected a prompt reaction to complaints of cattle spearing. The typical response was for two white policemen, accompanied by half a dozen Aboriginal police, all on horseback and all armed with Winchester rifles, to raid whichever Aboriginal camp was said by the pastoralists to contain the offenders. Extended chains of prisoners were brought in, sometimes as many as 30, both accused and witnesses, for a long walk through the scrub to town. Children as young as fourteen were also taken, usually only to give evidence against their parents. The chains were attached to the saddle of the mounted officer, and were not taken off when crossing rivers or creeks.

The reason so many prisoners were taken became abundantly clear to Roth. For each head seized the police received an allowance of two shillings and fivepence per day, supposedly to cover rations. Roth wrote:

> It is no secret that the police say, if the ration allowance was cut down or taken away they would not arrest so many natives. By their own assertions, every native caught means more money in their pocket; reliable witnesses have heard such assertions made. At present there is nothing to prevent the constable arresting as many blacks as he chooses . . .

Many women were taken as chained witnesses. Here is the evidence of John Wilson, a police constable:

> Have you any legal authority to arrest these women as unwilling witnesses? – No. Not that I am aware of.
>
> How do you detain them, with neck-chains? – They are chained by the ankles.
>
> Do you mean that their two legs are chained together? – No, I fasten the gins to a tree with a handcuff and then fix the chain to one ankle with another handcuff – one handcuff for each prisoner.
>
> Is it only at night that they are chained like this? – It is necessary to detain them sometimes in the day when going through scrub or rocky country where they might get away. It is very rare that they have to be secured in the day time.
>
> The commission has received evidence that these witness are

generally your gins, or young children. Is that so? – I have never brought in female children as witnesses, that is what I considered children.

Have you brought in young women? – Yes.

Do you allow your trackers or the assisting stockmen to have sexual intercourse with the gins whose relatives or friends you have arrested? – They might do it without my knowing it.

Do you take any precautions at night that these assisting stockmen or trackers do not have connection with the women when chained to the trees? – No.

Does such intercourse go on? – I suppose it does. It could go on in the camp at night and I would know nothing about it.

So far as you know, then, this sexual intercourse may go on with these female aboriginal witnesses? – Yes.[3]

Roth commented about this evidence: 'Accompanying the police may be the manager, or stockmen, who have volunteered to come, but as the manager does not prosecute and the stockmen are not called as witnesses, this voluntary action on the part of the station-employees may admit of another construction.'

In writing this Roth was talking of the white managers and stockmen taking part in the rape of chained witnesses, often the wives and daughters of the accused who were chained nearby. Another police witness, Constable Inglis, gave evidence that he did not have to chain the women as they always followed their men. Although he added that they were not reliable, therefore he took precautions to prevent them getting away. He was also asked how he selected his prisoners:

Do you ever bring in any witnesses for the defence? – No.

Is not this a rather one-sided kind of justice for the black? – It is in a sense. It is a queer country where I am. Every mother's son is guilty. It is only right that they should have a defence.

What makes you pick the women to give evidence against the men? – The grown-up men are those who kill the bullock.

There are no young boys in the tribes. The squatters have them all.

But you have admitted that these women are equally guilty as far as killing is concerned? – Yes.

Then these women are practically asked to turn informers? – Yes.

Who asks them to turn informers, the trackers? – They volunteer to tell themselves.

Do they realise the harm that they are doing to their husbands? – Not in the slightest. They do a lot of harm against their husbands, and do not know it.[4]

Roth noted: 'To secure a conviction the accused are accordingly made to plead guilty – at the muzzle of the rifle, if need be.' He recorded the testimony of one witness:

Boodungarry, Aboriginal Prisoner, the Gaol Wyndham

(This child is about 14 years of age, and is undergoing a sentence of two years' hard labour for alleged cattle killing. In reply to our inquiries, his English was very pidgin. Mr Hartrick, secretary to the Commission, took shorthand notes, and, omitting my questions, has compiled the following evidence in the form of a readable statement. – W.E.R.)

I was caught by Jack Inglis and Wilson [policemen] . . . Wilson asked me if I killed cattle. I said 'No'. Wilson and Inglis then talked together, and they said they would shoot me. Inglis put a cartridge in his rifle, pointed it at me, and said he would burn me at a rock. It frightened me, and I then said I did kill a bullock . . . He took me and some other blackfellows, who were also frightened. They all said they had killed a bullock because they were frightened. The policemen put handcuffs on our legs and hands. Two of us were chained by the legs. Then they caught some more blackfellows – a big mob – and some gins and took us away.

Wilson got a gin and took her into a gully. I have seen Policeman Wilson 'marry' plenty of gins. We were taken to Hall's Creek. At the Court House I said nothing, because Inglis told me not to talk. Wilson hammer plenty of blackfellows with nulla-nulla. I do not know why he 'wommered' [beat] them, but he frightened me and I did not talk in the Court House. The gins did all the talking. The magistrate only spoke to them. He did not ask me whether I killed a bullock.

Roth's cynicism about why so many female witnesses were brought in was understandable because, at the end of the day, witnesses did not seem to matter. No one giving evidence to the Royal Commission could remember an Aborigine ever being acquitted. Almost all were persuaded to plead guilty. Roth reported that some honorary justices he met were not fit to hold their appointments:

At Hall's Creek the whole brutality of the present system is brought into prominence when the acting Resident Magistrate sentences a child of 10 years to six months' hard labour for [unlawfully killing and carrying away one head of cattle]. The same magistrate has sentenced another infant of 15 to nine months for killing a goat and at least eight other children, between 14 and 16 years of age, to two years' hard labour for alleged cattle-killing. As already mentioned, four of the latter met with by your Commissioners in the Roebourne gaol have since been released.

Any Aborigine sentenced to prison was neck-chained – morning, noon and night – for the entire period of the sentence. Roth discovered that the chaining was enforced even if the prisoner was 'fairly civilized, and perhaps educated and working for Europeans for years'. Chains were never used on European or Asiatic prisoners, the justification being that they were not likely to run away into the bush. Roth heard much debate among prison officers as to whether neck-chains should be leather-covered or remain bare. The comptroller general of prisons said that since neither medical men nor the gaolers agreed on this topic, he left it to the discretion of individual prison officers. For his part the Broome gaoler said that the neck-chains should be without covering because it made the chain much cooler, and it reduced the chafing that occurred when the leather became cracked or the prisoner was working near sand. However, since he had no authority to remove the leather from the chains he received through government stores, he said, he had to wait until the leather fell off of its own accord.

The gaoler described the daily regime: 'The prisoners rise at 5.30. From 6 to 7.30 they are chained up, and at 7.30 they are taken out to work in gangs of three. They return at 12 and have a spell for two hours. They start work again at 2 and come in at 5.30. After tea they are chained up until the following morning. They have a swim in the creek.'

When Aboriginal people from the interior were imprisoned, the gaoler's first task was to teach them how to wear bloomers so they could decently be taken out to work in the streets of Broome. He told Roth, 'Owing to the change of diet they are sometimes sick and need special attention. When any of the prisoners, either black or white, are sick, my wife cooks them some little dainties, such as sago, etc.' He added that in his opinion, none of the Aborigines in his prison really understood why they were there.

Dr Richard Henry Wace, the resident magistrate at Derby, was asked about the effects of the pearling industry and responded:

> It is most thoroughly demoralising to the blacks . . . Several cases of supplying liquor to the blacks were brought down here. In every case I asked why the defendants had given the liquor, and in every case I was informed that the reason was that they wanted one of the women . . . It is the recognised payment. I have treated several cases this year of specific diseases amongst the pearling boats, and I know from my own knowledge that it is extremely prevalent amongst these crews and cannot but have

an extremely bad effect amongst the blacks . . . To my knowledge, girls have been taken from a mission station in accordance with the tribal marriage customs – young girls of 14 or 15 years, who have only just arrived at maturity and in perfect health – taken away and prostituted amongst the crews of the luggers, returning after some time suffering from specific diseases . . . I know also that members of lugger crews go ashore with guns, ostensibly for self-protection against the blacks. I refer to a case of a member of one of Mr Pigott's boats, Pedro Rodriguez, who was shot while stepping out of the boat. I elicited the evidence that he was taking a gun ashore for the purpose of 'self-protection'.

Dr Wace's comments about the carrying of guns for 'self-protection' would have surprised no one. In his *History of the Northwest of Australia*, published in 1915, Jas. S. Battye wrote that:

Men who undertook the burdens of pioneering and went into unknown country carried their lives in their hands, and to shoot quickly was often their only safeguard. Such men may have been technically guilty of murder, but even that was preferable to being stalked like game and treacherously slain by bloodthirsty savages.[5]

Even at the time Battye wrote, the death of an Aborigine at the hands of a white man would probably not be investigated with any vigour. Any policeman who might have felt the inclination to pursue a white murderer would have been deterred by town hostility and the knowledge that it was unlikely that a white jury would convict. As late as the 1920s it was recounted that a pearler brought back the skulls of four Aborigines he claimed to have shot while they circled his camp. He set the skulls up on the bar in a Broome hotel and, to the amusement of those present, demanded they buy him drinks to celebrate his skill with a rifle.

Roth made a number of recommendations to the government. At heart he saw that the cause of the clash between the Indigenous people and the pastoralists was the expulsion of the Aborigines from tribal lands. He wrote:

> The pastoralist gets a grant of land to raise sheep and cattle, and accordingly the kangaroo, the native food of the aboriginal, has to be got rid of. When these animals [the kangaroos] get scarce the blacks must kill the cattle or sheep . . . In the Sturt's Creek district, where a large number of cattle appear to be annually speared, the blacks can only get water where the cattle are watered; once they are driven from these places, they have nothing to live on; they could get food if they were allowed to stop where the cattle are, but blacks and cattle will not agree, and the blacks are driven away; they must live somehow, so they spear cattle . . . The climax of refined hardship and abuse has so far been reached in the recent Dog Act of 1904, Section 29, where the black is not allowed to have more than one male dog unregistered, the ultimate and ill-concealed effect of such legislation being to prevent aborigines using dogs for hunting purposes, and so limiting still further the supplies of native food otherwise available.

Roth believed that the solution lay in separating the Aborigines from the pastoralists. He urged the setting aside of large northern reserves for the sole benefit of the Indigenous people.

He made other recommendations directed to increasing the power of the Chief Protector and reducing the power of the police and the magistracy. He recommended that there be a requirement for employers to pay Aborigines for their work. He sought the abolition of neck-chains and their substitution by wrist-cuffs.

When it was released the Roth Report was vigorously criticised as being highly selective and grossly biased. Pastoralists and pearlers wrote letters to the papers denying allegations of abuse and stating that the bonds of affection between them and their black workers were deep. In some instances this was undoubtedly true and, as Roth noted, 'in many cases the squatters act with humane consideration, and that people who have always had natives as servants will not part with them'.

In 1905 the Western Australian Parliament, in a response to the Roth Report, enacted some reforms of questionable wisdom. The Chief Protector was given sweeping powers over the employment, property, marriage and children of Aborigines – sowing the seeds for the tragedy of the stolen generations which continued for much of the ensuing century. Police powers were curtailed but imprisonment for cattle-stealing remained, and Roth's suggestion of a mandatory wage was forgotten. Nor was his suggestion of large northern hunting reserves implemented. Instead, parcels were created in a patchwork across the state.

Despite Roth's urging, Aboriginal chain gangs remained a feature of the streetscape of all the towns of the north, including Broome, for decades. Wasted, angular men, naked except for a pair of baggy bloomers, with eyes seemingly blank from anger or humiliation, worked under the supervision of an Aboriginal policeman carrying a rifle. Linked by neck-chains a regulation 8 feet apart, they raked up leaves in a patient, slow motion, repaired footpaths or levelled the racetrack for the local turf club. Chaining was a humane method, so the gaolers argued, because Aborigines, being free spirits, could never have stood confinement in a cell. They were in the open air, shackled to their tribesmen for company and free to move about. Handcuffs, the gaolers claimed, were an impossible alternative because of their sinewy wrists, whereas chains around their necks allowed them to brush away flies and play cards during their leisure hours.

THE ARRIVAL of the missionaries added a bewildering complexity to the Aborigines' picture of the white man. Until then the white men they had met were violent and greedy for land, and their very presence seemed to bring a sickness to the community. Now there were others walking in their midst who said they came not to take but to give, who were prepared to live with them in the most desperate of poverty and stand with them against the worst excesses of the blackbirders and settlers. Yet it was at a price – the compromise of their souls and what they knew to be true.

The Aboriginal people were deeply spiritual, but they were not concerned with doctrine; it was a spirituality based on ritual – of dance, storytelling, corroborees, feasts and initiations. Christianity with its emphasis on the power of one external God ran counter to much of what the Aborigines knew about their universe. The nuns and priests who came from France, Germany and Ireland with the singular purpose of bestowing the blessings of Christian salvation on the Indigenous people discredited many of the Aboriginal rituals and disapproved of their customs. As was explained patiently to the black men and women again and again, their very nakedness was an affront to the Almighty.

The work of the missions was heartily supported, at least in words, by the government and the white communities of the northwest. Such was the decline in the numbers of tribal Aborigines that it was commonly believed that the present generation would be the last, and the difficult task of smoothing the pillow of the dying race seemed appropriate for the Church. As well as saving souls, the pearlers and pastoralists reckoned that Christian teachings served to take the aggression out of the men, and that the food doled out by the Church in isolated places kept the Aborigines well away from spearing cattle. And it could not be denied that the mission schools generally turned out employable servants. When it came to monetary support though, public and devotional aid was miserly and the missions were continually on the verge of financial disaster.

Despite their best endeavours, the missionaries were never successful in permanently holding the Aborigines. They would drift away from the mission, sometimes moving back to their traditional life of hunting and gathering, but more often gravitating into town or to the edge of the pearlers' camps, where women or work could be bartered for food or alcohol.

Both the Catholic Church and the Church of England conducted missions in the west Kimberleys. By force of the personalities involved, rather than by design, they displayed radically different approaches to their toleration of traditional Aboriginal life.

The Trappist Order set up a Catholic mission on Beagle Bay in the 1890s, but after losing heart with the isolation and difficulty of the work, transferred the mission to the German-based Pallottine Society in 1901. Father Walter, in charge of the Beagle Bay mission, told the Roth Commission that he had a staff of eleven lay brothers and one schoolmaster. Thirty-one students were taught reading, writing, arithmetic, music, object-lessons, and religious and Bible history. Father Walter said his principal aim was to teach the children the nobility of work, so after lessons he had them help in the gardens and in the various trade shops on the mission. In addition he had a number of Aboriginal men working in the fields and on the mission pearling lugger. When the lugger was in harbour, about one hundred Blacks camped around the site. Father Walter explained that the mission made a point of not feeding any of their charges who did not work, unless they were crippled or infirm.

The mayor of Broome visited the Beagle Bay mission in 1909 and reported to the council how impressed he was with what he saw:

> To see a boy of 16 welding a piece of iron together was marvellous; the carpentering was of high merit, the board and timber used being all cut from growing timber. In the bakery a mere boy would explain the heat of the oven, etc.; while the tin smith would turn out billy cans etc. as good as those turned out from a factory. The discipline was a notable feature of the Mission, one word from a father or brother commanding strict attention.[6]

The mayor said he intended writing to the Protector, as he thought the place deserved much more support than it was receiving.

At the entrance to King Sound lies Sunday Island, remote and difficult to get to. It was there in 1899 that the eccentric Montague Sydney Hadley established his mission. With the loose – and sometimes reluctant – support of the Church of England, Hadley ran a ramshackle, unconventional mission for more than twenty years. Hadley was the stuff of which legends are made. The son of an English peer, he amassed a modest fortune from pearling and blackbirding in the 1880s. He was one of those who conducted raids on the Aboriginal camps and after capturing young men and a few choice women, kept them on the Lacepede Islands, where he traded them to the pearlers for prostitution or as skin-divers. But then, so the story goes, Hadley underwent a divine revelation which convinced him that because he had committed so many evils against the black race, his only hope lay in devoting his life to their salvation. He embraced a belief that the Aborigines were an innately innocent and uncomplicated people, and if only he could find a tribe still uncontaminated by contact with white civilisation, he could gradually shepherd them into the protection of Christianity. A man of easy grace and impeccable manners, he inveigled Bishop Hale to support him in setting up his mission, first on the Forrest River (too late – the white man had already been there and the Aborigines were hostile), then, in 1899, transferring to Sunday Island.

Hadley also gave evidence to the Roth Royal Commission. He had only two staff, one an unqualified schoolteacher and the other a cook/storekeeper. The school taught the three Rs, general outlines of biblical history, drawing, singing and general instruction. He had 23 attending his school – ten boys and thirteen girls. All up about 90 people lived on the island.

Hadley was a mass of contradictions. He followed an awkward blend of thunderous adherence to old-style religion and relative indifference to personal morality. His church services were a raging delight of hymn singing and vigorous pulpit thumping about retribution and hellfire. He never urged the Aboriginal people to adopt the white man's ways or change faster than they wished. He was staunch in his protection of women from the predators on the luggers, but accepted as a tribal custom the right of men to demand their choice of wives. Some of the men had two or three wives, but Hadley still looked upon them as Christians and Hadley himself undertook a form of marriage with several young women during his many years on the island. He was a keen supporter of the preservation of Aboriginal culture and, in order to become initiated into the tribe, he was circumcised with stone implements and had his body scarified with tribal markings. He encouraged the wearing of clothes, but never seemed to worry too much if the people on the island chose otherwise. His respect for Aboriginal culture meant that he made few conversions. In 1903, after four years on the island, he said, 'I cannot say that I have been able to convert any native yet to be a true believer but I try my utmost and I must leave the results in His hands.'[7]

Hadley received little financial support from the Church and regularly made substantial contributions from his own pocket. He also had women dive naked for trochus and pearl shells off flat-bottomed boats, and gather bêche-de-mer (trepang) on the reefs. He was a controversial figure, regularly receiving adverse reports from government inspectors despite charming visiting dignitaries. When his elder brother died in the 1920s, Hadley suddenly became Lord Hadley. Still bearing his tribal scars, he returned to wealth and respectability to live out his remaining years on the family estate in England.

4 A White Australia

The Japanese belong to an empire whose standard of civilization is so much higher than that of kanakas, negroes, Pacific Islanders, Indians, or other Eastern peoples, that to refer to them in the same terms cannot but be regarded in the light of a reproach, which is hardly warranted by the fact of the shade of the national complexion.

The Japanese Consul to the Australian Prime Minister, in protest against
the *Immigration Restriction Act 1901*[1]

THE DAY BEFORE THE eleven Englishmen made their departure for Broome, a farewell in their honour was held in the dining room of the Royal Hotel, Perth. It was a small, airless place and so many well-wishers had insisted on coming that when James Davis rose to speak, he had to stand on a red leather settee to project his voice to those crowded in the doorways. The steamy smell of roast beef lingered in the air and several of the diners loosened their neckties.

Davis raised a glass of claret as he waited for silence. On this very day, he told his audience, in a British town on Australian soil, Japanese and Malays and Koepangers and Manilamen, and heaven knows what other races, were waiting for another pearling season to begin. They were preparing to take boats from an Australian port to seek wealth from waters adjacent to Australian shores. They were looking forward to stealing pearls from under the noses of their white masters and sending them to their own countries. But not for much longer. Their reign was about to end. The government of Australia had spoken – and the clear message was that coloured labour must be expelled. (Loud cheers.) Davis waved his glass to encircle the eleven men seated against the wall, then waited for the applause to die down before declaring that British Navy trained divers and tenders were the best in the world. These men were the forerunners of many others to come. (Hear, hear!) They were to bring to pearling the cold steel of competition. The Asiatic would be no match. (Hear, hear!) No match at all. (More cheering and stamping of feet.) Siebe, Gorman & Co. was proud to be involved in this grand venture with these men. The largest manufacturer of diving apparatus in the world. The sole contractors to the British Admiralty and the Crown Agents for the Colonial and the Indian Office. Siebe, Gorman would see these men through.

Davis called on those present to raise their glasses to the English divers and tenders and to their success in the great task before them. The diners stood as one, knocking chairs against walls and standing shoulder to shoulder. Someone started off on a chorus of 'For They Are Jolly Good Fellows' and the diners clattered cutlery in time with the ardour of the voices. When it was over, the singers reached across the linen to shake the hands of the eleven men, still seated with uncertain smiles on their faces. After more acclaim, the well-wishers sank back into their seats and a public-spirited benefactor came in from the saloon bar carrying a flagon of whisky, claiming loudly that it was all the more spirit with which to kick the Jap backside. (More cheers.)

WHEN THE states federated into the Commonwealth of Australia in 1901, the new Parliament was confronted with two industries dependent on coloured labour. One was the sugar-cane industry in Queensland, which imported Kanakas from the Pacific Islands; the other was the pearl-shelling industry, found across the top end of Australia from Western Australia to Queensland, which imported Asiatic workers from wherever the master pearlers could find them. A solution was readily found for the sugar-cane industry: the government placed a heavy duty on imported sugar and paid a bonus to those growers who certified they had produced the cane with 'white only labour'. The pearling industry was a knottier problem. Those running it claimed the work was too onerous for white men, and because that industry was conducted in a corner of the country no one went to, what did it matter? But it did matter. It mattered to the elected representatives of the people of Australia sitting in the Parliament of the Commonwealth. It offended the ideal of a White Australia. Festering like a sore, this was an industry being run with coloured labour on the very shores of the nation.

The White Australia Policy was the great unifying sentiment of national politics. All political parties supported it. No public figure of substance questioned it. The White Australia Policy went to the very foundation of what Australians thought of themselves and had been a motivating force for Federation. There was a national accord that Australians needed protection from the Asian hordes, the yellow peril, the threat from the north. No one who wanted to succeed in public life could doubt that an island state on Asia's doorstep needed to keep its drawbridge up.

This was a time when it was quite respectable to speak about inferior inheritance factors, racial purity and bad blood. Prejudice mossy with age was given a new shine by science. Schoolteachers taught eugenics, and simplified things by telling their students that mixing hereditary material was like mixing copper and tin to make bronze, and everyone knew that bronze was not a pure element. A crude form of social Darwinism helped out: the British race, through natural selection, was destined to rule – a glance at the pink areas marked on any atlas would demonstrate the truth of that. Political commentators sought to identify the servile nations of the world and academics debated whether Egyptians were civilised in the ordinary sense of the word. Phrenology was still a respectable discipline within the scientific community and professors from distinguished universities produced tables recording the dubious bumps on the skulls of the black races.

The 1907 census showed an Australian population of only 4.2 million, and in the vastness of Western Australia only 261,563 could be found. (The federal statistician did not count Aboriginal people – they were not fully included until 1971.) Editorial writers gained an immediate response by warning their readers that countries such as China, India and Japan increased their population each year by as many people as there were in the whole of Australia, adding that if an Asiatic force were to land at Port Darwin, it would be impossible for the Australian people, no matter how stoutly they fought, to protect a continent three times the size of Europe.

Trade unions shunned workers who were not white. Apart from old-fashioned racism, the fear was that Asians would work for a wage lower than a white man and his family could decently live on, and if you gave the bosses half a chance they would use imported labour to undercut conditions. Sir Henry Parkes, subsequently dubbed the Father of Federation, caught the essence of the common man's mood towards coloured immigration:

> We want no people here to form an inferior class – to form a class of hewers of wood and drawers of water for the rest, and these are the grounds in which I now, as at all other times, take my stand in dealing with this question. Unless you are prepared to permit these people to come amongst us . . . to intermarry with your children . . . to permit them to have the same rights and privileges as you possess to the full

measure of citizenship . . . then I say you are simply supporting them in coming here in order to establish a degraded class
in the country.[2]

The Minister of External Affairs explained the White Australia
Policy thus: 'No matter how high individual races may be either in
moral or physical standards – and we do not attempt to set ourselves
above other races in this matter – good results can never be attained
by the mixture of races disparate in blood and traditions.'[3]

These were the voices of moderate reason. There were other voices.
In Parliament, red-faced men exhorted each other to keep a white
Australia, a snow-white Australia, a pure and spotless Australia.
Public-spirited gentlemen set up anti-Chinese and Asiatic coolie
leagues, and roamed the streets armed with righteous indignation and
house bricks. The Anti-Chinese League claimed 20,000 members and
urged a total prohibition on Asiatic immigration and the segregation
of those already here. Popular journals including the *Bulletin*, the
Boomerang and the *Worker* put it plainly for the masses: the Chinese
were smokers of opium and they took white women into prostitution.
The Kanakas were lascivious, murdering savages and tainted with leprosy to boot. The Japs were devious, cunning and arrogant and, if
given the chance, would undersell and undercut the white workers.

Lurid cartoons showed the Chinese, the Kanakas, the Malays – or
indeed any race that was not white – as the propagator of syphilis,
typhoid, smallpox, cholera, and dysentery. Cross-hatched drawings
showed buxom white women gamely fighting off swarms of goofy
Chinese, armed to the teeth with knives and opium pipes. In 1910,
the *Bulletin* published a poem composed to mark the news that a
deranged white woman, married to a Chinese man, had suicided by
setting herself alight:

Chinaman's wife,
It was well you died.
Though poison, knife

Or river-tide
Give rest from shame,
Only by flame
Can such as you
Be purified.[4]

Public debate about White Australia, such as it was, was confined to details of implementation. The states had begun to pass restrictive legislation to curb coloured immigration from the 1850s onwards, but never in quite the same way. A hotchpotch of laws was passed over the next 50 years, full of enthusiastic prejudice, inconsistencies and anomalies. Some levied a poll tax of £10 for every Chinese landed, some imposed a dictation test, some forbade aliens from digging on goldfields, and Victoria forbade the passage of more than one Chinese for each 10 ton weight of the migrant ship.

Public perception was that these laws didn't work very well. It was impossible for one state to halt the flow. State borders were hundreds of miles long, and in the backblocks they were unmanned, unmarked and often unascertainable. Ships' captains would bring their human cargo into ports where the poll tax was not collected, or run them ashore on deserted beaches. The press warned of hundreds of Chinese jog-trotting from South Australia, where controls were lax, to the goldfields of Victoria and New South Wales, carrying their belongings suspended on poles.

There was a growing recognition that the proper administration of the White Australia Policy required a national approach, a commonwealth of the states with uniform laws to keep the coloureds out once and for all. A bill for the restriction of immigration was one of the first measures debated by the new Parliament in 1901.

The legislators looked for inspiration to South Africa, that great social laboratory in the conduct of racial relationships. By the *Natal Act of 1895*, an applicant for entry to that dominion had to write out an application in a European language, selected by the immigration authorities. In 1901 the Australian Parliament varied that model slightly and passed legislation prohibiting entry to those who failed to write out a dictation of 50 words in any European language. The requirement that the test be in a European language upset the Japanese, whose Consul wrote to the Australian Prime Minister protesting that:

> The Japanese belong to an empire whose standard of civilization is so much higher than that of kanakas, negroes, Pacific Islanders, Indians, or other Eastern peoples, that to refer to them in the same terms cannot but be regarded in the light of a reproach, which is hardly warranted by the fact of the shade of the national complexion.[5]

In an attempt to meet this complaint, the dictation test was altered to 50 words in any prescribed language, the intention being that when it suited the immigration officials, the test would be conducted in Japanese. The whole testing procedure was a matter for the officer's discretion. He might conduct it in French or Welsh, or even not at all. For those with white skins the test was rarely administered unless the immigrant at the gate was a political undesirable.

Not that the test was easy, even in English. One version in currency in 1908 read:

> Very many considerations lead to the conclusion that life began on sea, first as single cells, then as groups of cells held together by a secretion of mucilage, then as filament and tissues. For a very long time low-grade marine organisms are simply hollow cylinders, through which salt water streams.[6]

While the first government of the Commonwealth of Australia was busy erecting a racial barrier around its shores, the pearl-shelling industry remained exempt, and the passage of indentured workers (most of them from Japan) to the pearling grounds of Western Australia and Queensland continued unabated.

THE JAPANESE cemetery in Broome contains the bodies of more than 900 seamen, lined up in rows under slabs of red beach rock on which is carved the name, date of birth and friends of the deceased. Many more were lost at sea, or lost from memory, buried above the high-water mark on lonely beaches. The headstones record that half of those who died were in their twenties. Many came from the Wakayama Prefecture, a place of hills and mountains with little arable land and much poverty. Although Japan has a venerable tradition of naked *ama* divers seeking abalone, coral and bêche-de-mer in the chilly waters off its coast, this was not the source of the workforce for Australia. The influx of men from Wakayama had more to do with the Melbourne Cup. In 1890 several Japanese sailors were trying their hand at pearl-shell diving in the waters near Thursday Island in Queensland when they drew Carbine in the Tattersall's Melbourne Cup sweepstake. They won £22,500 and returned to build fine homes and buy up fishing boats and farming land.

From that time on, the villagers of the Wakayama Prefecture were convinced that the Australian pearling grounds were a place of untold wealth, and for the next half-century a steady stream of young men set off each year to Singapore and thence to Australia. A system of loans to finance their journeys was established. Villagers would cover a number of the men (so spreading the risk to take account of the inevitable deaths and crippling injuries) and advance amounts at the daunting rate of 27 per cent compound interest. Even as late as 1935, when a cyclone off Western Australia took the lives of 60 Japanese pearlers, seventeen of those were from a single village, Taji, in the Wakayama Prefecture. But for every fatality many more returned rich. To this day visitors to the villages of the Wakayama Prefecture note that some of the locals sprinkle their conversations with Australianisms like 'tucker', and it is the custom to put milk in tea and to prefer bread to rice.

The men from Wakayama paid dearly for their involvement in the pearl-shelling industry. As the shell in shallower water became depleted, the luggers moved into waters of 10 to 20 fathoms and a mysterious illness began to strike down the divers. As they were freed from their copper helmets at day's end, they complained to their tenders of strange aches in their arms and legs. Others were brought to the surface seemingly alert and free of pain, but during the evening meal they would suddenly collapse into a stupor and could not be woken for several hours. During the night divers would wake screaming with pain surging through their limbs. Sometimes the crew members dragging a diver to the surface were horrified to see the face glass of the helmet smeared with blood flowing from the diver's nose and ears. In 1889 the Inspector of Pearl Shell Fisheries wrote that several divers had died in depths of 20 to 25 fathoms. The first name recorded was that of a young Japanese man called Tanaka. He died of the bends on 26 August 1890 while on the schooner *Willie* off Ninety Mile Beach.

There was another mysterious killer both on the boats and among the population living in the Asiatic Quarter. It took almost as many lives as the bends. The limbs of the victims filled with fluid, their skin turned blue and breathing became laboured. Death occurred within hours. The disease was beri beri. At monthly meetings of the Broome health board it was the duty of the resident medical officer to report the number of cases and deaths since the last meeting. During 1910 he reported 199 cases of beri beri and 28 deaths; in 1911, 137 cases and 25 deaths; and in 1912, 153 cases and 19 deaths.

Beri beri hardly exists today and is confined to food faddists and alcoholics. It is a result of thiamine deficiency and it is easily cured by a proper diet, more particularly by eating unhusked cereal grains. Right up to World War I its cause was poorly understood, although increasingly health authorities suspected that a diet of polished rice was a likely culprit. However a competing view from the medical profession put its cause down to a contagion associated with cramped, moist living conditions. According to this theory, those with the disease needed to be kept isolated from others; the cure was rest and plenty of fresh air. It was seen as a particularly Asiatic disease, especially prevalent among the Japanese.

If beri beri was a problem for the town, it was deadly on the seas. The Commissioner of Public Health in Perth, Dr Hope, was convinced that the cause lay in the rations supplied to the crew. In this view he was influenced by a report that rampant beri beri among prisoners in the Hong Kong gaol had ceased once they were given rice with the husks retained. During 1911 and 1912 he advised the master pearlers that the crew aboard their luggers should be fed unpolished rice or a diet of peas and beans, especially soya beans. The master pearlers did nothing and in his annual report to Parliament in 1912 the commissioner wrote: 'It is regrettable that such callous indifference to their duties to their employees should be manifested. It is more remarkable that their sense of the material advantage to be gained by keeping the men in good health is as dulled as their moral sense.'[7]

The Pearlers' Association believed that such comments were unfair and protested in its annual report for 1913:

> Apart from the fact that high scientific opinion is divided on Dr Hope's theory that Beri Beri is due to the removal of the nutritious portions of the rice . . . your Committee considers Dr Hope's caustic remarks regarding master pearlers' neglect of duties unnecessarily severe. Both par-boiled rice and a ration of soya or other beans were included in the rations of many boats early last year, but, unfortunately, the crews manifested considerable opposition to their use and in many cases absolutely declined to accept such rations as being too unpalatable.

The Pearlers' Association favoured the views of Dr Blick, the district medical officer at the government hospital in Broome, over that of Dr Hope. Dr Blick warned that the disease was very infectious. He established three simple principles for its treatment which the Pearlers' Association circulated to its members. These were 'prompt medical treatment, strict segregation of patients, and careful disinfection of boats and clothing'.[8]

Dr Hope, convinced that the master pearlers were not going to follow his advice, gazetted a regulation prohibiting the sale of polished rice north of the 24th parallel of longitude. The Pearlers' Association, claiming that the regulation was quite impractical and an unwarranted interference in its members' affairs, activated its forceful lobbying skills and Dr Hope was told by the government to withdraw the new regulation. The deaths in Broome, and out on the boats, continued.

At the government hospital Dr Blick established an isolation ward for the treatment of beri beri. The whites of the town congratulated themselves on having some special racially-based immunity. (It was their diet, of course.) Those in the Asiatic Quarter seemed especially vulnerable, which the district medical officer put down to the crowded, unsanitary medical conditions.

In 1912 there were about 300 to 400 people living permanently in the Asiatic Quarter, most of them Chinese and Japanese. Facing discrimination and few employment opportunities in the rest of Australia, they had gravitated to Broome where they established a community to cater for the thousands of Asiatic sailors working on the pearling fleets. They had set up their own social clubs and temples. They ran stores, restaurants, boarding houses, sly groggeries and gambling dens – all designed to harvest as much as possible when the sailors came in from the sea.

They were called 'free Asiatics' in official publications, an odd name considering how many freedoms were denied them. These were people who had come to Australia prior to Federation in 1900 and, under various immigration restriction statutes of state and federal parliaments, were allowed to remain as a gesture of toleration. But they could never hope to become Australian citizens, they had no voting rights, they were prohibited from working in trades, forbidden from owning factories or ships and denied the old-age pension. Their numbers were declining, as Senator Staniforth Smith explained in a pamphlet he published on the West Australian pearl-shelling industry in 1903: 'The number in 1897 was probably double what it is now, as any that leave can only return under contract to the pearlers, and the sooner these remainder depart from our shores the better.'⁹

In 1900 police estimated there were more than 30 women working in the Japanese boarding-house brothels of Broome. These women, barely in their teens, mostly illiterate and the daughters of the rural poor, had been brought to Australia in the 1890s, ostensibly to work in laundries. The West Australian *Immigration Restriction Act of 1897* denied further entry, but allowed those already in the state to remain. One admirer wrote: 'The Jap women (very numerous in Westralia) totally eclipse their white competitors. They are particularly clean, modest, sober, exceedingly polite, don't thieve, and look upon their calling in a purely commercial sense. No white women can compete against those brown dots of humanity . . . '¹⁰ By 1912, the women were no longer young and the men from the luggers complained of making love to women the age of their mothers. They were seldom seen out in the streets, living as virtual prisoners in the boarding houses of the Asiatic Quarter. Their years of profitable work were drawing to a close and it was difficult to know what lay ahead for them. The most likely outcome of their return to Japan would have been shame and starvation.

The focus of the Japanese community was the Japanese Club, housed in one of the largest buildings in town, an impressive structure of whitewashed corrugated iron with two pronounced wind scoops in the roof, facing towards the sea. A high-pitched porch, held up by blackbutt beams, conferred a Japanese character on the entrance. The club was part welfare organisation, part trade union and part secret society. Its president for many years was Mr Imato Joe, and on the committee was Mr Yaksukichi Murakami. Both were storekeepers in the Asiatic Quarter, spoke excellent English and had lived in Broome since the turn of the century. From time to time the club made representations to the Pearlers' Association about increased wages and better conditions for the crews on the luggers, and threatened strike action, but these matters were usually settled without anyone withdrawing their labour and by the master pearlers giving ground.

In 1908 the members of the Japanese Club, who evidently had no great faith in Western medicine, or at least the variety that was practised by the government hospital, decided to raise funds for a hospital of their own. They executed their plans in secrecy and by 1909 enough money had been collected to guarantee a salary for a Japanese doctor and to buy him a fine residence, with consulting and dispensing rooms next door. By the time the white citizens knew what was happening, renovations on a house in the English Quarter, until recently occupied by the Dobson family, were going ahead and approval had been given for the doctor to enter Australia.

There was outrage among the white community. How had this doctor obtained an entry permit when all approvals for foreign indentured workers had to go through the sub-collector of customs and the harbour master? When bailed up by angry citizens, these two officials said they knew nothing of the matter. The mayor called a meeting of council which passed a resolution calling on the government to stop any Asiatic doctors entering the state. They also circulated a protest petition throughout the town. The executive of the Pearlers' Association organised a petition of its own. Both petitions were presented to the Premier, who promised to pass them on to the Prime Minister. By an uncomfortable coincidence, Mr T. Brown of the Labor Party was in town holding public meetings for a forthcoming election. Question time became diverted into a protest about the Japanese doctor. Men asked how a Labor government could allow such a thing to happen. 'Block him,' was a cry from the meeting.[11] Mr Brown took it upon himself to immediately wire the government asking for an explanation.

When the explanation emerged, it didn't help to calm things down in the slightest. The Japanese Club had organised it all behind the backs of the Broome community. The club had forwarded its request for an entry permit through the Japanese Consul in Sydney, who had approached the Department of Foreign Affairs directly. The department secretary, Atlee Hunt, had seen fit to hear the consul and listen to complaints that Dr Blick at the government hospital gave preference to the white population and was frequently unavailable to the Japanese sailors. It was also difficult for them to explain what the problem was to someone who did not speak their language. Hunt had consulted no one and had approved the permit while Minister Batchelor was visiting Papua.

The white community maintained that their objections to a Japanese doctor were substantial and reasonable, if only the authorities in Melbourne could be made to understand the situation in Broome. If the Japanese doctor took over the coloured patients, as presumably was intended, it would hardly be economic for the white doctor to continue. In the one-doctor town that would result, could it be expected that the whites would consult with an Asiatic doctor? What man's wife would allow herself to be examined by a Japanese? The master pearlers raised the point that a malingering sailor could obtain a medical certificate from the Japanese doctor. Surely this wouldn't be accepted by the magistrate? The local member of Parliament, Arthur Male, told the State Legislature that Chinese and Afghans would want their own doctors next. Before long, they'd be asking for Asian lawyers. There were jeers in the House. Where would it all end?

The master pearlers professed to be at a loss as to the reasons behind the plan for a Japanese doctor. After all, as part of the crews' indentures, they were entitled to free medical treatment from Dr Blick, yet seemingly the Japanese were prepared to turn their back on this and pay for their own doctor. And the pearlers were quite sure that the reputed £300 gathered to guarantee the doctor's wages had come from pearls stolen from them.

Despite the protests, the Federal Government did not withdraw Dr Suzuki's permit to enter, and in January 1910 he and his wife stepped onto the Broome jetty to be greeted with great formality and much bowing by a large assembly of Japanese sailors and shop-keepers. The couple were escorted onto the train to alight in front of the whitewashed consulting and dispensing rooms in Napier Terrace. Later Dr Suzuki presented his credentials to the state health department in Perth, which, after some hesitation, could find no reason to block his registration. The doctor commenced administering to out-patients from the start of the pearling season in 1910.

The competition, such as it was, came from the government hos-pital, located a few streets away. It was well recognised that no one would willingly become a patient of the government hospital and the locals judged that the best medical dictum was to stay healthy. The hospital was no more than a large house, under attack from white ants and sadly in need of paint. The isolation ward for measles and leprosy was beneath a palm tree in the grounds, there was no women's ward, and overflow patients were accommodated on the verandah, where the orderlies burnt coir rope to ward off the mosquitoes. Surgical pro-cedures were carried out by the light of hurricane lamps – this in a town where the billiard tables of the town's hotels were lit with acety-lene lamps, and most of the master pearlers ran electric lights.

Dr Blick, the town's medical practitioner, had been practising in Broome since 1900. In fact it was the only place he had practised medicine. Still in his twenties when he arrived from England, Dr Blick soon established himself as a hard-drinking, sporting man. He was president of the Broome Rifle Club and the Turf Club, a crick-eter, a tennis player, an archer and a horseman. Despite his busy life, he started investing in pearl-shelling, and Blick & Co. owned a schooner and four luggers. In 1908 he sold up his interest and announced he was going for a sojourn to the home country, but life had never been so good as it was in Broome, and he returned in early 1911, followed by his wife some months later. The townsfolk quickly noticed that he was a changed man, though. He was no longer well, spent periods confined to his bed, and was not always available to see them.

Meanwhile a few of the more flexible among the white community, disenchanted by the treatment received from Dr Blick, consulted Dr Suzuki. They would find, seated behind a wooden desk in his freshly painted rooms, a small neat man with a tiny moustache and an excellent command of English. Because he lived next door to the consulting rooms, he made himself available at all hours, even being prepared to visit patients in their homes and beyond, seemingly at any time of the day or night.

Dr Suzuki quickly attuned himself to the power structure of the town. He had only been in Broome a few weeks when he was visited by a Japanese sailor who wanted him to sign a certificate to say that he was too ill to work. This was a case that had already been to court in a preliminary skirmish. The man had been charged with malingering under the Merchant Shipping Act and a medical certificate had been obtained from Dr Blick to say that he was fit to work. No doubt Dr Suzuki thought long about the issue – the reality was that it was most unlikely that the resident magistrate, Major Wood, would prefer a Japanese doctor's opinion over that of a white doctor, and his involvement would surely excite the wrath of the master pearlers. Dr Suzuki politely declined to sign the certificate, and the sailor went back paperless to face the justice of Major Wood.

Within just a few months of his arrival, Dr Suzuki had a thriving practice which catered for people of all colours and creeds, suffering from the usual assemblage of medical problems from broken bones and stab wounds to runny noses and prickly heat. By August 1910 Dr Suzuki was one of the speakers at a dinner held in the Literary Institute to farewell the retiring mayor and mayoress, Mr and Mrs Archie Male, who were about to depart on an extended tour of the English counties. It was now forgotten that it was Mayor Male who had led the charge to block the doctor's appointment. Dr Suzuki spoke on behalf of the Japanese and Chinese business people and presented the couple with a purse of gold sovereigns. He then thanked

Mr Male for the manner in which he had looked after their interests during his term as mayor, and hoped that when he returned he would be prepared to carry on the duties from which he had been temporarily relieved. Dr Suzuki's speech was roundly cheered.

Dr Suzuki had reason to regret that Mr Male was no longer the mayor. The council, now led by Mr Hugh Norman, was in no mood to allow him to extend his consulting rooms into a full-blown hospital. The council refused the building application in September 1910, and when they could find no reason to refuse an amended application, ruled that the building could go ahead and be used to treat day patients, but it could not be used as a hospital until it had been considered by the health board.

When the health board met, it was discovered that no bylaws had been created about the conditions applicable for a private hospital, thereby giving an excuse for the application to be placed in abeyance until the bylaws were written. That took until May 1911, when the application was again adjourned by the board, this time pending a report from the state medical officer. What happened next is unclear, but presumably the medical officer's report was favourable because by the middle of 1911 the Japanese hospital was up and running. When the Japanese Club suggested to the master pearlers that a levy of £5 per boat be paid to the Japanese hospital instead of to Dr Blick for treatment of crew, many agreed, reckoning that where the money went made no difference to them.

Within months of the Japanese hospital opening Dr Suzuki had more patients than he could handle and he urgently required nursing assistance. He realised that in a frontier town like Broome, competent nurses would be difficult to obtain. The solution came from an unlikely source.

Several years earlier, the nuns of St John of God, led by Mother Antonio O'Brien, had begun to work at the Catholic Aboriginal mission at Beagle Bay, about a hundred miles to the north, and in 1908 they opened a little school in Broome itself. At first the school catered for the Catholics of the town – children of Irish pearlers, Filipino divers and Italian barmaids – but as its reputation grew, the children of the free Asiatics and white storekeepers attended as well. Despite the heat, the nuns taught in a pleated habit of heavy cloth and a stiffly starched cap and white collar. They were desperately poor, and distance seemed to mean they were largely forgotten by the Church. After a day of teaching some of the nuns, after just an hour's rest, would start a shift in the government hospital.

In 1909 one of the heroines of the story of Broome made her brief appearance. Sister Mary Immaculate Leahy, a 29-year-old nurse from Craddockstown, Co. Kilkenny, arrived during the hottest time of the year. She had understood that she was leaving nursing behind to be a schoolteacher. That was to be her new vocation and God's will, at least until the day Mother Antonio took her on a detour across town to the Japanese hospital to discuss something with Dr Suzuki. The doctor was in a desperate situation. During the week luggers had come into harbour one after another, with crippled divers moaning in unbearable pain. They were time-consuming and heavy patients, some still in their teens, far away from home, paralysed and fright-ened – some dying, some recovering, some never to recover full use of their limbs. He had no staff to assist. When Dr Suzuki next looked around, Sister Mary was attending to the needs of one of the immo-bilised men. After settling him, she moved onto the next one, and then worked ceaselessly through the night until the morning. She slept briefly and came back the next day, and the next. She was never to leave.

Sister Mary was a charismatic, pretty woman, cheerful, and ever sympathetic. The patients began to teach her Japanese. When an Asian man carrying smallpox was taken off a steamer from Singapore, because the quarantine station had been knocked over in the big blow of 1910, the police erected a tent on the beach and posted guards while Sister Mary nursed the patient. Meals were brought across from the Continental Hotel, and nuns visiting her from the convent had to call out to her from behind a line that the police had drawn in the sand. The patient recovered and Sister Mary began to be spoken of in tones of respect and reverence on the boats out at sea.

In January 1912, weakened by long hours of work, she contracted influenza and pneumonia, and died shortly after. The Japanese sailors erected a Celtic cross in her memory at the Broome cemetery. It is there to this day, one of the most elaborate stones in the graveyard. Other Catholic nuns took over from Sister Mary Immaculate Leahy and continued to nurse in the Japanese hospital.

While the reputation of the Japanese hospital increased over the months, the government hospital was experiencing difficulties maintaining its services. Dr Blick's health declined and frequently he was unable to attend to his duties. He was suffering from some vague stomach problem and seemed incapable of curing himself. When he did rise from his sick bed, he saw patients who looked healthier than he did. Matron James, who was now in charge of the hospital, could not cope. The *Nor'-West Echo*, after commenting on Dr Blick's absence, said:

> For months past the hospital, the matron, and the patients have been run by two domineering, lordly imperious and lazy orderlies, who took little notice of the matron's orders and less of the patients' needs; in fact if the complaints of patients are to be believed, the treatment meted out has been calculated to assist death rather than induce recovery. The only saving feature about the whole question has been the existence of Dr Suzuki's private hospital, where residents are sure of skilful medical attention and competent nursing. Look at the beri beri ward at the Government hospital, where the Government raised the fees from 2s 6d to 6s per day! These patients could have received far better attention if they were treated in a foreshore camp with a binghi in attendance.[12]

5 The Port of Pearling Luggers

Here was gathered together from all quarters of the earth the most heterogeneous collection of nations, creeds, languages, and races I ever saw, a veritable ethnological museum. Here was the morose looking, straight-haired Malays jostling the placid brachycephalic Chinese, the sturdy little Jap and the laughing South Sea Islander cheek by jowl with the treacherous and ostentatious brown man from Manila; while into this 'pot pourri' of humanity was stirred Cingalese, 'Klings', niggers, Javanese, Dyaks, aborigines, Koepang boys, Brazilians . . .

Senator Staniforth Smith, in describing the population of Broome's Asiatic Quarter in 1902 [1]

FROM DECEMBER TO MARCH each year, the monsoons bring unsettled weather to the coast of the northwest of Australia. During these months storms can turn the skies from cornflower blue to deepest black in a few hours, and winds spring up to whip the seas into a fury of sufficient force to easily overwhelm a lugger. Cyclones, called willy-willys or cockeyed bobs by the seamen who feared them most, had a history of sweeping through the pearling fleet. In 1887 a cyclone sank eighteen luggers off Ninety Mile Beach, and 140 men drowned. In April 1908 a terrific cyclone struck Lagrange Bay, concentrating its full force in the vicinity of Cape Bossut and sinking several luggers and drowning 50 crew. This was followed by another in December the same year, when the schooner *Kelender Bux*, the pride of Mark Rubin's fleet, was sunk along with 38 luggers.

In 1908 the Pearlers' Association issued a warning to lugger crews:

Hurricanes

Your Committee desires to draw your attention to the following observations that would, in their opinion, considerably reduce the disastrous effects of these hurricanes, if attended to in time:

(1) To carry on no pearling operations between the 1st December and the 30th April, except in those waters from which shelter can be easily reached.

(2) To carefully note the barometer night and morning during these months, as it is an unfailing guide to the weather in the tropics.

(3) The barometer has two tides in the tropics, just the same as the ordinary water tides. It rises about 1-10th from 4 a.m. to 10 a.m.; falls about the same from 10 a.m. to 4 p.m.; rises again from 4 p.m. to 10 p.m.; to fall again about the same from 10 p.m. to 4 a.m. High water by the barometer, 10 a.m. and 10 p.m. Low water by barometer, 4 a.m. and 4 p.m. Any variation from the above pearlers should view with the greatest care.

The normal summer reading of the barometer is 29.90. A fall in the barometer of say 2-10ths below normal should always be taken as a danger signal, and this more especially if the wind is in the east. During the summer months –

December to April inclusive – an easterly wind and a falling barometer is a sure indicator of abnormal conditions in the weather, and pearlers should at once seek shelter.

The one great lesson of the last two 'blows', however, has been not to work away from the place from whence shelter can be easily obtained, and, secondly, not to seek the shelter of an open beach because the wind is in the east.

Owing to Broome's position, the centres of these dreaded hurricanes have invariably passed to the westward, and this means that as the storm progresses the change of the wind will be from the east to north-east to north to north-west to west. This places luggers seeking shelter of an open beach (merely because the wind is east) in a position of grave danger, and has undoubtedly been the cause of the great losses the industry has suffered during the past year.[2]

Early in the summer of 1910 a spiralling cyclone curled in from the desert east of Broome and on through the township. It was the worst cyclone the town had experienced. An observer wrote:

Steady rain set in on Friday and lasted all day, but during the night the wind increased in force, and on Saturday morning had reached hurricane force, accompanied by very heavy rain . . . All the morning the storm kept increasing in fury. About 11 o'clock the more flimsy structures commenced to give way, and the wind increasing in force every few minutes, by 1.30 o'clock it became so serious that people were fleeing in all directions seeking shelter from falling roofs and buildings. Sheets of iron were driven before the wind like sheets of paper; and impeded by the blinding sand from the surrounding hills, the women and children, passing from one shelter to another were indeed in a precarious position. By 2 o'clock the storm was at its height, and the destruction of the town commenced with a vengeance. Roofs were lifted and carried hundreds of yards away, buildings fell in or were blown down, trees were uprooted or broken off; telephone poles were either snapped like carrots or were bent like wax matches, telegraph poles were blown over, flagstaffs and signboards were toppled over in quick succession, and today pretty Broome presents a scene of desolation.[3]

On that day the pearling fleet which had been caught in mountainous seas and torrential rain for two days made a run for port, not realising that the storm was centred in Broome itself. The fleet had just rounded Entrance Point when the cyclone swung across its path. Twenty-six boats were lost and 40 crew members died. Soon after, the Pearlers' Association committee made an addendum to its earlier notice: 'Since the above was written, Broome was visited by a severe "blow" on November 19th, 1910, proving the necessity of extending the application of the above-set-out precautions to the month of November.'[4]

Those foolhardy and greedy enough to ignore the warnings and venture outside during the cyclone season hugged the shore, anxiously keeping a lookout for clouds piling in the north, ready to scurry to safety in a tidal creek or a mangrove-shrouded bay. But even on a calm day, the water was often discoloured and shell was difficult for divers to see, so most accepted that the search for shell between late November to early March was not worth the risk.

So was born the lay-up – those tumultuous months when the weather turned humid, it was stinking hot, rain bucketed down every day and 300 luggers came to town. The boats were hauled into bays and sandbagged into an upright position where they rose and sank back into the mud twice each day with the running of the tide. The luggers stretched from the Customs House past the Star Hotel, either side of Streeter's jetty and around to Morgan's camp. And still they came, so the latecomers sailed around to Barred Creek, Normans Creek and Lagrange Bay to haul their boats up onto the mangrove banks. The crews were signed off, took their pay and fell into a wild debauch in the brothels, gambling joints, opium dens and sly grog shanties of Japtown. And between exhaustion and dawn, the men slept where they could – on board the luggers, in sheds along the foreshore, on the beach, or at one of the boarding houses and brothels tucked in around John Chi Lane. They were mostly young men, escaping hopeless, grinding poverty and all with the dream of returning home rich.

But Broome was no melting pot; there was a strict divide between the races. There was a hierarchy, a natural order determined by skin colour, and regulated by law. In the white quarter, over a rise in the sandhills out of view of the ocean and surrounded by gardens of tropical flowers, were the rulers of Broome – the master pearlers. They lived in large bungalows enclosed by wide verandahs which looked out across an expanse of green and on to the bungalows of their neighbours. Anyone who owned a lugger called himself a master pearler; there were no apprentice pearlers. Few had served at sea. Some were ex-policemen who had arrested ne'er-do-wells holding a pearl worth two years of a policeman's salary, ex-bank clerks amazed at the amount of money passing through their customers' accounts, publicans turning black money into green (for the Government of Western Australia had imposed an income tax in 1907), or pastoralists from the dry interior who detected ironic compensation in that the cyclones which sank their luggers also brought drenching rains to their pastures.

They collectively spoke of themselves as 'shellers', but to each other they were captains – Captain Biddles, Captain Richardson, the Captains Pigott (S.C. and S.P.), Captain Tilly, Captain Talboys, the Captains Gregory (A.C. and F.C.), Captain Hunter, and so on. There were so many captains, it was said that if you pitched a stone down Carnarvon Street on a Saturday morning, you were bound to hit at least one captain. Not that all captains were equal. While some had a dozen luggers out sailing the waters and were so busy in the sheds they had no time to go to sea, others were mere one-boat admirals. Some captains had formed themselves into companies that had many luggers and several schooners on their books, hauling up money in baskets. The richest, Mark Rubin, who never bothered about calling himself a captain, was the owner of more than 30 luggers and five schooners. He had become so wealthy that he was rarely seen in Broome. Instead he spent his time trading pearls on the London Exchange, leaving the running of his business to his manager, Abraham Davis, who lived in the biggest house in town.

Each morning, excluding the Sabbath, the shellers would leave the cool interiors of their bungalows in what was quaintly referred to as the English part of town and cycle, or take a buggy, to the packing sheds on the foreshore to supervise the business of shelling. There was something of a master pearlers' outfit which they adopted: white buckskin shoes, starched white trousers, a cream-coloured coat with detachable shell buttons, a celluloid collar held in place by gold studs, a coloured necktie, a pith helmet atop and a jauntily held Malacca cane. After a busy morning in the sheds, it was back home for the midday meal and a short siesta. Such was the humidity and dust of Broome that after the men emerged from their nap, servants had to have ready a fresh rig-out and nicely blancoed shoes for the afternoon's endeavours.

Although it was the white population that ran Broome, there were whites and there were whites. Much of the labouring work was done by dark-skinned people, but there were white labourers on the wharves and white guards in the prison, and those who ran plumbing businesses or worked in the abattoirs or for the council were also white. They lived on the outskirts of town, used upturned beer bottles for borders around their gardens, and sent their children to the local school run by the nuns.

Broome was like a plantation society, with the same rules as might be found in Burma or Borneo. Although discreet dalliances with coloured women might be overlooked, those few white men, on the skids, publicly fornicating with the Aborigines were shunned. It was social death to live in the Asiatic Quarter. Barmaids would not be welcomed at the lawn tennis club, but the newly appointed bank managers would be sent a formal invitation and the resident magistrate would neglect to join and be fawned over when he dropped in to have a hit. The racecourse fenced the whites into their special enclosure and naturally the rifle club was, for security reasons, restricted to Britishers. Most of the residents in the English Quarter kept a rifle handy against real and imaginary incursions by the Aboriginal people or the Asiatics. Apart from those occasions when the bishop was in town, the top dog was Major Wood RM, who dispensed justice assisted by his honorary justices in the police court, Monday through Friday, unless the business of the law was completed sooner.

A few of the wives of the master pearlers lived in the town all year round, but most departed during the humidity of the wet season, catching the steamer down south and settling children into boarding schools in Perth or even further away, thousands of miles distant, in Adelaide or Melbourne. The men left behind had their diversions. It was a manly, clubby life. The Continental Hotel and the Star held billiard competitions, the Star boasting two full-sized Alcock tables lit with acetylene lamps, and the Central had a Tattersall's licence. The Continental Hotel ran an outdoor Picturedome while the Roebuck Hotel screened the Empire Pictures at the Roebuck Stadium out the back of the hotel. There was a cricket club, a football club (of the Australian rules variety), a Glee Club (that is, a singing group), a literary debating society, a town band, an amateur dramatic society and a regatta club. The cricket club barely had the numbers for two sides and to create variety in the contests, the secretary jumbled up the players to form teams such as Singles vs Married, Stores & Banks vs the Rest, the Continental Hotel vs the World, Veterans vs Juniors, and Men Using Broomsticks vs the Ladies.

By the middle of each year the weather was settled and the worst of the humidity had gone. It was a climate tolerable enough for wives and children to steam up the coast to be with their husbands. And it was a climate tolerable enough for a man to be talked into dressing up like a penguin to prance around the Institute. For in July the ball season commenced in Broome.

Balls there were aplenty, held on Saturday nights in quick

succession – the Anglican Ball, with the same jolly crowd switching allegiances to be at the Catholic Ball on the following Saturday. The week after it was the Masonic Ball. Then the Fancy Dress Ball, prompting much preparation as rivals, vying for prizes, searched for a fair-haired woman to complete the Viking set, and a man with chaps to appear in the Buffalo Bill and the Indians set. Then it was the Cinderellas Dance for the hopeful, the Lady Mayoress' Ball for the aspiring and the Race Club Ball with card tables here and there so that those inclined could play a hand or two between items in the program, all with claret cup and punch for the ladies, and whisky and brandy for the gentlemen, served by brown men in white tunics.

The *Broome Chronicle* carried an extensive report of the Bachelors Ball of July 1909:

> The ball . . . proved quite a social function of the season. Inside the hall were flag and festoon decorations tastefully displayed; the floor was in excellent trim for those who desired to whirl away the happy moments, the verandah, hung with variegated Chinese lanterns from end to end . . . Captain Gregory received the guests at the main portico, and the chaperones (Mrs. Wood, Mrs. Cooper, Mrs. Grey, and Mrs. James), carried out their light duties with commanding effect. At midnight the supper tables were surrounded, and the space on the wide back verandah was taxed to its utmost. The tables were laid out in a most artistic manner, and reflected the highest credit of the caterer (Miss Wilson) for the ingenuity in the art of table decorations. Apart from this . . . the taste shown in the assortment and preparation of the viands was worthy of all praise when it is considered the difficulties here experienced in such an undertaking; and the choicest assortment of fruits, which had that day arrived, being specially ordered from south, was further evidence of the pride shown in placing before the bachelors of Broome and their guests such a sumptuous repast. The orchestral music, under the direction of Mr. Harper, was bright and tuneful, and added considerably to the pleasure of the evening.[5]

The article went on to describe the ladies' apparel, the married women bearing the initials of their husbands, and appearing in order of social precedence. The list commenced with the wife of the resident magistrate ('cream minon, trimmed with pale pink, blue ribbon, lace bertha), descending through the names of the wives of master pearlers, lawyers, publicans, bank officers, shopkeepers and council workers until, near the bottom, poor Mrs Beaumont, whose husband didn't seem to have any initials, was put down as: 'Mrs Beaumont, wedding dress'.

Women who could afford it ordered their finery from London or Paris. No woman of quality could possibly be seen in the same dress twice in the one season and there was so much on besides balls: bridge parties, dinner parties, quadrille assemblies, musical evenings, amateur dramatics and small-town adulteries – all requiring a change of outfit. And no woman of quality could appear wearing a working-class suntan so when out walking, accompanied by small boys in sailor suits and girls under lace-trimmed bonnets, they carried parasols and wore gloves. Women dressed in flowing skirts and broad-brimmed hats met men in cream suits and sola topis on the croquet lawns. Visiting cards were in use, and it was thought important to dress for dinner, lest standards should be seen to slip.

In January each year the master pearlers' attention was fixed on the Heinke Challenge Cup, a piece of silverware to the value of £130 awarded to the fastest working lugger sailing twice around the bay. The committee spent hours on the rules. No special gear could be used, the sails had to have been on the lugger for the past six months, no fins or special keels were allowed, the hatches and bulkheads had to be sealed, and no ballast or water could be shifted during the race.

Following the race, a program of athletics and novelties was organised by the committee. Events were classified into European, Binghi (Aboriginal) and Asiatic sections. The divers' boot race, the maidens' race, the greasy pole and throwing the cricket ball attracted large numbers of participants and spectators. The Indigenous people were not forgotten as this disparaging report from the *Broome Chronicle* about the festivities in 1909 shows:

> Binghi swimming races, dinghy races and greasy pole caused much fun, the natives not being able to master the knack of walking a well greased ships spar extended about 12 feet horizontally from the jetty, and about 8 feet from the water, and the many funny situations as the native's feet slipped and he would tumble into the water in every conceivable attitude caused much merriment.

The report added: 'Asiatics do not usually take to our style of sport, consequently there were no entries in the events provided for them.'[6]

THE WEST Australian Pearlers' Association, to give it its full name, was the association for the master pearlers. It was not a united organisation and there were continual tensions between the big operators who plotted the course of the association behind latticed verandahs, and the one-boat captains who sailed luggers mortgaged under lofty rates of interest.

The Pigott brothers were the power behind the Pearlers' Association. Sydney Pigott was its president and had been instrumental in setting up the association in 1901. The association had had only one secretary since its formation, and that was Sydney's younger brother Stanley. Stanley Pigott was acknowledged as a secretary of terrifying persistence. Night after night he would tap away at his Remington, writing to newspaper editors, ministers of state, the local council and men of perceived influence all over Australia. He wrote about the lack of facilities for cargo at the Port of Broome, the deplorable state of the government hospital, the inefficiency of the mail and telegraph services, the orderly marketing of mother-of-pearl, and the impossibility of introducing white labour to the industry. Most frequently of all he wrote to Atlee Hunt, the permanent secretary of the Department of External Affairs, located in Melbourne pending creation of a federal capital.

Stanley would make three strikes through the carbon: one for his files and one for each of the local federal and state members of Parliament. In this correspondence, one topic dominated above all others: government interference, and most particularly government attempts to stop the industry using coloured labour. Hunt became the personification of the enemy. A few pearlers had met him on visits to Melbourne and reported him to be a cold fish. Hunt never visited Broome but, as ministers came and went over the years, it was his signature which appeared at the bottom of letters and telegrams. And, as Stanley Pigott pointed out to him times beyond number, what unreasonable, wrong-headed, ill-informed communications they were.

Hunt didn't even have a proper representative in Broome. His man on the spot was the sub-collector of customs, Mr H.W. Huggins. He was a revenue man, with the added responsibility of trying to keep track of the whereabouts of the indentured workers up and down the coast and making sure there was no infringement of the White Australia Policy. The master pearlers regarded Huggins and his men with disdain. They might walk up and down the jetty in their blue uniforms, putting on airs and graces, but the pearlers knew they were just jumped-up clerks who knew nothing about real people trying to make a living, and even less about the sea and shelling.

At the bottom of the pile of Broome's society were the original inhabitants. By the turn of the century the Aborigines were a broken people. Decimated by disease and pushed from much of their lands, the Aborigines began to drift into the town, living an aimless existence on the fringes and getting by as domestic servants or on the scrounge, mission charity, prostitution and petty theft. The town

Aborigines were called Binghis by the whites. No one knew where the name came from. It bore no relationship to their tribal name of Jukun, nor was it a title of knockabout affection for a defeated savage – it was a term halfway between pity and contempt.

The presence of the Aboriginal people in town was a constant topic of complaint by the whites, and the situation never seemed to change. In October 1910 an editorial in the *Broome Chronicle* protested about:

> the number of indigent lazy natives that are allowed to roam about at their own sweet will, and do more to entice the industrious native from his quarters than any other cause. How often do we see a native in employment surrounded by a mob of his fellow countrymen, and when his meal is served out to him he will share alike with those who are his guests, not that day only, but for many days, and in the end the indentured native and his gin are persuaded to 'walk about' with what object is best known . . . Some little while back a native was sent to gaol as a vagrant, and there does not seem to be any valid reason why this could not be further tried, and then sent out of town absolutely, back to the sheep and cattle stations . . . If some firm and repeated action was taken in this connection, the country natives would soon regard Broome with a dread . . . [7]

Employment for the Aborigines, if it could be had, was limited to the menial and poorly paid. The resident magistrate regularly fined white men for employing Aborigines without a permit (the going rate was £5), and lectured them about their responsibility as employers for the good behaviour of the people camped around their premises. There were restrictions on the work an Aborigine could be given: in 1910 the state medical officer ruled that Aborigines should not handle dressed meat (even within special canvas bags), and local dairies ran advertisements assuring their customers that no natives worked in their establishments.

It was generally held to be undesirable to reward Aborigines for their labour with money. This view received support from the resident magistrate, Major Wood, who in 1909 commented on a case before him in which three men had been charged with being drunk and disorderly: 'They might as well give them drink as give them money, for when in possession of money it was an easy matter for them to obtain drink.'[8] He said that in future, a stipulation would be made when signing Aborigines on that no money would be given to them directly; if a master felt it desirable that his natives be paid, the money could be put in a savings bank.

The resident magistrate had the power to impose such conditions because he doubled as the local agent for the Protector. He also had the power to expel Aboriginal people from Broome. In one case a man called Yaram, described as 'an ex-missionary abo', was employed by Joseph Bush, a wine and spirit merchant, to work as a general hand around his business. Yaram was subsequently arrested for creating a disturbance and violently resisting arrest. The *Nor'-West Echo* reported:

> The whole neighbourhood heard the row, in which an abo. made free use of a bottle on police and civilians. The nigger freely exercised his right to cross examination in court, and put several pertinent questions. Sentenced to three months, and on his release to be ordered out of town, the Bench advised his employer not to employ niggers about his licensed premises.[9]

The resident magistrate generally took a broad brush to things, and in a case in 1909, he said he concurred with the view that Pacific Islanders and the Binghis 'should be treated as children'. Islanders might work well, but they 'should not have any more latitude than the natives'.[10] Exasperated by the failure of the whites to keep their Aboriginal servants under control, he announced in 1910 that he was 'contemplating proclaiming a native area so as to concentrate the natives and thereby have them more under control'.[11]

Laws forbade Aborigines from drinking alcohol, and white men and Asiatics from supplying them with it, but policing such laws was impossible and largely confined to arresting the most blatant of the drunks. The courts imposed fines which the Aborigines could never hope to meet, but rather than going to gaol, their employers, anxious to avoid the loss of their domestic servants, usually paid up. This is illustrated by a report in the *Nor'-West Echo* in 1912:

'Civilized' Natives

Drink, one of the whiteman's influential means of 'civilizing' niggers, was responsible for a devil of a row amongst the local binghis on Sunday last, spears, woomeras, killies, and other implements of warfare being effectually used. Nine of them were hauled before the beak on Monday, presenting a gory appearance. A gin was cautioned, and eight bucks, working for the following residents, were each fined, £1 or 14 days: Haines (2), J.F. MacDonald, Clarke Hall, Kennedy, Dyson, James & Pigott, Rev. Houston. All fines were paid excepting the last named, Rev. Houston preferring to see his nigger do time. Two Malays found at the camp during the fight were fined £1 and £2.

Ahmat Bin Ahmat was fined £20 or five weeks for supplying natives with grog; he's taking it out.

Its about time the Chief Protector, Mr Gale, came to Broome and did something to justify his receipt of his handsome salary.[12]

Control of the Aboriginal population was a continuing preoccupation of the Broome police court. Any danger of an Aboriginal uprising had passed years ago; now the concern was with sneak entry into the houses of white folk. Sentences for offences which threatened the security of white women were harsh. In one case:

Tommy, an aboriginal, was charged with being illegally on premises. It appears that one of Mrs. Hilliard's daughters was awakened by someone striking matches, and the accused was found upstairs on the back verandah. He was asked what he was doing there, and said he was looking for a native woman named Jinny. The R.M. said it was a serious matter to be found in a white man's house at night time, and but for the fact that he was looking for a native woman he would have dealt severely with him. He would have to go to gaol for one month.[13]

Eventually it was ruled that Aborigines could not remain in the town at night. At sunset it was the duty of Corporal Lamb and his constables to herd the Binghis along the streets of Broome to a camp of corrugated-iron humpies over the sandhills. Following representations from those concerned about unwashed dishes and other chores than hadn't been done, the Protector relaxed the rules a little – in a move described as a privilege, domestic servants were allowed to remain in the town provided that their employers accepted responsibility for their supervision and prevented them from obtaining alcohol. If an employer wanted to send his servant on a special errand during the night, the white master had to write a note to be shown to any policeman who bailed up the messenger.

In 1902 Senator Staniforth Smith estimated that about 55 Aborigines were employed in the Broome pearling industry as seamen, cooks or general hands – not a large number compared to an overall workforce of approximately 3000. He wrote that the coastal Aborigines were 'a superior class of men, physically and mentally' to the southern Aborigines and 'appeared as energetic and useful as . . . some of the Asiatics'.[14]

The tally of Aboriginal people working in the pearling industry did not increase and according to evidence presented to the Roth Royal Commission, by 1905 the number in Broome had dropped to 45. None of these were divers. A few Aborigines were employed as shell openers, the aim being to ensure that any pearl found was retained for the master pearlers and not seized by the Asian crew. It was a difficult job which provoked much hostility from the crew.

One shell opener, Paddy Djagween, told of the time when he was threatened with a knife by the Japanese crew demanding he hand over a pearl he had discovered. Pretending to meet their demands, he reached into the pearl box – but what he brought out was a revolver. With the gun in his hand he kept the crew standing on the deck as he took the tiller and steered the lugger back to Broome, where he delivered the crew to the police and the gem to his white master.

6 A Fine Stamp of Men

Of these men as a body, it may be a difficult matter to obtain in any numbers their equals in intelligence and good character.

West Australian Pearlers' Association Annual Report, 1912

THE STEAMSHIP *PAROO* OF the Ocean Steamship Company made the journey from Fremantle to Broome in eight days, stopping to pick up passengers and mixed cargo at Geraldton, Carnarvon, Port Hedland, and thence to Broome. In keeping with the employment agreements they had signed in London, the English divers and tenders travelled third class. Davis, who had no agreement but more money, travelled first class. On the promenade deck, the divide between the classes was no more than a wooden gate and decades of observance. On warm evenings first-class passengers, emboldened by a fine dinner and port, would click open the gate and walk a lap of the deck, smoking cigars and discussing important things in loud voices. The second- and third-class passengers never pushed the gate the other way. These things were accepted without rancour in those days, before World War I destroyed the illusion that their betters knew what they were doing.

Just before dawn on a morning in February 1912, one of the divers, Frederick Beasily, unable to sleep, rose and stood on the deck waiting for the sun to rise. The *Paroo* was due to arrive in Broome later that evening. Beasily had hoped to be able to see land to the east, but the sky was blanketed with low cloud. Instead a pearling lugger came into view. She lay at anchor on a flat sea, with a lamp on her mast twinkling like a star. It was the first pearling lugger Beasily had seen. A ketch-rigged vessel of about 30 feet, with a distinctive plumb stem. He had expected a larger vessel. The deck was covered with baskets and ropes, and as the steamer passed close by he recognised the stacked coil of the diver's air-pipe. The *Paroo* quickly left the lugger behind and slowly, over the next hour, the sky began to lighten. The sun cleared the horizon, bathing the corrugations of the sea in a pink glow. And there lay the coast of Australia – grey and flat, a long smudge between a watermelon ocean and the blue expanse of the sky.

The sun rose higher, it became hotter and Beasily could feel his face beginning to burn. The steamer ploughed on through a smooth, warm ocean. For hours he watched a shoreline of flat, yellow beach. He could see no hills or mountain ranges beyond. He was looking at the seaward fringe of the Great Sandy Desert, which envelops Broome for over 300 miles to the southeast.

Just after dusk the SS *Paroo* moored at the Broome jetty. The Englishmen stood on the deck peering through the gloom. Tea-coloured water lapped over mud flats. The wooden jetty, almost a mile long, curved to a shoreline of mangrove trees and corrugated-iron sheds. Along the foreshore as far as they could see were luggers hauled onto the beach, their masts silhouetted like dead trees against the gathering darkness. Not a movement stirred the air and even after the last glimmer of sunlight had passed, there was no relief from the heat. Around the bay, perhaps a mile distant, they could see the lights of the town. Coming clearly over the water were snatches of song and the laborious plonk of a piano, interrupted every so often by a yell and a short silence before the shouts and singing resumed.

On the wharf below, a number of men were gathered aft of the vessel. They climbed a gangway and shortly after emerged down another plank, under the flickering light of lamps, shouldering crates of beer which they stacked on a platform next to the rail-line. A train whistle sounded in the distance, and after a moment the glow of a locomotive could be seen, moving through the mangroves and puffing white smoke into the night air. The train halted near the shore. Passengers waiting there stepped aboard, the gate at the end of the jetty was opened, and the train chugged out along the tracks towards the steamer.

For the white population, the fortnightly arrival of the steamer was an occasion for a party. The steamer timed its arrival for the high tide and families would stroll down to the jetty, catch the train to its end and board the vessel for complimentary drinks from the Ocean Steamship Company. They would catch up on gossip, pick up newspapers from distant cities and collect their mail.

Davis and the English divers and tenders followed the crowds into the first-class lounge. The locals were anxious for news about events on the other side of the world: the Olympic Games about to commence in London, the dockers' strike in Liverpool, the belligerent German behaviour over Morocco, and Lindrum's triumphs on the billiard tables in England. Men with suntanned faces and bushy moustaches asked them about their training and when they were to start work and what they knew about gathering mother-of-pearl.

Davis introduced them to their new employers. Hugh Richardson had engaged two and Hugh Norman three. The Pigott brothers, Sydney and Stan, had taken three each. All four employers were likely to be demanding. They were tough men who had made their fortunes the hard way. None was known for his sentimentality.

Like every other white citizen of Broome, Sydney and Stanley Pigott had been born elsewhere. Their father, from a wealthy ship-owning family in Brixton, England, had settled in Melbourne in 1852. The Pigott boys had enjoyed a privileged upbringing, attending the best schools the colony could offer, but by the time Sydney was due to enter university, the family found itself experiencing severe financial difficulties. His father had died two years earlier and, to the consternation of everyone, an examination of his books showed that he had been close to bankruptcy. A university education for Sydney became impossible, so instead he took a position in the treasury department of the Victorian Government. He found that stultifying, and after four years he resigned to work in a merchandising business in the city. Hearing about the prospects for wealth in the pearling industry, he tossed in that job as well, arriving in Broome in 1890.

Sydney Pigott's life was seemingly devoted to the long haul of restoring the family fortune and his own self-respect. If that was his measure of life achievement, it must be said he triumphed. After arriving in Broome he signed on as a clerk aboard a mother ship for the pearling fleet operating off Ninety Mile Beach. After three years service, with a reliability and frugality which were to be his mark, Sydney Pigott was able to muster the finance to buy two luggers and commence pearling in 1894. By 1897 he owned four luggers and a schooner to service them. He ran his boats hard, and was one of those who carried rifles on board to quieten any Aborigines who ventured too close on a lonely shore.

Although Sydney had picked up a fair command of Malay, he preferred to listen in to his crew's conversations and speak only English, being of the view that this enhanced his control over them. With his increasing wealth he built a fine bungalow, not in the white quarter but on the waterfront, overlooking the tin shanties, so that he could erect a store and office next door. He started buying and selling pearls and established a business carrying cargo from the jetty to the town. Then he built a factory producing cordials and aerated waters, and began to import beer, wines and spirits from London.

In 1899, less than ten years after he had left Melbourne, Sydney Pigott made a triumphant return, a wealthy and respected man – and on the lookout for a wife. By February 1900 he had found one in the widow Jane Skamp, who had three children – Ethel, Alice and

Genevieve – from her previous marriage. The newlyweds and the children set sail for Western Australia. Accompanying them was younger brother Stanley, whom Sydney had persuaded to take leave from his job at the Union Bank and seek his fortune in Broome.

Everyone prospered. Jane Pigott married her daughter, Ethel, off to Stanley Pigott, and Stanley was made manager of the cordial factory and the wine and spirit import business. In 1901 Sydney was elected to State Parliament, in an anti-Labor coalition, as the member for West Kimberley.

Sydney Pigott's parliamentary career was brief – he lost his seat at the next election and returned to business in Broome, concentrating on pearl trading. The value of a pearl often depended upon the eye of the beholder, and the occupation of pearl buyer required a big bankroll and the nerve to back one's judgement. Sydney had those attributes. Soon after, he purchased 'Lucknow', a stately home with hand-cast iron lace in Claremont, Perth, where his wife and stepchildren spent the summer months avoiding the intolerable humidity of the monsoon season in Broome.

Once in Broome, Stanley could see what was plain to see: that the real money was to be made in the pearl-shelling business. He borrowed on his savings, purchased a couple of luggers and, like everyone else, became rich. Within a few years he was regarded as one of the town's leading citizens, becoming secretary of the Pearlers' Association as well as a justice of the peace.

Hugh Richardson was another employer of the English divers and tenders. He ran an auctioneering, shipping and land agent's business from a building on the waterfront. Although strictly speaking it was the firm of Moss & Richardson which engaged Webber and Reid, everyone knew that George Moss was the backroom boy, and if you wanted to do business you sought out Hugh Richardson. As well as owning a fleet of luggers serviced by two schooners, the firm was stockist and agent for Siebe, Gorman's diving equipment.

The fourth employer was Hugh Norman, who had lived in Broome since 1887. With his flowing white beard, he was regarded as the father of the town, having been everything from mayor (twice) and JP to coroner and president of the Pearlers' Association. He was known as Pa Norman to many, despite the fact that he was still only in his mid fifties and a vigorous man at that. He was originally from Sydney, the son of wealthy Protestant immigrants from Dublin. His business partner, William Robison, was also his father-in-law. William Robison was a Scottish adventurer who had the distinction of being a successful gold-miner on both the Californian and Victorian diggings.

After hearing there was money to be made in pearl-shelling, in 1887 Robison pulled his son-in-law out of his job as a soft goods salesman in Sydney, put him in charge of a schooner and four luggers, and set him off to sail to Thursday Island. Believing there were better prospects in the northwest, the youthful Hugh Norman picked up Aboriginal divers in the Torres Strait and proceeded on around the top of Australia to Broome. There he worked in the brutal business of getting Aborigines to skin-dive into several fathoms of water collecting pearl shell. He was fond of saying that since that day in 1887, he had never borrowed and all the money used to expand his business came from his own earnings.

After William Robison died in 1894, Hugh Norman continued to run the business with Boyd Robison, William's son, kept at arm's length as a director in faraway Sydney. Wealthy, respected and living proof of what hard work could do for a man, Pa Norman established a large general store on the Broome foreshore. He was a great sportsman. He was a cricketer and a familiar figure on the golf links, a popular singer of comic songs for the Broome Glee Club and a keen Mason. He was the agent for C.E. Heinke & Co.'s diving gear and owner of a fleet of 28 boats and two schooners, including the elegant *Ena*, and a launch with a new Evinrude motor installed which he used to chug around his fleet, picking up shell.

THERE WERE only two white boarding houses in Broome (only the most degenerate would consider a coloured house). One was Mrs McAlinden's two-storey establishment facing Napier Terrace. At 30 shillings per week it offered a sitting room and balcony bedrooms with views over the back yards of the noodle shops and brothels of Japtown and, beyond that, to the blue of the sea. The other was Mrs Gee's house for retiring gentlemen, where every room contained a porcelain pitcher circled around the top with painted miniature pink roses. After the evening meal the guests could join Mrs Gee around the piano to hear her splendid rendition of 'coon' songs.

The English divers and tenders probably took lodgings in one of these boarding houses. The alternative was one of the town's hotels. Daisy Bates, the eccentric friend of the Aborigine, once wrote of being 'marooned in a dirty room at the one decent hotel the town offered' and having her meals brought up 'in such moments as the passages were free of howling, drunken madmen'. She described the lay-up in Broome as 'a season of madness, in which white as well as coloured men went berserk'.[1]

Daisy Bates was not alone in her views. Many correspondents passing through Broome in the years before World War I described the foreshore pubs during the lay-up in exotic terms – a sort of Asian wild west. They wrote of oil lamps swinging from the ceiling, casting dancing shadows along the walls, and moist, warm air laden with the smell of bodies and stale beer. They described barrooms inhabited by Japanese seamen playing cards, South Sea Islanders singing to the accompaniment of a guitar, Manilamen clad in striped waistcoats with glittering gold buttons passing a rum bottle between them, Koepangers drifting back from the fantan tables, and white men with bushy, black beards smoking pipes. They wrote of brawls – over gambling debts and women – that spilled out onto the street, a crowd following to cheer the fighters on. Bottles, limbs of mangrove trees and knives were used as weapons and, when it was over, feet scuffed through a line of blood in the dirt outside.

There were six hotels in Broome. All were built of iron, wood and lattice-work, and contrived to look bigger than they actually were, with wide verandahs and high-pitched roofs facing the street. There wasn't a colour bar to entry of any of them – except for Aborigines, who were forbidden by law from consuming alcohol. The Continental, owned by Francis Rodriguez – who was also Captain Rodriguez, master pearler – was regarded as the best in town, advertising every convenience for boarders, travellers and commercial travellers. Its rival was the Governor Broome, run by Miss Cochrane, where civil receptions and formal dinners were held. The Central was where the Koepangers, Malays and Manilamen drank. It was continually under police surveillance and had its licence taken away for an extended period in 1910. It was run by Mr C. Bullivant who, during his period of enforced idleness as a publican, ran a bookmaking business on the premises – Broome races, and Caulfield and Flemington catered for. The Japanese frequented either the Roebuck Bay Hotel or the Pearlers' Rest on Dampier Terrace. The Pearlers' Rest was burnt down in 1908; as an indication of what a ramshackle affair it must have been, the insurance payout for both building and contents totalled £1550. The hotel was rebuilt in 1909, got flattened by the big blow of 1910, and was promptly rebuilt again.

The liveliest hotel in town was the Star. With a large five-cornered star painted on sheet metal atop to guide customers along, it sat on a small hillock at the end of Shiba Lane. Its design was pure Texan, with a horse trough out the front, regular horse auctions held out the back and two long bars where you never had to wait to get a drink. The annual Star billiard tournament was a big event, with huge bets laid on the outcome. Both the Continental and the Star showed movies, but the Star had Hyland's circus as well, across the road, under canvas in the natural amphitheatre of a sandhill. The publican, Tom Hyland, named the circus after himself, and at nights he became Professor Hyland, ringmaster. He put in tiered seating, his wife became a juggler and Professor Hyland did tricks with horses and kangaroos. But it was Hyland's eleven children who were the darlings of the crowds. Tom Hyland junior was billed as 'The Blind Jockey'.

Miss Maudie Hyland was stunning as a horsewoman. Agnes' educated ponies were a delight and Rose, scantily dressed upon a human pyramid, was always a popular figure. The children doubled as acrobats, tumblers, troubadours, wire-walkers and trapeze artists. There was £5 to anyone who could stay aboard Hyland's buck-jumping grey. The show concluded with a foot-stamping grand finale of a Liverpool steeplechase.

Professor Tom Hyland was the head of a remarkable family. Tragically, genetic eye problems bedevilled most of his children, and five became blind. Tom junior progressively lost his sight, becoming completely blind by the age of ten, but he remained a skilled horseman and continued to thrill the crowds. Sons Darcy and Stanley were the clowns of a thousand laughs despite their lack of vision. Both became blind in their twenties. Evelyn, the wire-walker, escaped blindness until after she left the circus. Maudie was a circus jockey and an acrobat. She too lost her sight. All Hyland's children played a musical instrument and they performed in front of the hotel on circus days, attracting crowds which they led, like pied pipers, into the big top. The circus season coincided with the lay-up and usually started in December, running through until the luggers set sail in the new year.

In November 1911 Tom Hyland took several of his prize horses to a race meeting at Fitzroy Crossing, and after the races wired back to his family that he was returning overland in time for Christmas. He never arrived. Darcy Hyland joined a party led by Constable Leonard, and with two black trackers they searched for some trace of his father. After three weeks of failure and frustration, they returned to Broome. They had followed two horse tracks (they could tell by the marks in the sand that one horse was being ridden and the other led) into Edgars Range for 7 or 8 miles, but then the trails were lost as they turned into Streeters Plain. It was widely presumed that Tom Hyland had perished from thirst somewhere in the arid country beyond.

But the show went on. The blind Tom Hyland junior donned Professor Hyland's outfit and strode through the sawdust to the centre of the ring. He knew his father's patter off by heart. A new program had been prepared by the children, including the comical pantomime 'Rich and Poor or Snuff Taking Extraordinary'. It was a tremendous success.

In March 1912, an Aboriginal man reported finding the dried carcass of a horse with an empty water bag around its neck, 8 miles from a government well near Streeters Plain. Tom Hyland organised a search party with a white man named Vivaish to be his eyes. Tom identified the horse he was led to: it was Black Bess when he rode her in the circus and Yardagarra when his father rode her at the racetrack. Tom Hyland and his party made an extensive but futile search in the surrounding countryside. It was assumed that after Black Bess had collapsed, Tom Hyland senior had set out on foot in search of water.

THE MORNING after their arrival in Broome the heat drove the Englishmen from their rooms early. The traditional Broome breakfast was fried steak (but not accompanied by eggs unless supplies had been topped up from the steamer overnight), salted bacon, tinned tomatoes, coffee and toast. After breakfast, puffing on their pipes as they stood on the boardwalk, it is likely they would have asked about the smell of bad fish in the air, and been told that the breeze was coming from the packing sheds where thousands of mother-of-pearl shells were waiting to be shipped to Europe and the United States. In 1912 Broome township stretched a little over 2 miles from just beyond the jetty at Mangrove Point to the Asiatic Quarter.

The work of repairing the boats had commenced in earnest after the New Year celebrations and would have been in full swing by the time the English divers arrived in February. There were only a few weeks left to get the boats ready for another year at sea.

Sails were taken down and spread across the sand to be examined for weakness or tropical rot. Patches were sewn on. After the rust had been chiselled away from them, anchor chains were run through hot tar bubbling in a drum. The rollers and bolts were replaced. On their hands and knees with the sun beating down on their bare backs and a nail can next to them, men poked oakum between the planks and then rubbed raw oil into the decking. Carpenters scoured the desert fringes for kadjebut boughs, knarled by time into a curve to match the pieces they needed to renew. Copper sheathing was fixed underneath and red lead applied to the exposed timber.

Another of the lay-up tasks was to rid the vessels of vermin. For this the crew relied on the sea. During low tide they would remove all the gear from their lugger, undo the stopcock and sit on the banks to witness vengeance on the rodents and cockroaches that had gnawed at them over the past months at sea. As the tide turned they watched water advance and flood into the lugger. Soon the deck was alive with hundreds of cockroaches, and as the sea rose higher they were swept away in the swirling water. If a rat attempted to swim ashore, excited crewmen standing on the bank competed to whack it with sticks until it sank from view. Presently, all that was left was an oil slick, shimmering across the deck.

Later that morning, James Davis took William Webber and his tender William Reid to meet the shellers, buy a few drinks, tell a few jokes and by the by mention that they would be using Siebe, Gorman gear, the best in the world, which incidentally could be purchased just up the road, at the Siebe, Gorman outlet run by Hugh Richardson. The shellers would have listened intently as Webber told them about the attempted salvage of the *Florencia*, the 56 guns aboard and the church ornaments left on board by drowned priests. On their tour of the town's hotels they met Pa Norman who, as the Heinke agent, was touting Beasily, Freight and Hanson to the locals.

The rivalry on the streets of Broome between Norman and Davis was no more than a reflection of an even greater rivalry between the two grand firms they represented. Between them C.E. Heinke & Co.

and Siebe, Gorman & Co. dominated the supply of copper-helmeted diving equipment to the world. The two firms competed like squabbling siblings, which was not surprising considering their origins. Both had been started by immigrant Prussians early in the nineteenth century, just streets apart in London, and had been in fierce competition ever since.

The Australian pearl-shell industry, conducted in Queensland and Western Australia, represented a huge market for diving equipment and both firms claimed the English divers as their own. While James Davis was greeting the English divers in Fremantle on behalf of Siebe, Gorman, a partner of Heinke, Mr Fred H. Sprang, was telling the Melbourne *Herald* that his firm was sending out the men and that he had no doubt that they would prove equal to the strain.[2] Sprang had also cabled the *Broome Chronicle* and advised that C.E. Heinke & Co. had more men on its register, all ex-naval divers, ready to respond when a call was made for them.

Pa Norman arranged a meeting for his men with Mr Green, the proprietor of the *Broome Chronicle*. This item duly appeared:

> On Thursday evening, at our request, the three men under engagement to Messrs Robison and Norman, (Messrs Freight and Brearly [*sic*], divers, and Hanson, tender) kindly called at our office for the purpose of being interviewed.
>
> 'We left London on December 23,' said one of the men, 'under engagement to Mr Norman.'
>
> What experience have you had in diving?
>
> 'In the navy. Men that volunteer for divers are sent to one of the gunnery schools at Davenport [*sic*], Portsmouth or Sheerness . . . '
>
> Have you any fear of success in pearl-shell diving?
>
> 'None whatever. We come here as trained certificated divers, under the latest system by experts in the best gunnery schools in England, and all we want to learn here are the local conditions . . . We are all thoroughly determined to make this white diving a success.'

Have you seen the luggers yet?

'Yes. They are better than we expected. On board we will have more room than on a torpedo boat or destroyer, and we are well satisfied with the accommodation.'

What is the term of your engagement?

'We are signed on for 12 months; but we feel sure we are here to stop . . .'

In further conversation we were told that there is a vast difference between diving in English waters and Mediterranean and other waters. In England the water is black, and one stands up to his waist in mud. With the clear water here we would soon pick up the necessary knowledge to make us competent pearl-shell divers.

Green's article went on:

Another interview was obtained with the three men under engagement to Mr. Stan Pigott (Elphick, Harvey and Andrews) and they spoke in much the same strain as Robison and Norman's men.

'We only have to learn the conditions,' said one, 'and then we will be as competent, or more so, as the Asiatic.'

'I don't see where we are going to fail,' said another, 'for our knowledge of diving, gained under the greatest experts of the day, and on the most scientific principles, must be far and away above the wretched system so prevalent on pearling luggers. Once we get a knowledge of the conditions below our system must tell. If the Asiatic can come here and make a success of it, surely a navy man can.'

Before qualifying do you undergo an examination?

'Yes, we all have to undergo a severe test by Dr. Hill, the diving scientist. To give you some idea of the scientific manner in which diving is demonstrated in the gunnery schools, Dr. Hill put a cat under a pressure of 200 lbs and then shut it off suddenly. The cat was apparently dead, but the doctor gradually put the 200 lb pressure on again and eased it off gradually. The cat was revived, and when we left was alive and kicking. It is the same with a man when brought to the surface in an unconscious state. He can be brought round instantly by putting him down again under the same pressure and then bringing him up gradually.'

Do many deaths occur in the Navy?

'Once in a blue moon. Paralysis. As we have said before, diving is taught and demonstrated on such scientific principles that such are almost unknown in the gunnery schools.'

The *Broome Chronicle* then added a note of its own: 'The general opinion is that they are a fine stamp of men, and they all seem pleased at the prospect of getting into harness and demonstrating that what the Japs can do in the way of diving so can a naval man.'[3]

For all their optimism there was no getting away from the fact that diving for shell was way beyond the previous experience and training of the English divers. In Britain they were specialists in engineering works. If the foundations of a bridge were under attack they directed stone blocks into support. They cleared the obstructed gates of locks, attached cables or buoyant cones to sunken barges, or recovered chains adrift from moorings. They raised cannons. They discovered sunken treasure. Not skills readily transferable to the monotonous search, day after day, for a nondescript shell strewn on the sea floor.

Mother-of-pearl is not easy to see. Inside the shell might look like the shimmering lustre of a rainbow, but the exterior is a washed-out brown, discoloured and blotched to match the hue of its surroundings, and is camouflaged even further by weed or coralline growing on its surface. It often has its own warning system – a small crab about the size of a fingernail lives within and when it senses any dangerous vibrations, it scampers inside, triggering the shell to clamp shut.

A diver searching for mother-of-pearl must recognise the type of ocean floor the shell prefers and recognise the type of fish likely to be flickering over a shell looking for particles of food. An experienced diver could follow the trail of a novice and sweep up bags of shell left behind. Shell must attach to something: rock, exposed sandstone, seagrass or coral cups. The only bad bottom was mud or sand where the shell cannot find a place to attach itself. During a storm, shell attached to rubble could be bowled along the floor and shifted to a new location. Sometimes it was banked together and was easy pickings for a diver. Meadows of thick leathery weed indicated the presence of shell, but if the vegetation had grown too lanky, the shell became hidden and an experienced diver would quickly signal to be moved on. A proficient diver watched for the glint of shell in the distance, and as he moved closer he watched for a sudden movement. He knew that when the tide was running, a shell would tend to face the flow of the water, fanning with its mouth agape and pushing the water though erect hairs on its gills.

The Japanese divers had developed a technique of sitting underwater astride a drifting anchor as the lugger sailed across the pearling grounds. When they saw likely shell country, they would signal via the lifeline for the anchor to be dropped, and the diver went with it, alighting just before it touched bottom. Some went so far as to construct an observation post on a swing suspended under their vessel.

If the tides were too great, a diver wouldn't dive. Battling against a tide to hold one's position over the floor quickly became exhausting. In a fast flowing tide the bottom became agitated, the water became turbid, and the rush of water running across a field of grass would flatten it, hiding the shell. But mostly the water was crystal clear, the sun shimmered through and the diver could see the detail of the sand, rock and the individual fronds on plants. On a good day a diver could see 30 or 40 feet before the terrain appeared distorted and fuzzy.

Another thing the Englishmen had to get used to was that pearl-shell divers did not walk the floor. It was too tiring to spend the day pushing against a wall of water in a lumbering, rubberised suit. A strong tide would knock a diver over if he attempted to fight it.

Instead, the diver planned his drop so the current pushed him across ground he thought was promising. The diver was slung almost horizontal in a flying pose, his brass-capped leaden boots inches from the ground. But it was a slow, awkward flight, for every now and then he had to bend over to pick up shell. If he came to an obstruction such as a rocky outcrop, he turned the air escape valve a couple of turns, slightly inflated his suit and rose, floating over the top. If the diver came into a barren patch, he would make a loop in the lifeline and sit in that, skimming above the floor as he directed the lugger in the search for more promising ground. A diver might have been able to see two clumps of shell 20 yards apart, but if he was being pushed by the tide or the drift of the lugger, he could not take them both; he needed to choose one and then decide if it was worth coming back for the other. An inexperienced diver could easily drift at right angles across a seam of good shell, while a diver with his wits about him would have signalled for the boat to turn and follow the line of shell along its length.

It was the diver who navigated the lugger from his position fathoms below. By a series of rehearsed tugs on the lifeline, the diver communicated to the tender, who then passed his orders on to the crew. The diver had to picture the scene above – the flow of the tides over the sandbanks, the currents, the distance from shore and the direction and strength of the wind. The rate of his movement depended on the skill of the crew above him and their ability to adjust the rigging and drop weights overboard, according to his instructions. Usually the lugger drifted stern first with the sails furled, and in smart weather was held back by an anchor with a chain hitched over one of the flukes. If the wind dropped away entirely, two crew men would take to a dinghy, pick up long paddles mounted on pintles, and in a sculling action move the lugger across the water. When a diver came across a good lie of floor, he would signal for the anchor to be thrown over and the diver would commence to fill his netted bag. The bag was woven onto an iron or cane ring, with an opening wide enough to take the largest of shells and a hook which allowed the bag to be placed onto the diver's corselet and dangle down his chest. A full bag would take ten to twelve pairs (one shell being a pair).

Over particularly productive ground, the diver would instruct the crew to drift backwards and forwards all day, like a harvester across wheat fields. They would repeat the process the following day, and the one after that, a buoy marking the position reached at the end of each day. Sometimes a boat would work no more than 5 miles of ocean in a month of repetitious sailing. There were few rules of navigation on the pearling grounds, but one was that a lugger should never trespass into an area marked with buoys, or drop anchor in the path of the drift of another boat. That sort of behaviour was likely to start disputes, occasioning shouting and threats. The offender ran the risk that the matter would be settled, months later, in one of the lanes of the Asiatic Quarter.

In England the engineering and salvage work the divers normally performed was over a fixed location, and it was standard practice to be guided in the descent by a line attached to a heavy sinker lying on the bottom. It was also common for a telephone speaker to be attached to the helmet so the diver could talk to those on the surface. Nothing like this applied on the pearling grounds. Communication was via tugs on the lifeline or the air-pipe. Although the British Navy had a time-honoured code of signals, there was no such standardisation among the self-taught divers of the pearling fleet. The codes were worked out between the diver and the tender on each lugger, and varied from simple ones such as drift slow, drift fast, more air, less air, slack out chain, haul in chain, bring me up and bring me up quick, to quite sophisticated commands relating to the sailing of the vessel. One diver had a signal telling the crew to start fishing if he saw a school of barramundi or bream swim past, and the diver then enjoyed the diversion of watching the fish take the bait and be yanked struggling to the surface. If a large and persistent fish appeared entranced by this strange copper-headed creature, the diver would sometimes call for a spear to be roped down to him and, lunging forward, would impale the fish for hauling up by the crew.

The diver could get much information about the world above him, but not by looking upwards, because that was no easy matter in a helmet. Instead he could hear sounds through the water, such as the propeller of a steamer in the distance, or the chug of a motor launch. He could hear the rattle of the anchor chain being raised or lowered. The air-pipe brought him the smell of the evening meal being prepared. He could hear the clack of the pump and with practice he could tell when the pump hands were slacking or when a new team had taken over. In still water he could hear the clicking of crayfish and the song of the whales vibrating from afar. He could see shadows flickering across the floor from storm clouds passing overhead. Divers said they could sense a cyclone hours before it arrived: the bottom became disturbed, underwater currents of cold water flurried the weeds, the water became foggy and visibility dropped to a few yards.

Yet for all this, diving for shell remained a lonely occupation. Some divers tried debating with themselves or commenting out loud on everything they did, or reciting love poems to their sweethearts, or singing or whistling in their tiny echo chamber as they worked. Diving also gave a man plenty of time to dwell on things. Divers were notorious for their bad tempers and, when they surfaced, for continuing quarrels long forgotten by the crew.

WHILE DAVIS was taking Webber and Reid around the town, Hugh Richardson, the man who paid their wages, sat at his desk in his packing shed of corrugated iron built atop concrete stilts driven into the mud flats. The front door opened out onto Napier Terrace and the back door onto Roebuck Bay. He was distracted by the sight of drinkers entering the hotel opposite for a lunchtime beer, but he stuck to his task. He was totting up the expenses of placing a white diver and tender on one of his luggers. Under the terms of the agreement, negotiated not by him but by some committee in London, he had had to pay their passage from England, admittedly at third class, and half-wages for the two months duration of the voyage. The cost of bringing them to Australia was £24 each. Now that they had arrived, Webber's wage was £13 per month. Webber insisted his nephew, Reid, work with him as tender.[4] Reid was costing £6 a month and Richardson had no idea if he would be a useful tender, but he did know that a coloured tender could be bargained down to less than £1 a month. He could also get a top Japanese diver for £3 a month and a Malay for £2. And then there was the food bill. He normally budgeted on £8 to £10 a year per man for crew's provisions, but that rice-based list would never do for a white man. He fiddled around with another list: golden syrup, tinned butter, canned beef, coffee, tobacco – no, he crossed out tobacco; surely that was their own outlay – canned vegetables, waxed eggs, tinned condensed milk, flour, jams. It was an expensive business, all right, and the most galling thing was that in order to take on Webber, he had had to discharge his perfectly competent Japanese diver, who was now refusing to return his advance. And there was talk that the Japanese Club would refuse to allow any of its divers to sign on with him next year as a protest. He would see about that. What about insurance? His firm was the agent for Liverpool, London and the Globe companies, but he knew they would never cover the risk on a pearl diver – not unless he paid an enormous premium. But you had to draw the line somewhere. He had never covered his coloured workers for injury and he had no intention of making an exception now, just because his new diver was white.

Further along the foreshore, Sydney Pigott was at work in his cordial factory, wine and spirits outlet and packing shed, all jumbled together next to his house. He was a small, thin man with a nose polished red after years in the sun. He sat behind an oak desk, alert to any customer who rang the bell of the liquor shop, and watched over the mountains of shell in his shed and beyond that to the bare masts of his luggers sunk into trenches dug into the bay. There was little he missed.

Sydney's wife and the children had travelled south to Perth just after Christmas to avoid the stifling heat of summer, and they were not due back until late March, but he had so much to do he rarely gave them a thought. It was his busiest time of year. He had to get in replacement labour from his agents in Singapore and lodge forms with the Customs House, showing that he could account for each indentured man and that he was not about to exceed his permit numbers. He had to check the returns of his cordial bottles from the hotels and work out why a consignment of syrup had been sent on to Derby and four cartons of beer had mysteriously disappeared from the wharf – assuming they had been consigned in the first place, but damned if he was going to pay for them. Shell harvested during the previous season had to be boxed and despatched to buyers in Europe and America. He had to ensure his luggers were repaired and sea-worthy, and that the diving equipment was in working order. And now he had three Englishmen in town about to commence work on his boats. Like Richardson, he was concerned about their cost. They would have to collect an awful lot of shell for him to recover his expenses, and he had more than a sneaking suspicion he would be out of pocket. Another risk he would have to take. That was the trouble with pearling – it was a business of continuous risks. All manner of things could go wrong. His best diver might become paralysed. Or the crew might suddenly decide to desert, or sail his lugger in an impossible journey back to Singapore. A cyclone could suddenly turn on a master pearler's fleet and send it to the bottom, just as it had to the unfortunate Captain Talboys, once in 1908 and again in 1910.

But the greatest uncertainty of all was the market. The value of shell fluctuated so wildly that many shellers gave up trying to present their product on a rising market and took the whole thing as akin to gambling. After hearing reports of shell fetching £180 a ton a sheller could despatch boxes to New York, only to have the prices dip mid Atlantic, and end up getting £110. London prices rode on a roller coaster. It was muttered that a Jewish cabal controlled the London trade and the auctions were a farce: two or three greybeards put their heads together and bought shell at prices of their own choosing. Others blamed French speculators, even going so far as to name the firm of L. Rosenthal Brothers of Paris, accusing it of despatching telegrams round the world in an attempt to push the swings even further.

Australia produced 80 per cent of the market's supply of mother-of-pearl and it was a continual lament that if only the master pearlers could work together instead of undercutting each other, they could dictate to the world. The Pearlers' Association held meetings every few years in an effort to get everyone to join in an orderly marketing scheme. Although resolutions were passed, nothing concrete seemed to happen. The main problem was that shellers were staunch individualists and when one heard of a bull run, the rush was on to get the shell there before the others did. And the more level-headed pearlers suspected there were no masterminds in Europe manipulating the auctions – economic catastrophes, disastrous wars and fickle fashion were more likely explanations for shell's gyrating value. Prices fell away to £85 a ton in the depression of the 1890s, picked up, then collapsed again in 1905 when, following the reversals in their war with Japan, the Russian aristocracy lost their taste for jewellery boxes. But prices were now on the move again, driven by the dictate that pearl-shell buttons were the fashion items in New York.

Sydney Pigott turned in his swivel chair and looked through the open doors at the piles of shell in his packing shed. With news from the cables that top shell was fetching £260 a ton, it was probably a good time to send a few boxes to auction. He'd have to act quickly, though, because just down the road Hugh Richardson, Pa Norman, Clem Gregory and all the others would have the same cables on their desks. He stood up and walked through to his shed. Already the sun was high, trapping the heat under the iron roof. The air itself seemed to sweat. Sydney Pigott loved the humidity and he savoured the scene around him. The shell grader was a Fijian of regal dimensions who sat overflowing on a stool, surrounded by piles of glistening mother-of-pearl. He was assisted by a thin, brown-skinned boy dressed in a pair of baggy breeches. The boy picked up a shell, chopped off the brittle fingers with a blunt axe and handed it to the Fijian. The man could tell its weight and width merely by holding it in his giant hand. The boy remained in attendance while the grader, in a stately, unhurried way, carefully held the shell up to the light and peered into its lustre. He rolled it over, looking for discolourations, and poked into holes with a piece of wire. After he had completed his deliberations, he reached for his pencil, noted figures in a book, handed the shell back to the boy and whispered to him the grade he had determined. Shell was sorted into five categories: wormy, defective, chicken, sound and medium, and sound and bold.

After receiving his instructions, the boy scampered between the piles to one of the wire-reinforced blackbutt boxes lined up against the wall. There he carefully placed the shells – one behind the other, like dinner plates – into parallel rows, taking care to save space by placing the top and bottom halves of the shells in separate rows. Each box was marked in stencil with the initials MOP (for mother-of-pearl) and with the name of a jeweller or dealer in New York, London, Paris or St Petersburg. And so it went on, hour by hour, hundreds of shells being graded and packed. Shell destined to be carved into buttons, buckles, brooches, bangles, boxes, fans and combs. To Sydney Pigott silently watching, each shell placed in its box was like a gold coin deposited in the bank.

It was the surge of the tide that fed the mother-of-pearl. Twice a day, as regular as a heartbeat, the tides moved enormous volumes of water along the coast, flushing food out of bays, harbours and inlets, past headlands and into channels far out to sea, washing out deep recesses, stirring up the floor and distributing nutrients up and down the food chain.

Because of the strength of the tides in the northwest, the master pearlers of Broome didn't think their pearling grounds would ever become exhausted. They believed that lying out to sea, in gloomy fathoms far deeper than a diver could ever sound, were large shells, continually releasing eggs and sperm to be turned into spat and uplifted by currents rising to wash all along the coastline. The fields were over 1000 miles long and in some areas were 40 miles wide. The Broome jetty had to be built jutting a mile out to sea because the rise and fall in the tide was 20 feet. Steamers on the northern coastal run were constructed with flat bottoms so at ebb tide they could sit snugly next to the jetty. Passengers loved to be photographed strolling on the white sand and inspecting the hull.

Once or twice a year king tides lapped into the streets of Broome and patrons on deck chairs at the outdoor movies had their feet washed as they watched the screen. Tides were sometimes so great that in places where no landing facilities were available, the skipper of a lugger would allow his vessel to be stranded in a purpose-built trench, to be unloaded by a bullock dray sent out across the mud. During king tides in some of the sinuous gorges of the Buccaneer Archipelago, pearlers saw, to their astonishment, the sea level dropping down the cliff face at the rate of a foot in ten minutes. In Talbot Bay the sea moving back to the ocean created a turbulent waterfall as it tumbled out through a narrow gap.

Concerns about overfishing had led the authorities in Queensland to impose a ban on the taking of shell smaller than 5 inches, but it was a law which was impossible to enforce. The ban may have meant that undersized shell was not brought back to port, but they were still picked up from the floor and opened on the deck before being thrown overboard – just in case there was a pearl inside. Any serious attempt to police the law would have required a public official on every boat.

With its great beauty, durability and resistance to discolouration, enthusiasts in the industry believed that mother-of-pearl would eventually replace ivory as the preferred ornamental inlay. Already in the United States piano keys were being made with the shimmer of the rainbow where plain white had been seen before, and the lustre of pearl-shell light switches helped fumblers seeking the switch in the dark. Cigarette boxes, jewellery boxes, pill boxes and containers for playing cards were all being made from pearl shell. The uses for MOP were endless: as decoration on fine furniture and walking sticks, as ashtrays in gentlemen's clubs, on ladies' spectacles and on the handles of dandies' revolvers.

However, the bulk of the shell still ended up as buttons. Large factories were established in Birmingham, Hamburg, Trieste, Le Havre and Iowa. Periodically the shellers toyed with the idea of setting up a button factory on the banks of Roebuck Bay. A report was obtained by the Western Australian Government in 1906 from a Birmingham expert who was generally in favour of the scheme, although there was concern about where the labour would come from. Nimble-fingered workers from countries such as Ceylon and China would have been ideal, but no one thought they would be allowed in. The State Government asked for federal money to get the project going with white workers, and the Federal Government said it was a state responsibility. The state authorities said it was up to the Pearlers' Association. There the idea lapsed and buttons continued to be manufactured overseas.

THROUGH THE open doors on the seaward side of his packing shed, Sydney Pigott saw a group of men pause to look at the mounds of shell on the floor. They were the English divers; some he recognised as his own, the others he assumed were engaged by his brother, or by Norman or Richardson. For a moment he thought they were going to come in. He knew that out in the sunlight they would not be able to see him within the shade of the shed and he made no move towards them. Eventually they strolled on, and after a minute he moved to the door and watched them looking at one of Gregory's boats. Their attention had been caught by a lugger skirted in grass matting like a hula-hula girl. He could have told them this was done to stop the sun drying out the hull while she was up on blocks, but he would leave that to others. Instead he returned to his desk.

Sydney had been ridiculed for taking part in the white experiment – possibly rightly so – but he was up to his neck in it now and somehow he had to work out how he could make the exercise pay. He knew that his brother Stanley had gone to the added expense of buying one of the new engine air compressors. Stanley argued that they were the way of the future, just as anyone could see that the motor car would eventually replace the horse and buggy. If the government was going to force them to take on a white crew, it was Stanley's view that at least he could reduce the numbers by getting rid of the pump hands. He also believed that with the new pumps, the shellers would be able to put divers into much deeper waters. Two good Malays turning the handle of a pump might be able to force enough air down a half-inch pipe to get a diver to 15 or perhaps 20 fathoms, but this amount of exertion was impossible to maintain. In practical terms, the limit was 10 to 14 fathoms. It was said that a team of six pump hands working in the Darnley Deeps in Torres Strait had forced air down to divers in 30 fathoms but that required a lot of unfailing back power, and it would only take a stumble or two for the whole exercise to end in disaster. Yet the miracle of mother-of-pearl was that it could be found at any depth and, seemingly, the deeper the better.

Sydney Pigott recalled a speech he had heard the previous April at the Broome Literary Institute, given by Mr Sprang of C.E. Heinke & Co. Sprang's firm had recently started manufacturing a Darnley pump, for use by the master pearlers in Torres Strait. There, said Sprang, in the Darnley Deeps, Japanese divers were lifting shell from 35 to 45 fathoms with the aid of the new pump. The shell was lying thick in potholes and the diver could collect several bags in a few minutes – so many bags they couldn't all be taken up by the diver but had to be marked by buoys and hauled up later. And, claimed Sprang, there had only been one death in the previous fifteen months.

The reference to the Darnley Deeps as a suitable place to dive surprised some of Sprang's audience. Although the Deeps were thousands of miles away and far from the reach of any boat sailing out from the northwest, such was their ominous reputation that they were well known to the master pearlers in Broome. They were called the Graveyards, and for good reason.

Sprang's suggestion that the shellers of Broome buy his firm's Darnley pump and dive deep was met with scepticism. Conditions were different in the northwest. The continental shelf slips away gradually from the shore so that at 50 miles the bottom is still only around 25 fathoms. There were thousands of places along the coast where the luggers could collect shell without trying anything new. An old Broome diver, Francis Rodriguez, wrote a letter to the *Broome Chronicle* scoffing at Sprang's claims. He doubted if diving in 40 fathoms could ever be safe. In order to avoid the bends the diver could only remain down for a few minutes at a time, so it was more like dipping than diving. How, he asked, could a diver ever find sufficient shell in just a few minutes on the bottom?

But there were at least two locations on the coast of the northwest where it was possible to dive deep. One was in the twisting channels of King Sound, several days sailing to the north. The other was in Roebuck Deep, on Broome's doorstep.

Roebuck Deep lay a few miles from the town; on a still night the lugger crews anchored above the Deep could catch the strains of dance music being played at the Governor Broome Hotel. Stories traded across hotel bars had it that, in the 1890s, shell stacked a foot thick was recovered from the fringes of the Deep. Divers, filling their nets as they went, were led into deeper and deeper water as they followed the channels twisting north towards Gantheaume Point. Near Escape Rocks, with two of the best pump hands in the fleet straining at the wheel, they halted at 15 fathoms. Much of the shell they collected was old, dead shell, faded and worth little, but there were also new shells the size of dinner plates, mouths agape and plump on the nutrients washing out of Dampier Creek. In 1908 two divers who ventured further were crippled with the bends after diving in 22 fathoms – and still they had not reached bottom.

In 1912 the state of knowledge of the life cycle of mother-of-pearl was so rudimentary that no one had any idea how long the shells lived, what their maximum size was, or how long they took to reach maturity. Uncertainty fostering fantasy led to claims that in the Deep huge shells, decades old, had tumbled into vast holes, there to grow even bigger and fatter, fed by the soup of particles falling in on them and with pearls the size of pigeon eggs tucked inside. These were shells with thick, ruffled crusts from which five thousand buttons could be made.

To Sydney Pigott, Roebuck Deep represented an opportunity. It was the claim of the English divers that they were trained to dive to any depth. Their boast was that so long as the Admiralty tables were followed, they were in no danger. For the Deep he would require an engine-driven pump and an extended length of pipe. He would have to act quickly, though, because he had no doubt that others, perhaps even his own brother, would have similar ideas.

That night *The Fall of Troy* was showing in the open air of the Continental Gardens just behind the hotel. It seemed that every white in town was there. They drove in flash cars, trotted up in sulkies, or rode on bicycles. The stars came out, the mosquitoes buzzed in delight, and overhead the flying foxes flew in from the mangroves in search of ripe fruit from the shellers' gardens. At the end of the first reel the projectionist had to wait twenty minutes until men and women came back from the front bar with frothing jugs of beer, carefully storing them under the deck chairs. It rained during the second reel, but no one cared because it was warm, misty rain and it got rid of the mosquitoes. In the third reel Troy fell.

DURING A tour of inspection of the Great Franco-British Exhibition of 1908, King Edward VII of England and the President of France, surrounded by aides, trade officials, reporters and a crush of sundry spectators, paused and then stepped forward, fascinated by what they saw. Before them was a large glass tank of water in which was suspended some sort of bloated cream-coloured device. Perhaps there was a man inside this thing – unquestionably there was something suggestive of an outsized human shape in the figure, and this became even more apparent as it clumped its way across the bottom of the tank.

The King and the President watched the apparition closely as, haloed by a stream of bubbles, it bent over and picked up a shell the size of a Windsor soup plate and held it up to the audience. Yes, it was clearly a human because they could see his hand, which the man, realising he was in the presence of his monarch and being an ex-naval rating, used in a salute, albeit a clumsy one because his movements were greatly restricted by the rubberised canvas. The King, somewhat irritated by this interruption to the demonstration, waved for him to carry on. The diver bent over, picked up the shell and, stepping forward to the glass, opened it to reveal to royalty the largest pearl anyone had ever seen.

Some legends say that pearls are created by bolts of lightning striking the water. Others believe they are the eyes of saints. The Chinese tell of mermaids weeping tears of pearls. The Hindus say that on still nights, dew dropping from overhanging leaves solidifies in the moonlight and rolls into the open mouths of shells gathered to collect them. So impregnated, the mother-of-pearl sinks gently to the bottom to nourish its embryo until it ripens into a pearl of wondrous beauty. To the Japanese divers they were the tears of Buddha, shed as gifts to look after orphans and widows.

The reality is less poetic. Pearls are created by an itch, by an irritant in the flesh of a mollusc – it could be a grain of sand, a piece of broken shell, or the tip of a crab's claw. At first the shell attempts to expel the object through its digestive system, but if that fails, the shell begins to secrete nacre around it, building up something smooth and hard that the flesh of the mollusc can endure. By this means, a pearl is formed.

There was no such thing as pearl-fishing. The crews on the luggers did not fish for pearls; they harvested shell and hoped, against the odds, that when the shell was opened a pearl would be found. It was estimated that the chance of finding a worthwhile pearl was one in five thousand.

Blisters, also called baroque, are an inferior kind of pearl, usually found attached to the shell rather than in the flesh. Most often a blister is caused by the boring of a whelk attempting to get a meal of oyster meat. But shell is hard and progress is slow. If the attacker gives up after a languid struggle of life and death, the shell exudes nacre over the hole, covering the rupture and making itself a bed of silky smoothness. Usually blisters are filled with a pocket of mud, but occasionally a skilful pearl-skinner can find a blister sufficiently rounded to allow him to lift out a pearl from within.

Most pearls have to be cleaned to get rid of surface imperfections before they are ready for sale. A pearl is made up of thin layers folded one on top of the other, like the leaves of an onion. The outer surface of each layer has a sheen, and the skill of the pearl-skinner is to file away an imperfect layer without damaging the sheen of the layer below. Thomas Bastian Ellies, a Cingalese who in 1912 ran a Broome jewellery and pawnbroking business from a single-fronted wooden shop in Carnarvon Street, was regarded as the best pearl-skinner in the world. He was universally known as TB. He could hold a pearl up to the light and seemingly see right to the core, where others were just dazzled by its lustre. (The pearl was impenetrable to Roentgen rays.)

By twirling a pearl between his thumb and forefinger, TB could feel whether a crinkle or ridge could be cut away or would only get worse the deeper he went, or whether a stain could be polished away. His equipment was rudimentary: several three-cornered files with handles made of champagne corks, a small pointed knife, thin-nosed pliers and a jeweller's eyeglass. No great conversationalist but a man of smiles and laughter with a black, waxed moustache, he worked while his clients sat opposite him. TB wanted his clients there because in less than half an hour the green felt of his table could become covered with worthless dust as a fortune was shaved away. A crease, barely noticeable on the outer layer, might, in a layer below, buckle into something larger – or it might disappear completely. A discolouration might be the start of a mud hole or it might be taken off in a few strokes of the file. These were the risks, and the client had to be there to accept them.

Jewish pearl buyers from Paris and New York would come to sit in his cramped shop with its Buddhist shrine in the corner and wafts of fragrant white incense smoke rising to the ceiling. Perhaps they were expecting the long slender fingers of a Balinese dancer; instead they would see TB hold the pearl between a short, muscular thumb and forefinger. Using his thin triangular file like a miniature violin bow, he would gently stroke the surface as he rotated the pearl, the tiny teeth of the file paring away layers as he sought the perfect dewdrop beneath. While TB smiled, the owners of the pearl perspired in nervous anticipation.

The pearls found around Broome were mostly milky white, but sometimes a pearl would be found with a gold or rosea tint; occasionally they were green–black, or perhaps whitish silver. The more exotic the shade, the greater was the asking price.

Something prized for its beauty but without any practical use was bound to be subject to wild fluctuations in price, and a smart operator could always talk up the value of a pearl. Nothing illustrates this more than the story of the most fabulous pearl of them all, the great cluster of the Southern Cross. In 1883 a sheller with the particularly Irish name of Shiner Kelly found a shell containing a line of small pearls which, with imagination, could be seen to be in the shape of a cross. Individually these seed pearls were not worth a great deal and, whatever their value, it was reduced even further when Shiner managed to break the cluster into three pieces. Back in Cossack, Shiner sold the assemblage to a pearler for £10 and a bottle of rum. The pearler sold it to a local hotelier for £40. After changing hands a few times more, and neatly repaired with diamond cement, it eventually appeared at the Colonial and Indian Exhibition of 1886 in its own display case with an asking price of £20,000. Where it is now is unknown, although the story around Broome is that in the 1930s British school children donated a shilling a head so it could be placed among the Vatican's treasures.

7 The Master Pearlers

Senator Dobson: Are these poor blacks to be allowed to do nothing?
Senator Pearce: There is plenty for them to do in their own country.
Senator Dobson: They are to be driven out of the stoke-hold, out of the sugar fields, and now out of the sea!

Australia, Senate, *Debates*, 2 November 1905, p. 4457

IT WAS NOT OPEN slather for the master pearlers to import as many coloured workers as they liked. There was a system of permits and it was the job of the sub-collector of customs, Mr Huggins, to ensure that the shellers didn't exceed their quota. The permit system had its origins in debates of Federal Parliament in 1905. In November of that year the Senate returned, as it frequently did, to the niggling topic of the pearl-shelling industry and a white Australia. Few in the chamber had been to Broome or Thursday Island, but they shared a repugnance towards having a few blocks of some Asian city, with its heady mix of open drains, exotic diseases and yellow faces, sited on Australian soil.

Senator Pearce, a Labor politician from Western Australia and a rabid supporter of racial purity, was one who was not prepared to allow this perceived infamy to continue. He took to the battle with gusto and moved a resolution calling for the cessation of the importation of coloured labour for the pearl-fishing industry. He attacked the master pearlers.

> A few rich men are reaping a harvest, but so far as concerns any benefit to the country itself – so far as concerns building up an industry which is conferring any benefit upon the Commonwealth – the pearling industry is of absolutely no use whatever. Nor will it ever be of value while it is carried on under present conditions. Personally I should rather have an industry which would return on the production only one-tenth of what it is at present returning, the whole of that tenth being produced and distributed amongst people who were good citizens of the Commonwealth, than have a larger production which conferred no benefit upon Australia as a whole, nor assisted to promote good citizenship.[1]

In Senator Pearce's world, it was not good citizenship to be Asian. He had also taken into the chamber a copy of the Roth Report on the condition of Aborigines in Western Australian. 'Revolting and unpalatable as the details are,' Senator Pearce told his fellow parliamentarians, 'I feel that it is my duty to quote them':

> Along the whole coast-line, extending from a few miles south of La Grange Bay to the eastern shores of King Sound, drunkenness and prostitution, the former being the prelude to the latter, with consequent loathsome disease, is rife amongst the aborigines. This condition of affairs is mainly due to Asiatic aliens allowed into the State as pearling-boats' crews by special

permission of the Commonwealth Minister for External Affairs
. . . The boats call in at certain creeks, ostensibly for wood and
water, and the natives flock to these creeks, the men being perfectly willing to barter their women for gin, tobacco, flour, or
rice; the coloured crews to whom they are bartered are mostly
Malays, Manillamen, and Japanese; they frequently take the
women off to the luggers . . . One magistrate considers that the
whites are just as much to blame as the coloured crews for the
prostitution going on where the boats land for getting wood
and water . . .

During about three months in the year the fleet lay up at
Cunningham Point, Cygnet Bay, Beagle Bay, and Broome, as
well as at other places: except perhaps at Broome, this laying-up
season is taken advantage of by the more unscrupulous of the
pearlers to swell the profits of the slop-chest by getting rid of
their supplies of opium and of liquor, no small portion of the
latter ultimately finding its way to the natives as payment for
prostitution. A still greater evil, and one which may have disastrous results in the future, is that both the Malays and the
natives, with whom they are at present allowed to consort, possess in common a certain vice peculiar to the Mahometan.[2]

The Senator read the report in a spirit of outrage. Images of Blacks
being buggered by brown-coloured Asiatics filled the Senate cham-
ber. The whole report 'is an indictment of the employment of
Asiatics in the industry', he said. 'The earnings go to Japan and the
Malay States, while the dividends go to a few rich men in Melbourne,
Adelaide, Sydney and Perth. If we are in earnest on the question of a
White Australia, can we allow this excrescence on our industrial life
to continue?'[3]

Opposition to Senator Pearce's motion, such as it was, was
restrained. A few senators argued that while they supported a White
Australia (of course), the pearling industry was a special case. The
main proponent of this line was the Western Australian senator

Staniforth Smith. In 1902 he had conducted a one-man investigation of the industry in Broome, spending several days on a pearling lugger, and in 1903 published a pamphlet on the topic. His approach to the Senate debate was apologetic:

> I shall be no party to any proposal to relax in any way the White Australia policy we have laid down. I go even further than Senator Pearce and say that if it were possible to sweep away from our northern shores the whole of the pearl-shell industry it would, in my honest opinion, be to the ultimate interest of Australia. Pearl-shell will always attract coloured aliens, no matter whether it be obtained from Australia or elsewhere.[4]

But then he went on to argue that the industry should be left alone because it could not support white wages, so any plan to ban Asiatics would force the master pearlers to move to Aru Island in Dutch New Guinea and conduct the industry from there.

Senator Staniforth Smith had few supporters in the chamber. Ultimately the best he could do was to avoid a complete ban on the employment of Asiatics. Instead, the Senate voted to support legislation that would freeze the number of coloured aliens allowed in the industry to the total presently employed. The Senate also proposed a bonus be paid 'to enable the replacement of coloured labour by white labour'.

Such was the tenor of the times that a resolution in support of a White Australia could not be ignored, so the Federal Government established a permit system for the importation of coloured indentured workers, designed to ensure that the numbers did not increase. The second part of the resolution was ignored and no bonus was ever paid. This was a constant complaint of the master pearlers. They never understood why the Queensland sugar-cane growers should be paid to produce a white product when they were not.

If Senator Pearce thought his resolution would punish those rich men in Melbourne, Adelaide, Sydney and Perth mucking in 'this excrescence on our industrial life', he was mistaken. In fact the reverse was the case – the permit system resulted in an immediate windfall to the master pearlers. If you were in the industry in November 1905, you immediately had an asset, a permit in perpetuity to import indentured coloured labour – and a potent means of limiting competition. A pearler who did not want to use up his full complement of permits could hire out his indentured labour to those who did. Luggers that had attached to them permits for indentured labour could be sold at a premium. There was a lot of money in permits. The sub-collector of customs at Broome wrote that because of the Senate resolution, boats worth £200 were now selling for £400 to £500.

Abraham Davis, the business manager for pearl king Mark Rubin, gave an interview to the Perth *Truth* explaining how the permit system worked:

When we want a man or a number of men we have to apply to the collector for a permit to engage him or them in Singapore. We have to say why we want the men, and what have become of those they are intended to replace. If I have a man die – they do, a big percentage of divers, from paralysis – [then] I must get another. I report to the collector, who wires the department in Melbourne detailing the circumstances and asking I have permission to obtain the help I require. He recommends the application, and in the course of a few days the reply comes that it is granted. Then I instruct our agents in Singapore to get me the class of man I want. The cost of getting him is about £14. There are a good many charges; first the medical certificate, then the fare, then, probably in advance, the agent's fees, and incidentals. Perhaps the man, after he is engaged and passed by the doctor, goes on a final razzle the night before he ships to come to us, and when he arrives is found to be unfit for work as a consequence of the night out with the boys – and girls.

> Then we have to send him back at our cost, first, because he is
> no use to us; and next, because the collector will not allow him
> to land.[5]

Photographs and the fingerprints of each indentured worker were
placed on file. When it was time for the worker to depart, the sheller
had to physically present the departing indentured worker to the customs office, hand the sub-collector a steamer ticket, and then both
would see the man aboard the steamer to make sure he left. A simple
one-on, one-off system, one would have thought. Each sheller
claimed a chain of replacements of his workers stretching back to
1905, and every time an indentured worker was sent home, or died,
the sheller would apply for a replacement. The system was designed
to be efficient and foolproof, and this was the way it was presented
to the public. The reality was somewhat different.

Soon after the Senate resolution, officers in the Department of
Customs were asked to work out the number of coloured indentured
workers in the pearling industry as at 30 November 1905 (the exact
day of the Senate resolution). This proved to be no easy task. Initially
the figure was 2321, but a recount several years later put it at 2542.
A confidential and apologetic memo from Atlee Hunt to the minister explained 'that proper records had not been kept for years of
indented men who arrived from other Australian ports, and vice
versa'.

And later in the memo comes this explanation:

> It is difficult to say how far the 1905 figures are correct. For
> instance, the return from Fremantle for 31/12/05 showed only
> nine indentured men for Cossack. The original return for that
> port cannot be traced at Fremantle, nor a copy at Cossack (it
> was not sent to this Department), but the Sub-Collector esti-
> mates that there were 153 indentured men employed on the
> date mentioned, his estimate being based on the number of ves-
> sels working at that time. The number of local men shown on

the return furnished to this Department was 6, and the
Sub-Collector estimated the number as 5, so presumably the
difference was not made up by local men.[6]

What all this really meant was that it was impossible for the department to say how many indentured workers there were in 1905. The
records were in a shambles, and indentured workers who landed in
another port – say, Cossack or Onslow – had sometimes been
counted again in Broome. Shellers who were determined to have a
recollection that in 1905 they had as many indentured workers as
possible thumped the table in Huggins' office in order to squeeze a
few more permits out of the system. The problem was compounded
by the fact that the Senate resolution spoke of 'coloured aliens'. Most
of the crew working on the luggers were coloured but were they
aliens? Some had been in Australia prior to Federation, a few had
been born in Australia, some were the offspring of a union with the
oldest inhabitants of all, the Australian Aborigines. Which of these
were coloured aliens?

After the embarrassment of having to inform the minister that
there were in fact many more aliens working in the industry than was
first thought, Hunt began to devise ways of cutting back on the numbers so that he could be correct after all. New rules were introduced:
indentured workers could not be replaced until they had reached
their home port, applications to replace men had to be made within
six months or else permits would lapse, and any permit granted had
to be used within six weeks of approval. Further, where a lugger had
been lost or disabled, a fresh application had to be made rather than
just relying on the old one.

The Pearlers' Association held protest meetings against this petty
regulation of their capacity to make money. All sorts of resolutions
were passed. Petitions were drawn up, members of Parliament were
written to, and a fund established to pay the passage of the minister
to Broome so he could understand the real situation. Stanley Pigott
wrote to the minister pointing out how unreasonable it all was. The

Pearlers' Association proved to be a very effective lobbyist. The government backed down and Hunt's new rules were scrapped.

But problems with the permit system were not confined to keeping a cap on the numbers allowed. In an article written in 1909 the *Port Hedland Advocate* claimed that the customs officers in Broome were corrupt and were letting in Asians without hindrance. The article also alleged that many of the coloured men claimed to be lost in two recent cyclones were very much alive and working under other names, and that pearlers were pretending to send their indentured workers home at the end of their three-year term when in fact they were staying. In response, Sub-Collector Huggins wrote long reports to his superior in Melbourne. Penned in a style as though recounting the activities of naughty schoolboys, he accused the master pearlers of rorting the system by fiddling their returns and hiring out their indentured workers to others. Senator Pearce became so concerned about the situation that he met the prime minister and told him that he had it on good authority that Japanese were entering Broome under the pretence of being engaged in pearling, but in fact were drifting into the permanent population. He claimed that there were 184 more Japanese in Broome than there had been six months previously.

Although all these complaints found their way into government files, nothing much was done. It was all happening a long way away, and it was recognised that it was not feasible to keep tabs on the indentured workers along the entire coastline. The State Government didn't seem to care and the Federal Government didn't have the resources. Huggins wrote to Hunt that 'during the lay up season at Broome, it would be impossible for me to even attempt to control the movement of those ashore, or to possess more than a superficial knowledge of the work the men were engaged at'.[7]

Huggins' reference to the impossibility of knowing what the indentured Asiatic workers were doing was a confession of his inability to enforce another of the government's edicts. Although the government was prepared to tolerate a violation of the White Australia Policy to allow Asians to work on pearling vessels at sea, on

no account were they allowed to work on shore. This was the territory of the white man. Public servants in Hunt's office provided
interpretations for the guidance of Broome's townsfolk. Stores were
not to be carried on board the luggers by coloured aliens – this was
the work of Australian stevedores. A coloured alien was not allowed
to cook his master's meal on the lugger then carry it to the shore, but
there would be no breach of the rules if the meal was eaten on board.
After some hesitation and consultation with his superiors, Huggins
advised that indentured workers might repair and renew a lugger, but
must not be caught building a new one.

As with many things in Broome, firm instructions from officials
in the cities were ignored. In storehouses along the foreshore, in sheds
at the back of bungalows in the English Quarter and on schooners in
the bay, the Asiatics whiled away the boredom of the lay-up by earning a bit of extra money on a range of activities, from cabinet-making
to shell-carving to sail-making. Every now and then Huggins would
write to Melbourne seeking specific dispensation for indentured men
to work on shore, thus implying that overall there was strict compli-
ance. In 1909 when the Japanese community erected a memorial to
the 200 lives lost in the cyclones of 1908, the minister formally gave
approval for the work and passed on his condolences. And after the
disastrous cyclone which cut a swathe through Broome in November
1910, the Commonwealth Government cabled that for a period of
one month coloured workers could help repair the town.

The annual intake of indentured workers took place in February
each year. It was Sub-Collector Huggins' job to meet any vessel
carrying indentured aliens as she tied up at the end of the Broome
jetty. The workers were kept below until the paying passengers had
disembarked, then they were escorted ashore on the train, more or
less under the guard of uniformed customs officers and several large
dogs. They were taken to the whitewashed Customs House near the
end of the jetty and placed in the back yard until the immigration
procedures had been completed. To the seamen from Asia it must
have seemed a strange place. Never would they have seen earth so red,

nor so many nondescript buildings of tin and lattice-work. They were now in the land of the foreign devil where red-faced men with large noses would order them around in an incomprehensible language.

Over the next hour, one by one, they were called from the yard into the Customs House where an officer in a blue uniform compared the flesh and blood before him with a photograph taken by the labour agent in Singapore. If there was a rough correlation between the two, the officer grabbed the worker's hand and pushed it, fingers extended, onto an ink pad, then used the hand as a stamp on the back of the photograph. These were not so much fingerprints (which was a science inadequately understood in Broome at that time) but palm prints, the idea being that three years later, when the worker was returning to his home country, the officials could check to see if the correct person was leaving. The formalities over, the worker was then directed out the front door. Standing on the street outside were a dozen white men – the master pearlers – and they were there to grab their men.

The master pearlers would take the indentured men to the accommodation they provided. These were the foreshore camps of canvas and tin sheds which lined up for a couple of miles facing the mangroves adjacent to the town. There were neither toilets nor running water, and whenever there was a storm or a king tide, the sea ran underfoot. The water of Roebuck Bay in front of the camps was fouled by the latrines and rubbish. Years later a retired crewman, Percy Fong, recalled these camps:

> Some of my friends, which came from Singapore, came here . . . all they slept on was a shell-shook, which is boxes they make the pearl-cases on. They just made it high enough, with a blanket on it. Sleeping on an old shed, and cooking, also, with an ordinary kerosene primus. And that's how they lived. And, you know, they wonder why the natives are so bitter against the Europeans. It's because they've been suppressed so much. And I think it's embedded in their minds; they haven't ever forgotten it, you know.[8]

Following a report from the health officer, in 1910 Broome council erected two public latrines – one opposite the Continental Hotel and the other near the Roebuck Bay Hotel – with the hopeful sign: 'Must Be Used by Crew.' Elsewhere the sea sufficed.

It was a fish-eating population down on the foreshore – fried, grilled, raw, in stews, curries and pancakes. The master pearlers supplied rice and flour and some kerosene for heating. Those indentured workers who could afford it quickly moved into one of the boarding houses in Japtown, and by the end of the first season the remainder, if they were not impoverished by gambling, had moved there as well.

Not only was the Federal Government concerned about the number of Asiatics working in the northwest, it also believed that there were too many Japanese. In 1910, an inspector of police, Mr W.C. Sellinger, wrote a five-page letter to the Premier of Western Australia about 'the arrogant and dictatorial manner adopted by the Japanese crews towards the Pearler and the Malay crew on the luggers and schooners'. His letter went on to warn that:

> the Japanese desire to see the boats manned entirely by their countrymen, and are resorting to every strategy to accomplish that end. At the present time the divers are principally Japanese, and they are frequently seen explaining to and teaching other Japanese the art of diving, but on no account whatever will they give the Malay any information or allow one to go down in the diving dress if they can prevent it.
>
> More than one Pearler has told me that White men in charge of boats are regarded with contempt by the Japanese, who take no pains to disguise their feelings. To use the expression of one of the men who told me – the White man is simply regarded as 'Mud' . . .
>
> Some time ago the Japanese diver on one of the boats insisted on the White man in charge of the boat giving up his berth in the cabin to the tender (another Japanese).
>
> On another occasion, a White man left his lugger to go on

to a schooner for something, when the Japanese crew set sail, and proceeded some miles away. On being asked for an explanation, he [the Japanese] replied that he was in charge of the boat and would allow no interference with his wishes as to where the boat should be taken.

In another case, the lugger came into Broome for supplies, and the White man gave instructions for the crew to be prepared to go out to sea again the next day. The diver would not go, saying he would be ready on the morrow. He was, but the boat went intentionally without the White man, and he had to wait for 5 days, before he could procure a passage in a schooner to the pearling grounds.

The letter, of which this is only an extract, concluded with this grim summary:

Briefly, the Malay is satisfied to work under the white master, quite content so long as he gets a fair deal, and is not molested or insulted. On the other hand the Japanese is ambitious. They apparently desire to see the fleets manned entirely by their own race, and their ability, energy, and wonderful organisation is unobtrusively but surely advancing in this direction . . . The possibility of such a result is, in my humble opinion, worthy of serious consideration, and I say without hesitation that the decision should not be left to the Pearlers.[9]

Alarming news from the inspector of police. So alarming that the Premier sent a copy to Prime Minister Fisher. It was referred to Mr Batchelor, the Minister of External Affairs, with instructions to do something about it.

Still in his mid forties, Batchelor was steeped in a Labor tradition born of his involvement in the trade union movement in South Australia. His determination to force the introduction of white men into the pearl-shelling industry would have surprised no one – the

Australian Labor Party was in power, and he was merely implementing his party's uncomplicated support for a White Australia.

The growing domination of the Japanese was not the only scandal brought to Batchelor's attention. In 1910 Sub-Collector Huggins wrote a long letter to Hunt advising that the master pearlers were now crewing their schooners with indentured workers. That Asiatics were working on the schooners was probably news to Batchelor and Hunt, who knew almost nothing about the practicalities of pearling. But they could quickly recognise chicanery when it was waved under their noses. The shellers might argue that white men could not be expected to work on luggers in awful, cramped conditions, but this could not possibly apply to the schooners tending the fleet. This was a clear case of coloured workers displacing the white man. To a government already harbouring grave misgivings about any coloured aliens working in Australian waters, the suggestion that indentured workers were required for what was, after all, mere coastal shipping seemed outrageous. As far as Hunt and Batchelor could see, there was no reason why white seamen could not be employed at normal Australian award rates.

The more they investigated the situation, the worse it appeared. It seemed that some of the master pearlers had invented fancy uniforms for the crews of their schooners and had bare-chested Malays in cream lap-laps with red fezzes atop serving gin and tonic to their white masters seated in wicker chairs. Minister Batchelor instructed Hunt to despatch a telegram to Huggins advising that, in future, permits to import indentured coloured workers would be restricted to working boats, and a working boat meant one actually employed in the process of recovering shell with the aid of a diver.

The Pearlers' Association went into protest mode. Meetings were held, local members of Parliament were lobbied and Stanley Pigott, as secretary of the association typed long and detailed letters to the minister and Hunt pointing out that the getting of shell required the conveyance of men and gear, and wood and water to and from the pearling grounds. It was a well-known fact that a fleet (even a small fleet) worked much more steadily and consistently when it had a schooner to service it. The luggers could work further away from port and did not need to return so often. The schooners served as a floating station for minor repairs of the luggers, and as a training vessel for those workers who knew nothing about seamanship. In an ingenious argument, Stanley Pigott tapped into what he perceived as the minister's aversion to having white men working in proximity to Asiatics:

> it is extremely doubtful whether Whites could be obtained who would associate with Asiatics in this way, but in the few instances where it has been tried on a small scale (as for instance on luggers) the mixing of Whites and Asiatics has resulted in failure and must always do so. Not merely do Whites and Asiatics require different foods and different methods for cooking, but the former lose caste in the eyes of the latter when they associate together at the same work.[10]

As the war of words between Stanley Pigott and the minister (despatched backwards and forwards across the continent by telegram) became heated, Hunt, now in a conciliatory mood, asked the master pearlers to advise on how they thought the permits should be distributed. A general meeting of the association, held in September 1910, gave its response. The members called for a sliding scale of permits: the larger the vessel owned by the master pearler, the more permits to employ coloured workers should be granted by the government. It was an audacious claim which sought to increase the number of permits overall. No doubt it only served to convince Minister Batchelor that the Pearlers' Association would do everything it could to frustrate his attempts to reduce the industry's reliance on a coloured workforce.

Meanwhile, Hugh Norman, who at that time was president of the Pearlers' Association, was visiting Melbourne and he met with the minister. The brief notes of the meeting state that the minister explained the government's desire to see the master pearlers making an effort to introduce white labour into the industry. He then went on to say that he would allow matters to continue on the existing basis until the end of 1910, when he would ascertain what steps had been taken to comply with the government's wishes. Pa Norman left the meeting victorious and returned to Broome. At the Pearlers' Association annual meeting in December 1910 there were debates on the perennial topics of advances to crews, the theft of pearls and the latest theory of what caused beri beri – but nothing of the minister's desire that this be made a white industry. It seems that the master pearlers took Batchelor's concession as proof that although the Labor government might huff and puff, it dare not jeopardise the pearl-shell industry by adhering to principle. It was a belief to be rudely shattered a few months later.

At the year's end Batchelor called for a report as to whether the shellers had done anything to meet his request to increase the number of white workers in the industry. Hunt asked his sub-collectors of customs in each port to advise urgently. Among the yellowing files in the Australian Archives in Canberra is the summary prepared by Hunt and given to the minister prior to the Christmas break. It must have unsettled his festive digestion.

PORT DARWIN: The Sub-Collector states that no change had been made in regard to the employment of white men in the industry. He says that at the present time there is no local labour either white or coloured, available at Port Darwin for pearling . . .

THURSDAY ISLAND: The Sub-Collector forwards a letter from the Torres Straits Pearlshellers' Association to the following effect:–

Anything in the way of immediate substantial changes in the industry would be fatal to existing interests and it seems to be impossible to at once bring about an increase in the number of white men engaged in the industry . . . Even if white labour be available it will take several years to train sufficient men to fill the boats now engaged . . .

ONSLOW: No change in the direction of the employment of more white labour has occurred at this port since the Government's wishes were communicated to the pearlers.

COSSACK: No change in the direction of the employment of more white labour has occurred at this port since the Government's wishes were communicated to the pearlers.

BROOME: No practical efforts have been made by the pearlers to meet the Government's wishes. Several suggestions have been made but they have not been carried out. It is understood that one pearler, Mr Norman, proposes to man his schooner 'Mina' entirely with European labour but this has not yet been done.

PORT HEDLAND: As this port is not the headquarters of any pearling fleet, and as men are only occasionally discharged or engaged there, the Sub-Collector is unable to furnish any information regarding the matter. He states, however, that he duly acquainted pearlers with the Government's wishes.[11]

Mr Batchelor took the Christmas break to ponder what he could do to bring the master pearlers to heel. He would have known that it wasn't going to be easy. The issue of the use of coloured labour in the pearl-shelling industry had been troubling governments for twenty years. There were many reports, inquiries and commissions all identifying the moral dangers of importing Asiatic workers, but they were short on solutions. Batchelor would have realised there would be a storm of protest from the master pearlers if he forced the introduction of the white man, and he knew that the Pearlers' Association was adept at galvanising public opinion. An election was coming up in Western Australia and Labor had a good chance of gaining office. Labor politicians in Western Australia were staunch theoretical supporters of the White Australia Policy but were painfully aware that pearl-shelling was the state's fourth biggest industry and brought in substantial revenues in port taxes and charges, and licence fees. If the industry was crippled, Broome would shrink to the size of a fishing village and the vast area of the Kimberleys would revert to occupation by Aboriginal tribes and scattered pastoralists. The Fremantle dockyard had a thriving industry in the construction of luggers, and hundreds were likely to lose their jobs should this activity cease.

But Batchelor was a White Australia man through and through. What particularly stuck in his craw was that this was skilled work, which should have been the preserve of the white man. He regarded the whitening of the sugar-cane industry in Queensland as a triumph of government intervention. He was Minister of External Affairs and he was not prepared to have it said that Australia welcomed the Asiatic because its own nationals couldn't do the job. If he was to leave a legacy, it would be that he had cleared the last area of coloured employment from the nation.

In January 1911 he decided to act against the master pearlers. After catching a steamer for a trade conference in New Zealand he left it to Hunt to send off the appropriate telegram. Dated 9 January 1911, it read: 'All future approvals for the introduction or re-engagement of indentured labour for pearling industry are to operate only until the first January, 1913. (Signed) Atlee Hunt.'[12]

Mr Huggins no doubt read this telegram with astonishment. This would mean, in just two years time, the devastation of the pearl-shelling industry. And the demise of Broome. A shipload of Japanese workers was due in Broome on 14 January, each of them holding indenture papers for a three-year term. What would happen to them? Was he supposed to turn them back or tell them they could only stay for two years? Huggins immediately wired back to Melbourne seeking clarification and decided to keep the telegram to himself until he knew what it all meant. But perhaps he carelessly left the telegram on his desk while he went out for lunch, or perhaps he told a few of the master pearlers in confidence, or perhaps the telegram office leaked the communication, but somehow the news got out, and a large crowd, including Mr Green from the *Broome Chronicle*, bailed up Huggins in his office.

At first Huggins told them that he could not reveal the content of the telegram as it was purely a departmental instruction, and when they howled that down, he said he needed the minister's consent, so Green suggested he get that, and the protests grew and grew, and finally he handed the telegram over. It was promptly printed in the *Chronicle* and the town went into an uproar. Talk in the hotels and homes of Broome continued long into the night. They were ruined. It was the end of their livelihood. Didn't the government realise that this industry couldn't exist without Asiatic labour? The next day, traders declared they would cease investing in the town and at the weekend no bids were received for a prime block of land in the town's centre. The price of luggers tumbled.

A few days later a second telegram was received:

> Melbourne, January 13th, 1911. To the Customs, Broome. As intimated in telegram of 9th, permits lapse after two years. They can only be renewed on condition that diver and tender in the boats on which they are to be employed are white men. Letter following. (Signed) Atlee Hunt.[13]

This message, on the surface a clarification, in fact represented something of a backdown. The number of crew required on a lugger varied depending on the size of the vessel, but the average was seven, made up of a diver and his tender, two pump hands, a cook and two seamen. Whereas the earlier telegram meant the whole seven had to be white, the second limited that restriction to the diver and tender. Not that this wasn't also greeted with howls of alarm from the master pearlers. Stanley Pigott fired off telegrams in protest. Some shellers pointed out, yet again, that since most of the diving was conducted in international waters, they could easily up anchor and conduct their operations from Aru Island in Dutch New Guinea. The president of the association (by now Sydney Pigott), relied on his parliamentarian connections to persuade the Premier of Western Australia to lobby the federal authorities and ask for the decision to be reconsidered.

Batchelor was unmoved. Upon his return from New Zealand, he called the press together and told them that Broome and other pearling stations were outposts of Asia in existing circumstances. 'With the exception of a few pearlers and those who supplied their requisites, the Pearling Industry gives nothing to Australia. If it were possible to make it an industry that gave occupation to White Australians it was the duty of the Government to do so.'[14]

Hugh Richardson, who was in Melbourne, called on Hunt, protesting against the bans. A note of the meeting kept by Hunt shows that Richardson pointed out that in order to keep shelling alive, something like 700 men would be required in Broome alone, and it would take at least twelve months to train them as divers. This would be an expensive and difficult exercise and they would welcome a concession from the minister of at least another year before the change was implemented. Richardson proved persuasive. Although with some reluctance, Minister Batchelor scribbled a note in the margin of the file: '12 months extension for Cabinet.' But the sting was that the government had extracted a promise from the Pearlers' Association that it 'would make an honourable effort to obtain and work with white divers and tenders'.

Mr Batchelor was not to see the year out. One day in October 1911, he took a hike with the Wallaby Walking Club from the Warburton chalet in Victoria to climb Mount Donna Buang. He had barely tackled the first rise when he complained of a pain around his heart. He collapsed. A team of runners hurried him down the mountain, but they knew he was already dead. He was 46 years old. When Federal Parliament assembled a few days later, Batchelor was eulogised. He was described as a kindly, gentle man, tragically cut off in the prime of his life. Members from both sides of the House spoke of his honour, wisdom and unfailing courtesy to all.

The elections for the Western Australian Parliament were held in October 1911. The Pigott brothers campaigned strongly for the anti-Labor candidate, Mr Arthur Male, squatter and pearler, who said he was against the coloured man entering Australia as much as the next person, but the pearling industry was a special case and should be left alone. In this he was repeating the views of the industry. No one in the Pearlers' Association ever argued that the White Australia Policy was wrong. Privately they may not have cared whether the workers were black or white so long as they brought up the shell. Some may even have thought that a hundred or so servants from the Indian sub-continent might have made life in the tropics more bearable, but these thoughts could never be expressed, even in jest. Publicly and repeatedly, the pearlers went out of their way to assure everyone how strongly they favoured the ideal of a White Australia – but the cost would ruin the industry, and since the coloured aliens spent most of their time at sea, they were not likely to have much opportunity to degrade the purity of the white race.

The Labor candidate for the seat of the Kimberleys, Mr Brown, was in an awkward position – after all, it was his federal colleagues who were determined to destroy the most profitable industry in the electorate. Brown asked the voters of the Kimberleys to consider federal and state issues as separate, and not to hold decisions from Melbourne against him. A rather forlorn plea. Brown was unsuccessful, but Labor was triumphant overall, and John Scaddan became the state's premier.

As part of the bargain in obtaining a twelve-month extension from the government, the Pearlers' Association had agreed to make an honourable effort to place white men in the industry. Much to the surprise of the master pearlers, obtaining divers and tenders from England was not difficult. This was not altogether welcome news, but there it was. James Davis, who was running the Broome office for Siebe, Gorman, contacted his brother, who was the managing director in England. Siebe, Gorman advised that the firm had 300 experienced divers on its register. Heinke said that it had a similar number.

Back in Australia, squabbles took place as to who should pay for the recruitment of the Englishmen. Stanley Pigott, remembering that in 1905 a bonus for using white labour had been promised by the Senate, wired the Prime Minister. The new Premier of Western Australia, Mr Scaddan, supported the idea of a Commonwealth bonus, or failing that, a sharing of the costs, but the Commonwealth wasn't having any of this – it was a state matter. In the end the only support for the scheme given by either government was that the fares from England were made available at the assisted migration rate.

Securing master pearlers to take on the Englishmen proved to be the difficult part. Stanley Pigott placed an advertisement in the *Broome Chronicle* on 18 November 1911, inviting 'Pearlers desirous of obtaining the service of white divers and tenders for employment on their vessels next year, to make early application for such numbers as they may require.' He repeated the advertisement the following three Saturdays. The response was disappointing. Stanley Pigott heard all sorts of excuses. It was too expensive. His colleagues doubted if the whites could match the Asiatics – although they suspected that the whites would demand better food. In the end Stanley Pigott had to take three of the men himself and cajole his brother Sydney into taking three. The others were engaged by Pa Norman, the Heinke agent, and Hugh Richardson, the Siebe, Gorman agent. All four employers were committee members of the Pearlers' Association. The original plan had been to bring in twenty men, but it soon became apparent that no other members of the Pearlers' Association were interested.

Batchelor's replacement as Minister of External Affairs was Mr Josiah Thomas. He was determined to carry on the vision of his predecessor. The member for Brisbane, Mr Findlayson, rose in Parliament to give the new minister some advice.

Mr FINDLAYSON – I warn the Minister of External Affairs . . . I found that the members of the Pearl Shellers' Association do not intend to make the slightest effort to prepare for the time when the alien must go and the white man take his place; there must be some training, something done to insure that the white man will be ready to step in. The pearl-shellers, however, are living in the hope that the Labour [*sic*] Party will not always be in power – that, perhaps, before the time arrives, this party will have left office; and that they will be able to get an extension of time.

MR RILEY – Do they think there will be a 'black-labour' party in power?

MR FINDLAYSON – They apparently think so.

MR RILEY – Nonsense![15]

Findlayson was referring to the situation on Thursday Island, but he could just as well have been speaking about the pearlers of Western Australia. The occasion of this exchange was during a debate in Federal Parliament in October 1911 on a motion proposed by Mr Frederick Bamford, MP to hold a Royal Commission into the pearl-shelling industry. Bamford was the Labor member for Herbert in Queensland, and was well known as the man to rid Australia of coloured labour. Not only had he decided that what was needed was a Royal Commission but, not to leave anything to chance, he wanted it to be composed of members of Parliament with himself as chairman. The House agreed, and in April 1912, in the formal way such things are done, he and the five other members received their appointments from Thomas Denman, the Governor-General. The terms were to:

inquire into and report upon the Pearl-shelling Industry as carried on in Australian Waters or from Australian ports, and more particularly in relation to:–

The classes of labour at present engaged;

The reasons why white labour had not been hitherto more generally employed;

The practicability of white labour being introduced;

The employment of machinery in connexion to the diving pumps;

The cultivation of the pearl shell oyster; and

The means to be adopted to encourage employment of white labour (a) wholly, (b) partially.[16]

In early April 1912 Bamford and his parliamentary colleagues, their personal assistants, several amanuenses and Mr H. Farrands, secretary to the commission, packed their bags in wintry Melbourne and embarked on a two-week cruise up the coast to Cairns in tropical Queensland. The commissioners would have to take several long sea voyages, one to the pearling centres in North Queensland, Thursday Island and Port Darwin, then back to Melbourne, before undertaking another to Perth, and north to Port Hedland and Broome. Thousands of miles, weeks at sea and months before a report could be written. It promised to be the junket of a lifetime.

8 The Deep

The divers live not to a great age. Heart disease, surfeits, sores, blood-shot eyes, staggering limbs, and bent backs — these are part of the wages. Sometimes they die on reaching the surface, suddenly, as if struck by a shot.

The Oyster, 1863[1]

WEBBER AND REID EMBARKED on a search for shell on 20 February 1912, just two days after their arrival in Broome. They sailed on the *Eurus* with stores for eight weeks and the tanks full of water. Their employer, Hugh Richardson, of course, was well aware of the risks of venturing to sea during the cyclone season and it must be assumed that Webber was as well. Perhaps, after the inactivity of a sea voyage of two months, Webber was keen to get started. He may have wanted to show that an ex-navy man was prepared to risk the weather while the Asiatics were still holed up in the foreshore camps. He may have wanted to show what a Siebe, Gorman trained diver could do. Webber came with the endorsement of those at the top of

Siebe, Gorman and prior to his setting out from London, the firm had written to the Pearlers' Association in Broome:

> You will notice that I have included Webber. I have sent him not only because he is a deep water man but he is a very loyal servant to the Firm and I think we ought at least to have one man that we know and can trust to look after our interests amongst the Fleet. He is most enthusiastic about the work and very anxious to show the pearlers what he can do.[2]

Richardson had not installed one of the new engine pumps on board the *Eurus*; instead, the diver's air was supplied by a couple of coloured workers turning a wheel. In Britain Webber had been used to an engine pump with an air compressor; Richardson had none on any of his boats. They cost almost £200, a high price when it is considered that a lugger could be purchased for £600, and a pump hand could be hired to turn the wheel at a shilling a day. It is also likely that Richardson didn't trust engine pumps. To keep an engine pump in working order required someone with mechanical ability and, before Reid, there was no one with those skills on any of Richardson's luggers.

Richardson gave evidence to the Bamford Royal Commission when it finally visited Broome in 1916. He said that Webber and Reid went out with his best coloured crew and an 'experienced old diver to choose the ground for them'. Richardson had plenty of crew to select from. The firm had 40 Japanese, 29 Malays and six Manila-men working on its fleet. Because there was no engine-driven pump aboard, Reid's job was to be a tender to the diver, and not an engineer. He spent the day leaning over the side with the lifeline to Webber in hand, watching the bubbles rise and learning how to get the boat to drift over the pearling grounds.

Records do not show who the 'experienced old diver' was. He probably guided Webber south along the expanse of Ninety Mile Beach. Here boats had been gathering shell for the past 30 years and the supply seemed inexhaustible. Considered a floor of dreary flatness along a coastline deserving a similar description, it stretched southwest from Cape Missiessy to just north of Pardoo Station. So undistinguished was this coast of white beach, barely visible above the horizon, that in 1909 the Public Works Department erected five iron beacons with a finger sign pointing to show those at sea where fresh water wells could be found. In this setting the *Eurus* had the seas largely to herself. Apart from a few shellers prepared to risk the weather, it would be another fortnight before the rest of the fleet would tempt fortune.

Then, on 7 March 1912, disembarking from the SS *Gorgon*, another English diver arrived in Broome. His name was Reginald Vernon Hockliss. He was an ex-naval diver and, like the others, had no experience as a shell collector. Sydney Pigott could find no master pearler willing to employ Hockliss, so he had to add him to his own list. Sydney Pigott now had four divers, when what he really needed was a few tenders who knew how to sail and look after the pumps. But he consoled himself by thinking that if he was right about the amount of shell to be found in Roebuck Deep, four divers who knew how to get beyond 30 fathoms might be very useful indeed.

So keen was Sydney Pigott to have his English divers search the Deep, he arranged for welders at McDonald & Low's Engineering Works in Broome to fix a small engine to a hand-pump and install it on his schooner *Muriel*. At depths of 25 fathoms, the pump had to work hard to provide the enormous pressure to send air to the diver – 120 pounds to the square inch. The plan was that Hockliss, Noury and Rolland would dive in rotation, two recovering on the surface while the third went below. Each diver would be on the bottom for only a few minutes, but Sydney Pigott expected so much shell to be found that it would be worth it.

Captain Herbert Sewell, a witness to the Royal Commission, said he and a few other master pearlers, at the invitation of Sydney Pigott, went out to watch the Englishmen making this dive. He described Sydney Pigott as standing on the hatch of the *Muriel* with an alarm clock and the Admiralty tables in hand. He said that Pigott had one of his Malay divers, Ahmet Penang, along to explain to the Englishmen what the shell looked like underwater. There must have been a great deal of interest in what Pigott was up to because Hugh Richardson also gave evidence that he motored out in his launch to have a look.

Broome is located on a peninsula which protrudes into Roebuck Bay. Most of the bay is quite shallow, 2 to 4 fathoms, but at the end of the peninsula is the Deep, about 7 miles long and shaped much like a banana, even to the extent of having a bend which curves gently around the peninsula. The edge of the channel is marked on modern hydrographic charts by a 50-metre line, the edges of which are hatched to indicate underwater cliffs, and then at the western end is a circle indicating a depth of 100 metres. A fathom is roughly 2 metres, so the fall away to the bottom is 50 fathoms or more. In 1912 much less was known. Maps marked Roebuck Deep from 25 fathoms to a depth unknown. Certainly the men Sydney Pigott brought with him that day never found the bottom.

Hockliss took the first dive. Dressing for a dive was a slow exercise. At the surface the water is a tropical bath, but as the diver goes deeper it gets colder, and Hockliss had been warned about the Deep, where beyond 15 fathoms the water, in still pockets, could become frigid. He tugged long stockings over his feet and halfway up his thighs. He pulled on two woollen singlets and a pair of tweed trousers, then two heavy sweaters which he buttoned onto the top of his trousers. He placed a red woollen cap on his head. Then he sat down on a stool before an outsized canvas suit and a water-greened copper helmet the size of a bullock's head.

Noury held the canvas diving suit gaping open in front of him. Hockliss shoved his legs inside and pushed his feet into rubberised shoes. Then he stood up and held out his hands as Noury rubbed soapy water around his wrists to allow him to force his hands through the tautness of the india rubber cuffs of the sleeves. Noury tied a coir lifeline around his waist while Rolland knelt before him and strapped on boots laden with 14 pounds of lead. Noury placed a copper corse-let over Hockliss' shoulders, taking care to align its holes over the brass studs set into the canvas dress. Rolland placed heavy plates of lead over his chest and back, then fixed them into special buckles.

Swaddled so completely, Hockliss began to overheat and ran his fingers across his brow, flicking drops of sweat onto the deck while he waited for Rolland to get the pump going. At last the clack-clack of the engine began to sound. Rolland put his hand in front of the out-let pipe to check there was a good push of air, then he and Noury guided Hockliss across the deck to where a coir-rope ladder fell over the side. The two men manhandled Hockliss onto the ladder. His feet caught the wooden slats and he swung there with water up to his waist, neck extended, while Noury gently lowered the helmut over his head and screwed it onto the cleats of the corselet. For a moment the circle of Hockliss' face, visible only from eyebrows to chin, peered out in a wry smile, then Noury swung the glass port of the helmet shut and screwed up the butterfly nut holding it in place. Instantly the glass fogged up.

As always, it took a few seconds for the air to come through and, as always, Hockliss listened anxiously for the sound of its first hiss. It was slightly tainted with the smell of oil from the compressor, but it was air and gratefully he took several deep breaths. Noury gave the all-clear by tapping on the top of the helmet, Hockliss released his grip on the ladder and pushed himself backwards in a standing posi-tion into the water. For a moment the top of his helmet was visible, then he reached up to adjust the escape valve and he disappeared from view in a canopy of bubbles.

Hockliss entered Roebuck Deep from the east of Escape Rocks. He signalled by tugging on the lifeline for Noury to drop him a few fathoms then hold him steady until he got his bearings. He fell through a cloud of small silver fish which flashed around him before abruptly turning as one in a shining wall and disappearing. At 15 fathoms he looked downwards, over a chasm with no floor. He sig-nalled to be taken lower. He halted at 20 fathoms. He was aware of the immense pressure on his body, which squeezed breath out of his lungs and made it difficult to breathe. His throat felt dry. The thump of his heartbeat, transmitted by the compressed air around him, echoed in his ears. He swept an arm through the water and, like a top on the end of a string, he half-swam, half-spun in a slow circle. A sheer cliff came into view. He saw a ridge where tufts of washed-out weed grew. A jagged battlement of rocks extended to his right. But he could see no mother-of-pearl.

Noury signalled to him. He signalled back that he was okay. He decided to drop another 5 fathoms and the line was played out further. He had never been at this depth before. The line went taut. He had expected to see something below: a gloomy hollow, perhaps, where he might have glimpsed the flash of firefly or the spark of fish which carried lights of their own – but he saw nothing. There was no bottom. He began to feel cold. He signalled for the lugger to drag him along the line of the cliff, but for some reason he was taken lower. He jerked the lifeline; he was held steady. He felt a sharp pain in his eardrum, and then a buzzing noise deep within his skull. Stupidly, he tried to poke at his ear with his hand, but it bumped helplessly against the helmet. As he dropped his hand, he fingered the canvas of his suit, stretched smooth under the pressure. Of course it wouldn't split, he told himself. It was best Heinke rubber. He had checked it himself. A new suit, only months old. He held a breath before expelling slowly.

He was next to the cliff face. He had to take care; if the lugger pulled him into it, he would be scraped across rocks. He looked carefully for shell, as Ahmet Penang had described them, covered in growth but seen by the ruffle of their lips. Instead he saw a large, green crab with long spindly legs, so long it was hard to reckon that such a creature was feasible. It scampered down the precipice. Some other thing, of grey ooze and with a pair of glistening black eyes, stared at him out of a narrow fissure.

Hockliss received a signal from above. It was time to come up. He was taken to 10 fathoms and held for five minutes, then 8 fathoms for ten minutes and 3 fathoms for twenty minutes. Time seemed to crawl as he swung in a blue void, the only sounds being the hiss of the air in his helmet and the faint reverberation of the compressor. Eventually he surfaced and, as he clambered up the ladder, Noury reached for the shell bag. It was empty. Noury and Rolland glanced up at Sydney Pigott standing on the cabin roof. Pigott glared back at them but said nothing. The crew pulled Hockliss aboard and unscrewed his glass. There was a small gust of released air, and his suit collapsed into wrinkles, falling off his shoulders. Hockliss looked up at Pigott and shouted that he hadn't even seen the bottom. Pigott told him there were shells there, for sure. Then, with an edge to his voice, he added that Hockliss couldn't see them – that was the problem. He turned to Ahmet Penang and ordered him to take the next dive instead of Noury. Ahmet Penang would show them.

Hockliss and Rolland helped the Malay dress and go over the side. Pigott, standing above them on the cabin roof, yelled out for them to watch what Ahmet Penang could do. They would see Ahmet Penang fetch some shell. Hockliss shouted back that he'd bet a fiver there was no shell there. Pigott ignored him for a moment, then added, 'You just wait and see.'

After twenty minutes Penang returned to the surface. He had nothing in his bag. The Englishmen looked up at Sydney Pigott with broad smiles on their faces. Pigott glared at Penang but said nothing.

Then it was Noury's turn. Noury dropped to 30 fathoms. He brought up three shells and waved his bag at the man standing on the cabin roof, but his efforts didn't seem to satisfy Pigott in the slightest. He motioned to Rolland and watched sullenly as Rolland clumped across the deck and climbed overboard.

While Rolland was below, Noury sat on the deck with his back against the cabin and watched Hockliss play out the lifeline and airhose. Next to Hockliss was Ahmet Penang, wearing only a pair of half trousers and smoking on a gurgling pipe as he explained something about the bubbles from the helmet agitating the water underneath. Penang was a small, wiry man with a smile of a thousand wrinkles. He gabbled in broken English with such speed it was difficult to know what he was saying. Noury felt the heat bouncing off the sea-whitened boards of the deck. There was no wind. A trickle of sweat tumbled under his shirt and over the folds of his stomach, yet strangely he felt cold. Suddenly, a shooting pain rippled along his right leg and shot into his knee joint. Noury gasped in the agony of it, but no one heard him. No one turned to him. Slowly the pain ebbed away. He rubbed at his knee and straightened it out. It felt fine. Strange that it had happened, though. He sat deep in thought, quietly massaging his knee.

In 1905 the Lords of the Admiralty, concerned about the number of crippling injuries to navy divers from the bends, had set up a deep diving committee to investigate the causes and to recommend preventive measures. Led by Professor J.S. Haldane, it conducted a series of experiments in London, and then with divers off the HMS *Spanker* in the lochs of Scotland. As a result of the committee's work, tables were published in 1907–8 (known as the Admiralty tables) showing the staging times a diver should follow after being exposed to extremes of air pressure. The Admiralty tables were intended to ensure that no man would ever again suffer from the bends.

The master pearlers of Broome were suspicious of the Admiralty tables. They had all heard the analogy about the fizz of nitrogen in the bloodstream being like taking the stopper off a bottle of soda, but there was no getting over the fact that if a diver followed the tables, he would spend most of his time suspended in mid water rather than collecting shell. The tables specified that if a diver went to 15 fathoms and remained below for an hour, he should ascend in three stages, taking a total of 30 minutes to come to the surface. If he went to 30 fathoms for an hour, he should spend 111 minutes coming up. All that was impossible. And as if that wasn't bad enough, in 1908 Surgeon N. Howard Mummery of the Royal Navy made a further astounding recommendation about recovery times between dives: 'as a rough rule . . . a diver who has been down in 15 fathoms for one hour should remain on the surface for three hours, and one who has been down in 25 fathoms or more for a quarter of an hour or less should not go down again on the same day.'³

This the master pearlers ignored. It would mean the end of their industry. Instead they took the view that the whole system was too complex and, besides, safety was up to their divers. The Heinke Company issued a simplified table for the pearling industry but even this version was thirteen columns wide and 65 columns deep, and incorporated bewildering concepts such as 'half-times', which proposed decompression for much longer periods for the second half of the ascent. Most of the divers from Asia didn't understand the tables; those who did complained of the tedium of hanging on the end of a line, and also that, in rough weather, being jerked up and down made them sick.

Hockliss, Rolland and Noury returned to the hotels of Broome and told the locals that they hadn't seen the bottom, only a slope to deeper parts. Sydney Pigott might have expected them to see shells on the side of the Deep laid out for the picking, but they weren't there. However, the men had been trained in deep-sea diving and they must find an end to that hole eventually. They'd try again in a few days.

Sydney Pigott spent three days of the next week on board the *Muriel*, drifting up and down Roebuck Deep, dropping Hockliss, Rolland and Noury into depths of 30 to 35 fathoms. Once Pigott dropped a plumb line to 40 fathoms. He wasn't sure if he had reached bottom because the tide began to pull the line across the bow of the boat. He suspected he hadn't.

Each evening as the sun set, they sailed back to Broome. The English divers agreed that it was important that they face the drinkers in the hotel bars wanting to know how they got on. There was no shell there, they declared.

At the end of the third day, Sydney Pigott gave up. Back in Broome he told his divers to wait until the danger of cyclones had passed then, in a few weeks time, they would be sailing out with the fleet. He went back to the tasks mounting up for him in his packing shed. It wasn't often one of the Pigott brothers failed, and the town enjoyed being witness to it.

Meanwhile, news from the cables was that the London market for mother-of-pearl remained buoyant and buyers were anxious to place orders at £230 a ton. There was money to be made and the shellers were anxious to get their boats to sea, but the weather was against them. Each morning, rolling banks of black clouds lined the horizon to the northeast. By mid morning they had drifted in, dumping warm water on the town, causing gutters to overflow, flooding creeks and sinking gardens in squelch. Then by afternoon the clouds had gone and the sun was large overhead.

Roads became gluey with mud, steam rose from paths, flowers bloomed and millions of insects came out from nowhere. Mosquitoes became the terror of everyone's life. People found it difficult to get the energy to move. Seeds sprouted on muddy boots left on verandahs, black fungus began to climb up walls and mildew appeared on the bed linen. Men and women developed prickly rash in pendulous places. The slightest cut refused to heal. And in the gardens of the master pearlers, wives complained that the bougainvilleas, scarlet and aggressive, were taking over.

So the town waited. The Englishmen – Beasily, Freight, Hanson, Andrews, Elphick, Harvey, Noury, Rolland, Hockliss and Sanders – were still picking up their pay in small brown envelopes at their employers' packing sheds every week. They told each other that the failure to find shell in Roebuck Deep meant nothing. There was no shell there. They waited for the weather to clear. Then they would show the locals what they could do. With their improved pumps the Englishmen believed they could fringe the outer limit of the beds, beyond the reach of the Asiatics – out where large, mature shell could be found on banks which hadn't been picked over before. More than a thousand miles of coastline lay in a band from 20 to 30 fathoms. That would be the province of the white man. Out where Webber and his tender, Reid, were now. They had not been heard of since they left on 20 February, but Webber was a top diver and they were sure he was doing well.

The days stretched into March. The weather remained hot and stifling. During breakfast each morning the Englishmen watched the mercury that hung on the dining-room walls of their boarding houses climb steadily towards 100, and listened to the creak of tin being stretched. They wondered what they were doing there. In the hotel bars they had seen the number of crippled men with legs that dragged behind them as they walked. They had all noticed the top Japanese divers, men who could bring up 5 tons of shell a year, absent-mindedly poking their fingers into the bones of their wrists to relieve the pain as they chatted to friends.

The Englishmen filled in the hours as best they could: doing a bit of fishing, catching the coach to Cosy Corner and walking for miles along the flat, golden sands of Cable Beach, never encountering another person. They swam naked in the sea and then sat in the shade of the sand dunes as a breeze from the Indian Ocean blew hot across their bodies. They went to the Asiatic Quarter, gambling and drinking, getting to bed late and rising late, waiting for the weather to clear.

The Asiatic Quarter was an area of a couple of blocks hemmed in between the foreshore camps behind Streeter's jetty and the mangrove swamps on Dampier Creek. All manner of business was carried on there: laundries, restaurants, tailors, billiard saloons, coffin makers and monumental masons. Hundreds lived and worked there in whitewashed buildings of wood and corrugated iron, huddled together in a self-supporting jumble intersected by a few crooked lanes. The smell of steamed rice and sweet sewage gusted through the area. Fresh air was in such short supply that few of the windows had glass; instead they were set with iron bars behind which there was a lace drop.

During the lay-up, as soon as there was a break in the rain, the lanes and alleyways were crowded with crews from the luggers: Malays dressed in bright silk shirts and sarongs of trade store cloth, groups of Manilamen with sovereigns sewn on their jackets, and Japanese in white jackets and peaked hats of vaguely naval design. Aboriginal people carrying large fish suspended on sticks made their way to the restaurants and noodle shops hoping for a sale. Street vendors sold iced lime drinks. It was a milling throng, perpetually on the move, but in no particular hurry as there was nowhere to go.

The medical officer consistently reported to the Broome council what a menace to public health the Asiatic Quarter was:

> The whole area is very congested, the drainage is often very primitive and in some cases does not exist. Owing to the cramped spaces, closets and urinals are in a great many cases very close to kitchens and sleeping rooms, a very undesirable state of affairs. I note with surprise that they have been allowed 50% of verandah space in an apportioning of lodgers. I cannot agree with them having any verandah space allowed. Some houses are carrying as many as 26 . . .[4]

On another occasion the medical officer complained that two of the boarding houses had no obvious entrance and he had to climb fences to get into them. In March 1912, Dr Blick reported to the council that the area is

> already over populated and it is your duty to see that every endeavour is made to depopulate this area rather than grant any extension of premises here. Please remember that practically every house on this area contravenes your by-laws most glaringly – in want of yard space, in the placing of privies, and in the matter of height of floors above the ground.[5]

Nishioka's Emporium and Photographic Shop was located in John Chi Lane, set deep past a shady verandah and a large awning. In the window was a display of all that was sold inside: boots, toys, bolts of linen and silk, Japanese tea sets, tennis rackets, clothing, reels of wire and cans of nails, and, designed to catch the eye of passing seamen, all sorts of useful and useless trinkets and gewgaws imported from Singapore. A sign said that sheet glass could be cut to any size, and pictorial postcards of Broome were always in stock, at sixpence each.

Customers entering the cool interior of the shop would find behind the counter a handsome, ever-smiling Japanese man wearing a white apron. His name was Yasukichi Murakami. He was born on a farm cut into the misty mountains of the Wakayama Prefecture on Honshu, Japan. It was a region of extreme poverty and in 1896, when Murakami was sixteen, his parents had sent him, under the care of a relative, to a place where they had heard gold nuggets could be found. This was Cossack, now a ghost town but in the 1890s a lively port on the edge of the Pilbara, catering to the miners scratching a living on the inland goldfields and the pearlers using Cossack as a base for supplies. The town's general store was owned by Tomasi Nishioka, who sold shovels and picks to the miners, and anchors and diving hose to the shellers. Nishioka was elderly, childless and failing in health. The young Murakami never searched for gold; instead, Nishioka took him on as an employee in his store, then as an apprentice, and finally adopted him.

By the early 1890s, Murakami and his new father could see that the Pilbara gold was petering out and Cossack was doomed. They sold up and moved to Broome, two days sailing to the north, and established an import and merchant business in the town's centre. Then Nishioka brought out his wife, Eki, who had been waiting for him all those years in Japan. Eki had packed her camera and, sensing an opportunity, persuaded her husband to allow her to place some of her shots of Broome in the store window. They attracted many curious passers-by and before long Eki had established a photographic studio in a corner of the shop. She took photos of the indentured workers to send back to relatives, portraits for the master pearlers and their families, and tinted picture postcards of scenic Broome for sale to passengers on the steamers.

Nishioka had planned to live out his remaining years with Eki and his new son in his shop near the warm waters of Roebuck Bay, but it was not to be. He died suddenly in March 1901. After the death of her husband, Eki decided to remain in Broome and continue as the town's photographer. Like Eki, Murakami had also spotted a business opportunity. Most of his countrymen who came to the pearling fields were young and ill-educated, and they found the banks run by white tellers to be intimidating. He offered to keep their money safe and, as an added convenience, they could go around to his shop whenever they wanted and he would show them the entries in a stiff-backed notebook, in a language they could understand, showing how much money they had. Murakami himself had no anxiety about banks, and took his countrymen's money to the Union Bank's Mr Smythe, who advised on the best rates of interest. In July 1908, when the town luminaries met at the Governor Broome Hotel for a valedictory dinner for Smythe, who was returning to Perth, Murakami attended and took a grand flashlight photograph of all the attendees.

Murakami could read and write English fluently, and he became adept at untangling the convoluted communications between the white establishment and the Japanese workforce. To the whites he was a Japanese they could understand and, up to a point, was prepared to see their position. To the Japanese he was the man to smooth things over with the white community when a crewman pushed too hard. He was a leader in the Japanese Club and instrumental in the establishment and management of the Japanese hospital. Somewhere along the line he learnt to ride a horse and was picked up as a jockey by Honest Ted Hunter, a master pearler who owned a handful of luggers and quite a few horses, which he ran regularly at meetings of the Broome Turf Club. The combination of Hunter and Murakami was a favourite of the punters.

One who frequented the races, and anything else going on in town, was Captain Ancell Clement Gregory. He was born in Caswell Bay in Wales, and after leaving school became apprenticed to a shipping firm on the South American route. In 1906 he arrived in Broome as the chief officer on the SS *Charon* of the Ocean Steamship

Line, and was instantly struck by the excitement and apparent wealth of the place. Never short on self-promotion, he persuaded one of the larger shellers, C.N. Murphy, to make him master of his boats, and shortly after, when Mark Rubin expanded his empire by buying out Murphy, Gregory found himself in charge of the biggest fleet on the coast – 29 luggers and five schooners, including the grand *Kelender Bux*.

Gregory was a tall, elegant man of athletic build, a favourite with the ladies, an extrovert, gregarious, and one largely unconcerned with the opinions others held of him. He always dressed in unsullied, pressed whites, smoked Egyptian cigarettes and, when drunk, took bets on whether he could kick the looping fans on the ceiling in the Governor Broome Hotel. He usually won. In her book *Full Fathom Five*, Mary Albertus Bain quotes a pearler who knew Gregory: 'In forty years of meeting people from many countries, I have never met so brilliant a person as Gregory. He was always six steps ahead of everyone. The problem was that he had commenced a second lot of steps before you were aware that there had been a move at all.'[6]

During the cyclone of 1908 Gregory had made something of a hero of himself in the popular press. Gregory was the skipper of the *Kelender Bux* which, after being buffeted by furious seas for four days, was rolled over near Ninety Mile Beach. Several days later he was found wandering along the sand exhausted, dying of thirst and clutching a dead gannet by the neck. He recounted a harrowing tale of the anchor parting in a storm the likes of which he had not seen in fourteen years experience at sea. His crew of 30 perished, save himself and the cabin boy, but he carried pearls worth £2000 to safety.

Despite his projected image as a robust hero, Gregory was a man with his hat tilted over his face. To the misgivings of the white establishment, he was noticed in huddled conversations with Japanese merchants in hotel bars and seemed to be in Murakami's store more frequently than mere shopping would require. In fact Gregory had discovered that it was easier to catch pearls on land than at sea, and that most of the Japanese money in town was in Murakami's hands, just waiting to be used somewhere. By 1908, in a scam to get around laws prohibiting Asiatics owning or having an interest in pearling luggers, Gregory began to buy luggers in his own name using Murakami's money. By April 1909 his interests were so extensive that he gave up the sea. He left Rubin's employ and somehow got himself appointed to the multiple positions of harbour master, marine surveyor and inspector of shipping. He manoeuvred around any objection to a government servant owning luggers by transferring them to a company called Gregory & Co., nominally owned by his brother, Clem Gregory. Not that Captain Ancell Gregory was prepared to relinquish control. His brother ran the business at his behest, and Murakami, who by this time was referred to as 'Gregory's shadow', worked behind the scenes, recruiting the best divers for Gregory's luggers, which were crewed entirely by Japanese.

The transparency of these arrangements was exposed in a case heard at the Broome police court in January 1911 and gleefully reported in full in the *Broome Chronicle*. Clem Gregory brought a charge of wilful disobedience against an indentured worker named Tommy Kitchie. When the case was called on, the accused, to the court's surprise, had a lawyer defending him (we can only presume that he was paid for by Gregory's enemies) with a marvellously technical argument. Yes, Captain Ancell Gregory may have transferred his boats to Gregory & Co., but had he transferred the permits to employ indentured workers as well? Sub-Collector Huggins was called to give evidence. He was an extremely reluctant witness, but eventually he had to admit that customs records showed that the immigration permits had never been transferred. At the lawyer's urging, the magistrate then held that Tommy Kitchie could not be guilty of disobeying the lawful commands of his master because Clem Gregory's commands had not been lawfully made.

But this was no more than a mildly embarrassing setback. No doubt the paperwork was corrected. Gregory and Murakami continued to run the fleets of Gregory & Co. The company bought a building for its pearling business across the road from Bedford Park, and Gregory built himself a large bungalow in the white quarter of the town. While Gregory was away in Britain assisting with the fit out of two government ships in 1912, he allowed Murakami and his family to live in his house, to the consternation of the white community.

ALTHOUGH THE weather remained threatening, some of the boats started to move out. Elphick and Harvey, working on one of Stanley Pigott's luggers, were at sea by mid March. They headed north to Cape Leveque.

The more cautious master pearlers kept their boats in port. Two cyclones of whipping winds and torrential rains, just days apart, swept in and blew out in the Great Sandy Desert: the first just to the north of Broome, the second to the south. No lives were lost and no ships were sunk, but people warned each other that along this coast cyclones came in threes.

9 The *Koombana*

If the hurricane actually comes on, it is best to leave the ship and get up on the sand hills, as the tide rises considerably above high-water mark, and the low land is flooded: on these sand hills both white and black men are huddled together, but the exposure is very severe. The vessel will probably be driven inland some distance or lodged amongst the mangroves.

Edwin Streeter, sheller[1]

ON 20 MARCH 1912 Webber, 15 fathoms deep, moved across fields of broken coral, breathing in air smelling of stale rubber. The insistent drag of the lifeline from the *Eurus* moved him on. He was surprised how flat it was. In all directions, to the very reach of his vision, he felt he could see for miles. He had been working since first light and was beginning to feel weary, but he knew he must keep going. He had to find more shell. He had to improve. Suddenly he noticed a puff of sand just in front of him. He placed his foot on it and, to his satisfaction, felt the lump of a shell under his boot. He picked it up and placed it in his bag.

Far above him, in the hold of the lugger, two rice farmers from Surabaya, one on each wheel, turned a hand-pump cased in a wooden Siebe, Gorman box. The hold was a confined cell and the backs of the men glistened with perspiration.

When he came up for afternoon tea, Webber got out of his diving gear and lit his pipe. The deck was so hot that he had to jump around looking for a shaded spot to place his bare feet. He lit a cigarette and noticed that the Malay crew were walking on the deck shoeless. Another thing to get used to, it seemed. He turned his gaze to the shells he had collected. There were only seven. They were a recrimination to him after the hours he had spent below, pushing through water, dragging coils of black pipe behind him, looking incessantly backwards and forwards across the sea floor. Reid brought him a cup of tea and a piece of dried fruit cake. It wasn't a good spot, Webber explained. He suggested they should try further out the next day. His nephew nodded, but Webber knew that Reid had no more idea than he did.

The two pump hands climbed out of the hold and sat with their backs resting against the tiller. They smiled at Webber, perhaps wanting recognition for the air they had sent down to him. Webber waved at them. They were just boys. He had not given them a thought while he was below – which was curious, because his life depended on their labours. They waved back. Handsome, lithe, brown-skinned boys with sparkling eyes and teeth red from chewing betel nut. He waved again to them, and they giggled and chatted to each other in their own language. Exhausted, Webber leant back against the cabin and closed his eyes: what uncomplicated lives they led, he thought, turning the wheel of an air pump, on a boat bobbing around on a warm ocean.

Then it was night and through the open scuttle he could see the moon bathing the cabin in soft light. The lugger rocked gently. With alarm he realised that he had been unconscious. Something of the previous hours came back to him. He remembered Reid attempting to pour brandy down his throat. At one stage he was doubled over the side of the bunk from the pain in his shoulder. He had never realised pain could be so bad. It was as if someone had reached inside his body and attempted to wrench the bone away from the muscle. He recalled the relief as it gradually subsided and Reid putting him to bed and placing a blanket over his body. He sat up and swung his arm around in an arc. It seemed fine. He lay back in his bunk and for a long time worried about what had happened. It seemed impossible that he should have got the bends. He had been so careful to stage properly. How could this have happened to him? Was there something different in the waters here, in warm waters, which negated the rules he had learnt in England?

When he awoke the next morning, he noticed forbidding black clouds gathering in the northern skies. Some way off, he reckoned. He watched them as he ate breakfast. They seemed to billow upwards in a threatening manner, but he was not sure they were getting any closer. Before he took to the water, he asked Reid to keep an eye on them. When he came up for morning tea the clouds had not moved, and when he examined them through the glasses he thought he could see sheets of rain falling from their underbelly. He went down for another hour, came up and decided to take another dip before lunchtime. He had collected only a few shells.

After twenty minutes on the floor, he noticed a large, reddish object some distance away, faintly visible in the swirl of water. An outcrop of rock, he imagined. He decided to head towards it. At least it was something with substance, something to fix his eyes on, something to trudge towards, giving a semblance of logic to what he was doing. Perhaps shell would be found there, clinging to its base or fixed in crevices.

He signalled to Reid to have the *Eurus* drift with him and, when that was done, began to half-float, half-walk across the floor, his eyes staring intently through the port of his helmet, looking for some sign of shell – anything, really, to break up the frustration of hours and hours below. He felt tired, and there was a clammy, chilled atmosphere within his suit. It was colder today. He seemed to have been down for a long time. He was dependent on Reid keeping time according to the Admiralty tables – perhaps Reid had forgotten to look at his watch or had mistaken the hour. The lugger began to veer off course so he yanked angrily on his lifeline and waited while the boat came around. The outline of the rock seemed more indistinct than before, as though an underwater haze was obstructing his vision. That was odd, losing visibility in the middle of the day.

Then he heard a low moan. He stopped, listening intently as the sound turned into a melancholy dirge, repeating a scale over and over. Then behind him, vibrating through the water, came an answering call, as deep as a church organ, the answer taking up passages of the first call. The moan now seemed to come from another direction. The sound enveloped him. The helmet made it impossible for him to glance behind, so he stumbled around in a tight circle. He thought he saw huge shapes hovering in the distance, but it was hard to see. There was no reason for a whale to attack a diver – although he had heard the story, told in the pubs, of a diver perishing when his life-line was caught in a humpback's fluke and he was dragged across the ocean floor until the air-pipe snapped. The song from the first whale returned, echoing through the water, as lonely as a train whistle but this time further away. He decided that if any whales appeared, he would signal to be pulled up.

He turned back to the search for shell and found to his surprise, that he could no longer see the rock. It should have been there, just in front of him. He shuffled around to make sure he hadn't lost orientation or moved past it. No, it was gone. The low rumbling sounded again. Something indistinct and large moved slowly to his right. The hairs on the back of his neck stood up. The water had become milky. An icy current swept along the sea floor and it had become darker. He peered upwards. A stream of grey coloured water seemed to be hovering between him and the surface. He jerked the lifeline to tell Reid to pull him up.

It would take at least 30 minutes to stage to the surface, even if he cut a few minutes off at each level. He staged at 12 fathoms. The

water was not noticeably warmer. He began to count away the seconds as he waited. Eventually, after an eternity of waiting, it was time
to surface. The crew pulled him aboard. He sat on a stool, waiting
impatiently while Reid fiddled with the bolts on his helmet. Immediately it was lifted, Webber searched the horizon. The clouds he had
noticed earlier now covered the northern sky and were swirling in an
ominous, tumbling motion towards the lugger. To the south, closer
to the beach, were three of Gregory's boats and, further out to sea, a
fourth lugger which hadn't been there when they had started that
morning. All of them were set in full sail and making to the north.
With growing alarm he realised that the *Eurus* was several miles off a
beach which offered no protection and no firm anchorage. Webber
asked the crew if there was any shelter nearby. There was a saltwater
creek, they said, pointing to the north. It meant sailing further along
an exposed beach and towards the storm. Each time he glanced at the
horizon, the clouds seemed to be more agitated and darker. Suddenly
there was a low whistling in the wind and above his head the canvas
began to flap. They would have to make a run for the creek. As the
crew got the boat ready, Webber got out of his diving suit and went
to the cabin to get changed. By the time he was back on deck, the
lugger was speeding through the water and in front of them were
restless black clouds spreading across the sky.

That night there was a tremendous storm to the south of Broome.
From the town people could see distant flashes of lightning jumping
within huge clouds, and they were kept awake by the rumble of
thunder. It seemed that the third cyclone of the season had come,
but, to the good fortune of the town, it had passed far to the south,
somewhere between Port Hedland and Lagrange, and frittered itself
away in the pindan country. The citizens of Broome breathed freely.

The SS *Koombana* was due to dock at the Broome jetty with the
evening tide the next day. On board were 156 passengers and crew,
including many of Broome's leading citizens. James Davis from
Siebe, Gorman, the man who had met the English divers in Fremantle, was aboard. So was Abraham Davis, no relation of James,

who worked for Mark Rubin, and Keenan, a King's Counsel who was on his way north to prosecute a murder trial. Also on board was the matron of the government hospital, the Reverend Main of the Presbyterian mission, Captain Stewart, Dean Spark and Mrs Jane Pigott, the wife of Sydney Pigott, and her two daughters, returning home after spending Christmas in Perth.

Sydney Pigott was waiting on the jetty to greet the steamer, along with a number of others, as dusk began to fall. They searched for a telltale trail of smoke against the sunset and then, rising over the horizon, the distinctive funnel of the *Koombana*, painted in the colours of the Adelaide Steamship Company. But the *Koombana* failed to arrive.

The next day a steady stream of people climbed the only sizeable hill in town, at the end of Dampier Terrace, to peer out across Roebuck Bay. The general presumption was that Captain Thomas Allen had taken the precaution of going out to sea to give the cyclone a wide berth and would be steaming into harbour any time now. It was inconceivable that something could have happened to the *Koombana*.

She had been built in Glasgow in 1908, and was designed especially for the tropics. Passenger accommodation was arranged to run fore and aft with large alleyways between, so that no matter how oppressive the weather, air could circulate throughout. The cabin doors were louvred with detachable button-on curtains, and electric fans were installed in all public areas. The vessel was lit by electricity, with back-up oil lamps and the latest Graham patent telephone switch allowing communication all over the ship. There were smoking rooms, music rooms, a library and numerous private studies. Ice was available to all who desired it, 24 hours a day. She was the most modern and expensive steamer of the coastal fleet. Like the *Titanic*, which at that very moment was taking bookings for her maiden voyage across the Atlantic, the *Koombana* was the very latest in British maritime engineering.

Then the wires at the Broome post office began to run with news about the damage caused by the cyclone which had ripped along the coast two days earlier. The captain of the *Donna Matilda* reported finding the wreckage of the cutter *Kooki* broken in half and ten bodies in the nearby mangroves. Three lifebuoys were found in the cabin, so it was concluded that the storm fell on the crew so quickly they did not have time to put them on. The luggers *Elsie* and *B19*, belonging to Ward and Price, had not been seen and it was feared they were lost. All seven witnesses in a murder trial at Balla Balla had drowned while being transported to shore in a longboat. The two Italians accused, Joseph Saleno and Laurence Cappelli, sound and dry in the police lock-up, began to think that acquittal was a good prospect.

Next, a story swept through Broome that the *Koombana* was safe at Derby. No one knew where the rumour had started, but everyone had heard it. The *Koombana* was safe; she had merely gone straight on to Derby to avoid the weather. The wires to Derby had been blown down, so it wasn't possible to ascertain the truth. Men crowded into the postmaster's tiny office, drinking beer brought over from the Roebuck Bay Hotel while they waited for the wires to be reconnected. Arguments broke out and the postmaster ordered everyone to wait outside, but they ignored him. Every few minutes he jiggled the key, but there was nothing there. It might take hours for the men he had sent out on horseback to rejoin the wire. The heat rose in the room, but no one left.

At last, near sunset, the wire came alive. Those in the room fell quiet, listening to the taps of the keys. The operator at Derby didn't seem to understand. The message was repeated. There was a long wait while Derby made inquiries. The tapping recommenced. A brief answer came: 'Koombana not at Derby.' Silently the crowd left the office. The postmaster typed the words on a black-bordered page he kept for death notices and hung it on the board outside.

The next morning a steamer was reported heading towards the jetty at Cossack, but those who rushed to the foreshore could quickly see that she was not the tall-funnelled *Koombana* but the SS *Bullarra*, a cargo steamer. The *Bullarra* had left Port Hedland twenty minutes ahead of the *Koombana*. Captain Upjohn on the *Bullarra* said the weather was as rough as he had ever seen it but, although they had passed through the centre of the cyclone, the 'old *Bull*' had behaved splendidly. The *Bullarra*'s funnel had snapped in two and the 50 head of cattle in pens on the deck had been swept overboard. No, he hadn't seen the *Koombana*.

WEBBER AND REID, on board the *Eurus*, gained shelter along a thin, reedy creek emptying into the waters off Ninety Mile Beach. There were six luggers lined up on the banks and the Malay, Japanese and British crewmen had set up three separate encampments on a nearby sandhill. They sat huddled around fires blazing in old oil drums as all night the winds roared around them and the rain, gusting in horizontal sheets, never let up.

At daybreak the storms continued. Winds rippled the canvas and tugged at stays. Cooks from the luggers carried out pots and pans, bags of flour and their cabinets of spices, and began to prepare breakfast. The men listened to the boom of the waves dumping on the beach just over the sandhills, grateful they were not out there and wondering if anyone they knew had perished.

For two days and nights the boats were trapped. The sea rushed up the creek and gushed and gnawed at its banks. The men dragged the boats up as high as possible along the creek and moored them by several stout ropes to trees even higher up. The wind howled around the camp, and overhead a tempest tore clouds apart. Some walked to the top of the sandhills and stood looking at the wild sea. White caps lined up to the horizon and jostled each other on their way to the shore. Men went down to the beach and walked across cakey sand to make their selection from the hundreds of fish washed up along the high-water mark.

When the men awoke on the third day, the air was still. They climbed out of damp blankets to watch the sun rise like a crimson ball against a deep blue sky. Suddenly it was hot, the air was soggy, there was a shrill drum of bush insects and low-skimming birds tried out their wings. The men got ready to depart. Boxes of stores, stoves and bedding were taken back on board. Sails, already infected with the musty smell of tropical rot, were unfurled to dry. Blankets and clothes were spread out on the deck. By mid morning the boats were ready to sail. The men were anxious to catch the high tide giving them passage down the creek to the sea, but still they took time to gather in groups and say goodbye. It might be weeks before they saw each other again. They shook hands because they were the survivors.

Still there was no news of the *Koombana*.

The harbour master at Port Hedland said he had warned the captain of the *Koombana* about the falling barometer, but he had replied: 'I am going straight out to sea.'[2] This had a nice determined ring about it, but even as the *Koombana* passed the breakwater, the harbour master said he had seen her propellers beating out of the water. Normally a steamer is out of sight in 35 minutes, but the seas were so choppy that day the *Koombana* took two hours to clear the horizon.

The ship's designer, Mr McDonald, wrote to the papers defending the design of his creation against rumours that she was top heavy. She was capable of carrying 900 tons of water ballast and had watertight doors in every compartment. She could withstand any sort of weather and if she was disabled she had a workshop capable of effecting almost any repair.

Sydney Pigott cabled Premier Scaddan in Perth and demanded that the government commence a full-scale search. The *Bullarra*, minus half her funnel, was promptly turned around and sent to steam through the area of Bedout Island. The cattle ship *Moira* joined in the search from the Lacepedes to the Montebellos. The *Gorgon* crossed from Surabaya to Rowley Shoals to search there. The *Minderoo* patrolled in the vicinity of the Montebello Islands. Sydney Pigott sent out his schooner *Muriel* and a fleet of luggers under the command of Captain Dalziel, the harbour master.

During the days of the search the sea was flat, the sun was fierce and the air was fat with moisture. The *Bullarra* had to return to port to pick up coal, and Captain Upjohn said that although the light-house flame on Bedout Island had been extinguished, the glass was not encrusted with salt, from which he concluded that the island had not met the full force of the gale. He set off to join others in a zigzag along Ninety Mile Beach. Captain Dalziel on the *Muriel* landed on Bedout and was struck by the hundreds of maimed birds scattered along the beach. He concluded that Captain Upjohn didn't know what he was talking about, and set the vessels under his command in a patterned search centred on the island.

Every day was an agony for Sydney Pigott. He locked himself in his packing shed, constantly looking up, hoping to see through the windows, as if by magic, the *Koombana* steaming into port. He drew blue, yellow and green lines across a chart of the coast showing where the different vessels were searching: the *Gorgon* steaming across to Broome from Rowley Shoals, the *Charon* out near Lynher Reef, the *Minderoo* now approaching Cossack, the *Bullarra* back from Bedout Island and the *Una* west of Rowley Shoals. The lines crisscrossed and tangled with each other until it looked as though skeins of coloured yarn had been unravelled over the paper.

It was difficult to understand what could have happened to the *Koombana*. The latest theory was that she had become disabled, a rudder smashed perhaps, the boilers blown up, and she was some-where at sea, and all the passengers, bored with waiting, were sitting on deck chairs expecting to be rescued. The *Broome Chronicle* recalled that this had happened to the *Wyachato* a few years back. She had been towed into Fremantle Harbour after being posted missing for months.[3] But Sydney Pigott knew this was merely hope speaking.

Then, about 70 miles west of Bedout Island, the watch on the *Minderoo* saw several red leather cushions bobbing along in her wake. They were hauled aboard and, amidst great excitement, were identi-fied as being from the smoking lounge of the *Koombana*. Other vessels rushed to the area. The *Bullarra* found a billiard cue, a piece of ceiling panel and part of a wicker chair. Then the splintered remains of a door were collected. The lugger *Kathy* found an empty tin of cooking oil, the bottom board of a dinghy and a first-aid kit in an old cigar tin. Were these from the *Koombana* or from one of the luggers sunk by the storm? Who could tell? All these prizes were taken back to Broome and displayed in the hotel bars. They were picked up hundreds of times and passed from hand to hand like religious relics.

There is no record of the English divers taking part in the search for the *Koombana*, which is not surprising given their lack of knowledge of the seas around Broome. Besides, they were divers, not seamen. Still, they must have felt uncomfortable to be stuck in the hotels of Broome, delayed yet again in the search for shell, and being paid by the master pearlers to do nothing. There were no moving pictures shown in the theatres because the new program of films had disappeared along with the *Koombana*. And Mrs Hyland, proprietress of the Star Hotel, hung a notice on the hat stand stating that the billiards tournament had been cancelled 'Out of Respect'.

While the people of Broome had spent anxious hours waiting for news of the *Koombana*, a police constable was stabbed to death on the verandah of the Roebuck Bay Hotel. The victim was Constable Fletcher who, after twenty years in the force, had taken temporary leave of absence to devote himself to the work of the Presbyterian Church. This was the same Constable Fletcher who in 1905 had given evidence to the Roth Royal Commission that whenever he saw crewmen coming ashore from the pearling luggers, he would go down to the camps and put the Aboriginal women in chains for the night. He had been waiting in Broome for the past week to meet the Reverend Main, who was journeying by sea on the *Koombana* from Perth. The two had planned to then sail to Cockburn Sound to select a site for the establishment of a mission. When the *Koombana* failed to arrive, Fletcher had spent many hours with the local congregation praying for the safe deliverance of the Reverend Main and all on board.

On Saturday night Fletcher was working late on the mission boat, moored opposite Dampier Terrace, with Hayi Said bin Abbas, who was a member of the crew. About midnight, as he was carrying supplies stored at the Roebuck Bay Hotel to the vessel opposite, he noticed a man and a woman seated in the dark on the verandah, carrying on a whispered conversation. They were John Freeman, a barman at the Pearlers' Rest Hotel further down the road in Dampier Terrace, and Helen Fimister, a barmaid at the same hotel. At the end of their shift at the Pearlers' Rest they had walked to the verandah of the hotel, followed by Thomas Bilheeba, a Manilaman who regarded Miss Fimister as his woman. Fimister told Bilheeba he wasn't wanted. When this didn't work, Freeman lost his temper and attempted to push Bilheeba into the street, but Bilheeba clung to the verandah post and the two men swung round on it until Freeman, deciding to end it quickly, hit Bilheeba in the face. At that Freeman found himself attacked by several Manilamen.

Fletcher, walking past, put his parcels down on the darkened verandah and joined the fray. What happened next was subsequently the subject of confused and conflicting testimony at the inquest. Who was carrying the knife remained unclear, but it ended up in Fletcher's throat. He broke free, clutching his neck as blood poured through his fingers and down his chest. He staggered down the stairs into a horse cab waiting in Dampier Terrace and was rushed to the hospital. He lingered on through Sunday and died at six on Monday morning.

The police arrested Bilheeba and four other men in the vicinity, including Hayi Said bin Abbas, who protested, to no avail, that he was merely a crew member on the mission boat and had nothing to do with the fight.

On Monday afternoon a large crowd of sombrely dressed men and women alighted from buggies hitched to the railing of the Broome cemetery, and moved through the eucalypts to stand next to a freshly dug grave. The Reverend Rolland told those who had gathered that it was a time of sadness and peril for the whole community. He asked

William Webber was one of the English divers who took part in the white experiment. After his discharge from the Royal Navy in 1903 he became a leading commercial diver. In 1912, at the age of 32, he came to dive for mother-of-pearl in the waters off Broome. Courtesy Angela Stevens and Bill Webber.

The photographer captioned this picture 'W.A. Natives waiting for rations'. By the turn of the century in many areas of the northwest of Western Australia the Indigenous people had been driven from their lands and depended on the pastoralists who had displaced them for work and sustenance. Courtesy Battye Library 76963P.

A pearling lugger on the northwest coast of Western Australia – an image which captures both the romance and isolation of the life of those who searched for pearl-shell. Courtesy Battye Library, A. Richardson Collection 28077P.

A view along Shiba Lane with the Star Hotel at the end. Although now known as Sheba Lane, prior to World War I it was called Shiba Lane after Mr K. Shiba who ran the Bay View Restaurant there. Courtesy Royal Western Australian Historical Society R3193.

The Continental Gardens Theatre in the quadrangle of the Continental Hotel. In the evenings a screen was set up on the stage and moving pictures were shown to an audience seated on deck chairs. Courtesy Battye Library 26191P.

Broome jetty had to extend almost a mile into the sea because the rise and fall of the tides are so great and Roebuck Bay is so shallow. It was demolished in the 1960s. Courtesy Battye Library 70963P.

Workers, supervised by master pearlers, pack pearl-shell and load it onto a trolley pulled by a horse along rail tracks on Broome jetty. A steam locomotive replaced the horses in 1910. Courtesy Battye Library, A. Richardson Collection 28048P.

Master pearlers pose with their indentured workers, who have unloaded baskets of pearl-shell from a dinghy in preparation for carrying it to the packing sheds. Courtesy Battye Library 54725P.

Broome, looking towards the foreshore camps and the packing sheds of the master pearlers. Courtesy Battye Library 212992P.

During the cyclone season, between late November and early March, over three hundred luggers came to town for the lay-up. The boats were hauled into bays where they rose and sank back into the mud twice each day with the running of the tide. Courtesy Battye Library 62141P.

ABOVE LEFT: Pearling luggers anchored in Roebuck Bay. On the shore is one of the camps provided by the master pearlers as accommodation for their indentured workers. Courtesy Battye Library 52274P.

BELOW LEFT: Streeter's jetty with Streeter and Male's packing sheds on the Broome foreshore. Courtesy Battye Library 52277P.

As a diver struggles to obtain a foothold on the coir rope ladder, his tender hauls him up by the lifeline. Courtesy Battye Library 25098P.

The diver's netted bag could hold ten to twelve shells – this one holds only a few. Courtesy Battye Library 27243P.

A diver and his tender face the camera. Preparing for a dive took so long that the diver would usually remain in his dress during breaks for lunch and tea. Courtesy Royal Western Australian Historical Society and Battye Library 24324P.

A diver in his full suit with his tender standing beside him. From *Forty Fathoms Deep*, Ion L. Idriess.

The shell-strewn deck of a pearling lugger. Courtesy Royal Western Australian Historical Society R1966.

LEFT: An Aborigine and a Malay man opening shell. Courtesy Battye Library 25856P.

Once the lugger returned to port the crew brought the shell onto the deck and packed it in wicker baskets for transportation to shore. Courtesy Battye Library 94P.

Japanese women of the boarding houses. Women were brought to Australia in the 1890s, ostensibly to work in laundries, but the reality was quite different. The *West Australian Immigration Restriction Act of 1897* denied further entry, but allowed those already in the state to remain. Some of the women continued to work at their profession through to the 1930s. Courtesy Battye Library 60855P.

Manilamen in Sunday attire. The pearling industry brought wealth to many indentured workers who had formal photographs taken of themselves to post to friends and relatives at home. Courtesy Battye Library 52318P.

The Broome Japanese cemetery, in which over 900 seamen are buried, most under headstones of coloured beach rock. Courtesy Battye Library 70967P.

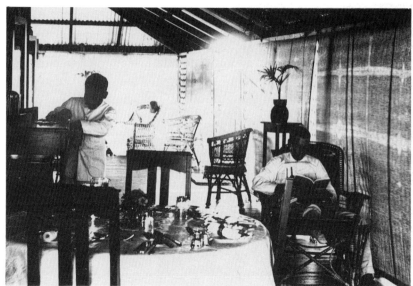

A Malay servant waits on a master pearler and his wife. Broad, shady verandahs enclosed by lattice, such as this one, encircled most homes in the English Quarter of Broome. People took their meals, entertained guests and in the summer months slept on their verandahs. Courtesy Battye Library, A. Richardson Collection 28043P.

The Broome residence of Abraham Davis, who managed the pearling empire of Mark Rubin until he was lost at sea when the SS *Koombana* sunk in 1912. Courtesy Battye Library 70968P.

When Europe plunged into war in August 1914, the Japanese Emperor declared on the side of the British Empire. This patriotic float in the Broome Red Cross and Appeal Day Parade displays the Union Jack and the Japanese flag united over the one roof. Courtesy Battye Library 66513P.

Indentured workers on Broome jetty at the end of a pearling season, preparing to leave by steamer for Singapore and ports further north. Courtesy Battye Library, A. Richardson Collection 28085P.

them to pray for the soul of Bertram Henry Fletcher and all those missing on the *Koombana*, including their own Reverend Main. Constable Fletcher and the Reverend Main had given their lives in the service of others and to the task of relieving the suffering of the natives of the inland. It was very difficult to accept what had happened, or to work out the reasons for it. Nevertheless as two good men took their leave, he asked the congregation to pray to God that there would be others to take their place. There was so much to be done.

A subscription was taken up and today a visitor to the Broome cemetery may find a fine sandstone monument to Constable Fletcher. The inscription on the headstone reads: 'Thy will be done. Sacred to the memory of Bertram Henry Fletcher, aged 39 years, Constable of Police, who was killed at Broome in the execution of his duty April 1st 1912.'

The first step on the way to a hanging was to hold an inquest. In the case of Constable Fletcher, the coroner was Pa Norman, assisted by a jury of three, and the inquest concluded on 6 May 1912. The jury took fifteen minutes to consider their verdict. It was unclear to the jury whether Thomas Bilheeba or Candido Colestrom had stabbed Fletcher in the neck, so both were committed to stand trial for murder, and the other two involved in the fight were sent to trial as accessories after the fact. There was, said the jury, no evidence to implicate Hayi Said bin Abbas, so he was released back into the care of the Presbyterian Church. He had been in prison for over a month.

The *Koombana* was never found. Early theories were that she had sailed westward into the Indian Ocean in an effort to skirt the cyclone and had struck Bedout Reef, crashed over it and sunk in the deep water on the other side. Many blamed Captain Allen, who after all was only a holiday stand-in for Captain Rees, who had been taking steamers up and down the coast for years. However, it was probably not Captain Allen's fault at all. There is little doubt that in the push for luxury accommodation, the designers had made the

Koombana top heavy. She was built like a multi-layered wedding cake. The most likely scenario is that the *Koombana*, pounded by mountainous seas and smacked by winds of unimaginable force, had simply toppled over and flooded.

In April 1912 news of the sinking of the *Titanic* reached Broome by cable. As the stories emerged of the passengers and crew assembling on the deck on a frosty night to guide the women and children into lifeboats, those who had lost relatives on the *Koombana* thought of the wild, storming terror aboard that vessel as she had toppled over and water flooded down the passageways. It was hard to imagine there was any dignity attending their deaths. No one had survived, no bodies were recovered and no one knew where the *Koombana* lay.

The white tribe of Broome had lost about 10 per cent of its population in that single storm. Everyone knew at least one person who had perished; some knew many. Sydney Pigott had lost his wife and two of the children he had taken into his house. Stanley Pigott's wife had lost her mother. The bishop conducted a memorial service in the Church of Annunciation for those lost in the cyclone and the overflow crowds, unable to fit in that tiny building of weatherboard slats, spilled out into the garden and listened through the louvred windows.

The death of his wife and stepchildren weighed heavily on Sydney Pigott. He spent many hours on the verandah of his bungalow late at night discussing with his brother what was left for him in Broome. Sydney was 44 and had lived in Broome for 22 years. He had made a substantial amount of money. He was respected and successful. He had been the parliamentary representative for the area and was president of the Pearlers' Association. He spoke of selling his fleet. He spoke of selling everything – his house and his business. It was time to let go.

Around him, though, life went on. Broome was like an island, hemmed in by desert and by sea. The only access to the outside world was via a fortnightly steamer. Although the whites were prepared to spend money on their comfort, at heart they knew that the only justification for living in that solitary outpost was to work, make money and get out. Already it was April and most of the luggers still lay in ditches along the bay. The year of 1912 saw the latest start to the shelling season that anyone could remember.

10 Sail-out

Such is the craving for 'more shell' when it has once got possession of a diver's imagination – I held an inquiry a few days ago into the causes connected with the death of one Wattanabi, an old and experienced diver. His last remark was . . . 'I'm sorry I am going – the water is clear, and I could have got plenty of shell'.

Report on the death of a Japanese diver, 1894–1895[1]

FINALLY, IN EARLY APRIL 1912, the fleet took to the seas. In their own way everyone marked its departure. Brahim Sa Maidin, the imam from Jahore, drew his followers to the tin mosque set in the bush on the edge of town and prayed for deliverance from the tempest of the winds and the deep of the seas. The Japanese went to the Buddhist temple, and on Sunday evening had a dinner at the Japanese Club and drank sake to the health of the Emperor. Father Bachmair conducted a morning mass at the Catholic Church for his congregation of Irish and Manilamen. The Reverend Needham at the Church of Annunciation scheduled a seafarers' Sunday evensong, and

Mrs Needham pumped out 'Abide with Me' on the organ. And the irreligious (not to be forgotten) toasted themselves into a state of sweaty exhaustion in the foreshore pubs. After midnight, those who could raise the energy went down to Shiba Lane for their last visit to the ladies of the boarding houses for weeks.

On the morning of the sail-out, Beasily was aboard Robison & Norman's *Ena* by six am. Hanson, his tender, met him there. The two men stood on the deck and lit a cigarette while a warm sea breeze blew into their faces. They were in high spirits and they talked and joked. Beasily realised that it had been five months since he last dived – under grey skies in the waters off Portsmouth, shivering on the deck of a tug manoeuvring over a wreck sunk in the mud of the Solent. Now he was on the other side of the world, on a morning sparkling with light, and the search was for pearl-shell.

On the schooner *Muriel* were Noury, Rolland and Sanders, under instructions from Sydney Pigott to dive deep beyond the outer limits of the fleet where few had dived before. But it was a subdued Pigott who gave his orders and then left them to it. The men had heard the rumour that everything Pigott owned was going on the market, including his fleet of luggers. There had been debate in the pubs about how much each of his boats was worth.

Further around the bay, Harvey and Elphick sat on upturned boxes next to the tiller of Stanley Pigott's *Fram* and watched Andrews fiddling with the air compressor. He had the engine in bits and was cleaning the pistons. He blew the air nozzle free of oil. The three of them had been told by Pigott that the navigation of the boat should be left to the Malay crew. Pigott said he had given instructions to the crew to sail further from the coast than the main fleet and look for shell there.

Just after first light, the boats began to move. The crew of each vessel stood on the deck, shouting goodbye to friends they wouldn't see again for weeks. Hundreds of luggers, with white sails heeling over in the breeze, moved through the mangroves and past Entrance Point. Like pigeons released from a loft, the boats scattered across the vastness of the waters of the northwest.

Each skipper had his own theory as to where shell was to be found. Some were heading for King Sound where the rush of the tide made diving dangerous but the shells were large and thick on the ground. Others believed that mother-of-pearl sank to the deep to spore and then rose at the end of the cyclone season, so it was best to wait for them at the edge of uplifted areas off Ninety Mile Beach. A few reckoned on searching in the reed beds near the blood-red sandstone cliffs of Cape Leveque, or in the coral-fringed islands of the Lacepedes. Some consulted charts of channels around islands and estuaries where turtles swam, because turtles were a sure guide to where shell was to be found, while others relied on places where they'd been successful the previous year, or the year before that. Most sailed all night. The crew, exhilarated by their first night on the ocean for months, remained on deck and, as wind filled the sails, watched the lugger cutting through phosphorescent seas.

There is no note of where the English divers spent the first few weeks of April 1912. Certainly some of them would have followed the fleet, a day's sailing to the south, to the regular shelling grounds standing off Cape Du Boulay, Cape Latouche Treville, Lagrange, Cape Missiessy or Cape Jaubert (names sprinkled along the coast by the French explorer Nicholas Baudin in 1803) and down to Ninety Mile Beach. No coral gardens along this coast – seaward was a flat expanse of faded sandstone topped by a thin layer of sand, dun-coloured rocks and an occasional bed of weed, sea squirts, sponges and fan coral.

THERE WAS no such thing as a standard lugger. They were built to multiple designs in shipyards in Fremantle and Broome, Singapore and Sydney, in the back yards of home builders, and next to cattle sheds in the Kimberleys. What was required was a vessel large enough for a crew of seven, with room for a diver's pump, 60 yards of air-pipe and lifeline, provisions for several months, 400 gallons of fresh water and room to store 2 or 3 tons of shell. Sleeping quarters and facilities for the crew were of secondary importance.

By the 1900s the typical lugger coming out of the Fremantle dockyards was 10 to 15 tons and 30 to 45 feet in length with a draught of about 5 feet. The frame was of hardwood timber bolted together. Local timbers were favoured – jarrah, or the tough kadjebut – often warped and suitable for curving into ribs. Imported Burma teak, oregon or ash, fastened with copper nails, was used for decking. They were lumpy, plumb-stemmed boats which were used for their hardiness rather than for their grace. They had to be built strong because they were often grounded in creeks and inlets with holds full of shell while waiting out a storm, and during the lay-up season they sat sandbagged in trenches for months. At sea they endured snubbing at anchors as they steadied themselves over patches of shell.

They had a low freeboard to reduce the effect of the winds on the hull, enabling the crew to keep a steady position over the pearling ground and to make it easier to haul the diver and his shell aboard. In any sort of rough weather the decks were constantly awash. Some claimed that this made the luggers susceptible to flooding during cyclones, but the shellers justified the design by saying their boats laid low when the willy-willys arose and their shallow draught meant that they could hide away in creek beds. The decking was alternatively wet and baked by the sun, and required constant oiling and the seams recaulking with oakum and pitch.

A well-built lugger had a 40-foot main mast – an 8-inch pole of clear, grained oregon, ideally without a knot in its length – and a short mizen mast. The mast extended through the deck and was stepped on a keelson. A ratline, made out of notched and lashed mangrove sticks, ran along the shrouds. A ladder made of coir rope with outsized gaps between its wooden slats (designed to take the height of a diver's lead-weighted boot) hung over the side.

They were steered by a tiller. There were no portholes. Speed was not a consideration. The sleeping quarters aboard a pearling lugger have been described as rat holes shared with the rats. There was a small cabin aft, used by the diver and tender; forward in the peak were four bunks for the crew – all under deck, hot, claustrophobic and smelly. The bunks were made of wooden slats on which were placed straw mattresses. There was barely shoulder space between them, and a hand flung out in restless sleep was likely to strike the other sleeper. Harry Talboys, a master pearler whose evidence was received by the Royal Commission, said the cabin was so cramped that 'a man had to stand out[side] in order to put his trousers on'.[2]

On smaller luggers there was only one cabin, by tradition and rank reserved for the diver and the tender, while the rest of the crew curled up somehow, somewhere. Clothing and personal belongings were usually kept in a tin trunk under the bunk, and it paid to have it watertight because in rough weather sea sluicing over the decks flooded into the cabins. A person climbing out of bed in the morning could easily step into a couple of inches of water. On a wall of the cabin might be a tinted postcard of a Tokyo street scene, or a picture of mountain valleys and snow-capped peaks steamed off a can of tinned peaches from California. On the ceiling would be a nicotine stain, a result of the diver puffing on his pipe as he lay in the bunk. As the weeks went by and shell mounted up, the boat began to smell of rotting fish, but the stench so permeated the vessel that after a while it wasn't noticed at all.

Cooking was done on a cut-down 44-gallon oil drum, set on an iron plate or an earth box, with steel rods as a grille and a fire fed though a jagged hole cut in the metal. On this stove, despite at times a rollicking boat and wild winds, the cook, juggling several boiling pots, performed the miracle of serving three meals a day for a crew of seven – almost without fail. Next to him on a table sat a small wooden case filled with tiny jars of coloured sauces, pastes and spices, capable of disguising the most obnoxious brew with a fiery taste. The ideal slow-charring fuel was sticks cut from mangrove trees. Mangrove wood gave off a minimum of smoke which was important because air drawn into the diver's pump had to be as pure as possible. Mangrove wood would catch even if it was almost green, and certainly a week in the sun was sufficient to get it going. The flame would burn down to a white ash, which, if a swell was running, made mangrove wood less of a fire hazard than charcoal.

Stores of food and cooking utensils were secured under canvas in the ship's dinghy. A record survives of the victuals master pearler Hugh Richardson supplied on his boats for an Asian crew of seven for a month:

> 20 tins of 2 pounds meats at two shillings and fourpence each
> 2 tins of dripping at one shilling and ninepence each
> 4 tins of Jones Jams at one shilling each
> 4 tins of 1 pound condensed milk at ten shillings
> 2 tins of half a pound of curry at eightpence each
> 4 tins of 1 pound salmon at tenpence
> 4 tins of large sardines at eightpence
> 2 bottles of pickles at ninepence
> 2 bottles of vinegar at sixpence
> 2 pounds of tea at one shilling and twopence
> 2 pounds of coffee at one shilling and threepence
> 1 bar of soap at eightpence
> 56 pounds of onions at total cost of ten shillings
> 4 bags of rice at twelve and sixpence a bag
> 2 bags of flour at ten shillings and sixpence a bag
> 28 pounds of sugar at four and h'pence each
> 10 pounds of salt at one and h'pence each
> 4 pounds of chillies at one shilling each
> 4 boxes matches at total of eightpence.[3]

The crew were expected to supplement their diet with fish. In the waters of the northwest, all kinds of fish – barramundi, bream, catfish, garfish, mackerel, trevally – all starving, it seemed, snagged themselves on the hook almost as soon as a line was thrown overboard. The Japanese prized the soft-fleshed bonito, which was eaten raw with uncooked onions. The Malays loved the sweet flesh of the small yellowtail, which they parboiled then pulled between their teeth, throwing the bones overboard. There was fried fish with rice for breakfast, fish chowder made with ship's biscuits, onions and pepper sauce for lunch, and fish with noodles, fish in batter or fish cakes for the evening meal.

Every mother-of-pearl hauled aboard held an adductor muscle which had a fishy taste and slightly chewy texture. They were fried with limes and belacan, or curried in peanut sauce or chilli paste and served with noodles, or batter-fried in oil. Those not eaten were strung around the boat to dry. They might have looked like a clothesline of ears, but back in Broome they would fetch two shillings a pound from Chinese merchants who exported them as delicacies to Hong Kong. Bread was only baked on a Sunday; it took too long during the working week and, besides, bread was an affectation of the white man, the Asian crew preferring rice.

Fresh water was a problem on long voyages. Rain during the months of the dry was scarce, and creeks running into the sea were few and often briny. Drinking water was strictly rationed and couldn't be spared for anything else. There was no toilet. Everyone had to sit on a bucket on the deck, unless you were prepared, during an early morning swim, to become adept at bending over double and clutching at your ankles. Bathing was done under a bucket of saltwater or by plunging over the side.

If the crew was desperate for water, it was occasionally possible to purchase some, at an exorbitant price, from a schooner owned by one of the big firms. Failing that, it had to be collected on shore. The lugger would be run into a creek at high tide, then it was a walk upstream until a spot was found where the water was flowing fresh. It was bucketed into large canvas bags, dragged back to the boat and manhandled into the opening of the tanks. It was hot, hard work. The wells sunk into Ninety Mile Beach in 1908 also involved a long walk inland for the doubtful benefit of cloudy water stinking of minerals.

Fresh water could not be spared for washing clothes. The recommended method of cleaning them was to place them in a bucket of water half-in and half-out of the sea, and the rolling of the waves would do the job by morning. After 30 minutes slung over a line between the shrouds, the garments would be crusted stiff and ready to wear.

If the lugger was anchored close to shore, the sandflies and mosquitoes would come out in swarms as evening approached. Most luggers carried a supply of the skipper's favourite repellent, be it joss sticks, pine shavings, cattle dung or frayed rope. But the most persistent tormentor of the crew were the cockroaches. Although the boats were flooded during the lay-up season, after a few weeks at sea the cockroaches were back, hatched from eggs left by their drowned parents, or transported in with the stores. They found a vermin heaven – tropical humidity, abundant scraps of fish as they scurried among the piles of shell, and plenty of cracks in which to hide. They were inquisitive, fearless and they bred recklessly. At night they nibbled on exposed toes and ears – so gently that although they drew blood, the victim rarely awoke. In the morning it was a good idea to check inside the teapot before using it.

The cockroaches came in two varieties. The grey ones were about half an inch long and could squeeze into crevices the thickness of a fingernail, coming out in brazen bunches when food appeared. The others were large, black and several inches long, and would fly around the boat on whirring wings. When the cockroaches became too much to bear, a wash of oil of tar and kerosene was poured down cracks. Others used a swill of cyanide and sulphuric acid.

Rats and mice also found a sheltered home within the confines of the luggers, but a rat-free boat was thought to be a disaster because rats kept the cockroaches down. If a boat had no rats, the crew might moor the vessel at a certain creek where, on a quiet night, a few might be enticed aboard.

After the evening meal there might be an hour of daylight before nightfall, which in the tropics is sudden and early. The crew might read – if they could, and if they could find something unread – or jump overboard for a swim. There was no great space for a stroll. It was a deck of obstacles, with a mountain of diver's air-pipe, shell strewn across it, the cook's oil-drum stove and a dinghy lashed forward. On many luggers there was such a shortage of space that a square platform for extra storage was built hanging over the stern. The only stick of furniture on deck was a stool reserved for the diver.

Every lugger seemed to have at least one crew member who had a guitar and a desire to sing about languishing love. Others might play a game of cards while the diver quietly drank black tea and gently rubbed the joints of his knees as he prayed that the pain wouldn't come that night. As it darkened, the mother-of-pearl, after an afternoon stewing in its own juice on the deck, would mistake the evening for cooling waters and open to take a last gasp.

The crew usually turned in early. The cook handed around sugared pastry and coffee, then threw wood on the stove to keep it alive till morning. They would rise at dawn the next day.

After a couple of seasons each lugger took on her own particular smell; hard to describe, but distinctive just the same. Something of the pitch laid between her planks and the smoke from the wood-fired stove. And as all who sail the seas know, a boat is much more than wood, canvas and iron. Some are built with good fortune, and some are cursed from the moment they are launched. Some run sweetly with the wind, float over reefs and pass through the quiet heart of storms. On such boats when at rest on a still night, the crew can hear the timbers fretting in care of those on board.

It was into this environment that the English divers and tenders were dropped. Doubtless some of the Englishmen adopted the usual practice of white fish out of water and kept to themselves. Some erected a tarpaulin aft of the cabin, a place where dark skins were discouraged and where, on a shelf fixed to the wall, they stored a selection of teas in small bottles, porcelain pots of relish from Fortnum & Mason and several pipes in a rack, all caged down to resist theft and rough seas. In this tiny canvas sanctuary, protected from the burning sun, they read, for the hundredth time, back copies of *Pall Mall*, told the same old stories, rationed the whisky and kept an eye on the coloureds, while being acutely aware that they held the only key to the rusty rifle, locked in a clamp over the cabin door.

Some white men delighted in the new. They padded around in bare feet, justified as the only sensible thing to do when you had a deck continually underwater. They threw aside their shirts so their skin colour became indistinguishable from the crew's, save when white and yellow bums were exposed during a Sunday afternoon frolic over the side. Such men were said to have gone native. Their hair became bleached to flaxen. They joined the guitar player in singing love songs, played cards with men from Solor, and lay on the cabin roof under a sky of a million pinpoints and smoked opium. They looked forward to Malayan stir-fried fish followed by flapjacks and jam served on chipped enamelled plates with coffee in pannikins.

Not all took to their new environment, though. One of those who quickly became disillusioned with the life of a pearl-shell diver was John Noury. Years later he recalled his experiences on a pearling lugger:

> There was I, mind you, the only white man on board and miles out to sea . . . The Japs and islanders had too strong a hold. They were good workers, and cheap. They put up with conditions that none of us could stomach for a minute. Yes, and they died, too. But who cared? For every one who passed out of the game there were twenty willing to take his place . . . The whole trouble was that the poor devils knew practically nothing about decompression. They would come straight up from a long dive and collapse in front of you with the bends. Not all, of course, but a damn sight too many . . . It's a game for the yellow boys. They like it, so let them lump it.[4]

Noury could also have mentioned that, in addition to being dangerous, diving for shell was hard and repetitive work. About 1500 pairs had to be collected to make up a ton and a master pearler counted on one of his luggers collecting 4 to 5 tons of shell a year, more if they had a decent diver on board. With shell bringing up to £230 a ton, a tidy profit could be made if costs could be held at, say, £130 a ton. Additionally, there was always the chance of picking up a pearl. If he had a good season and his lugger wasn't sunk by a cyclone, a sheller could pay off his vessel in a year.

The English divers were paid £13 a month. They could also expect 2½ per cent on the price fetched for any pearls and a bonus of £40 a ton for shell, but only if they lifted in excess of 2½ tons a year. The tenders were paid £6 a month, a small bonus on the shell collected and 5 per cent on the price of pearls found. These were wages well in excess of the Asiatic crew, but not so generous when compared with what an Australian workman could demand. If a man was keen on a seafaring life he could work on an Australian coastal trading vessel at £7 to £8 a month, under much better conditions and with less chance of dying. Wages in Broome tended to be higher than the rest of the nation – for example, Mrs Prentice was hired by the Broome Municipal Council as pound-keeper at £5 a month and the man watering the grass in Bedford Park was paid £7 a month.

Prime Minister Andrew Fisher showed a close interest in the white experiment. He asked for the names of the men, the dates of their landing, and what they were being paid. The Labor Premier in Western Australian, Mr Scaddan, sent a telegram supplying this information, adding that a highly capable man may earn £250 a year in addition to keep. It is not known who supplied Scaddan with this information. To earn that amount a diver would have needed to collect 5 tons of shell. This was possible, but in his first year even a promising diver would be fortunate to collect 3 to 4 tons. A top Japanese diver would require two years experience to consistently lift 5 tons a year.

One thing the English divers did not get was an advance on income. The shellers had been fighting the Japanese Club over this for years, and it is understandable that they did not wish to extend the benefit to the newcomers. In 1908 the master pearlers were complaining about having to pay an advance of £100 to the best Japanese divers. By the end of 1909 the amount was £150. In July 1910 the inspector of police at Broome wrote to his superiors: 'The Japanese diver demands exorbitant advances before he will sign on – as much as £170 being asked for and received in many cases.'[5] By 1912 amounts ranging up to £300 were being paid to crack divers. But the shellers only had themselves to blame because they would continually bid against each other to obtain the best divers. This curious note, which appeared in the minutes of proceedings of the annual general meeting of the Pearlers' Association in December 1910, gives an indication of the extent of the persuasive pressure placed on the shellers by the Japanese:

> In a very heated discussion . . . members deplored the practice, fast becoming prevalent, of divers having their shell weights falsified in their slop chest and shell books, in order that their take of shell for the year may appear larger than it actually was and might delude pearlers into engaging them at heavy advances. The responsibility of these falsified entries in most cases lay with the diver, but occasionally pearling masters themselves were to blame by allowing entries in the books which gave a wrong impression of the diver's real take of shell.

Discussions among the pearlers about the evil of advances went in seasonal circles, reaching their pitch during the haggling over new contracts which accompanied the lay-up. All agreed that it would be a sensible thing to place a limit on the amount of advances but it never happened. Resident Magistrate Major Wood suggested that in order to discourage gambling, the Pearling Act should be amended to prescribe that not more than one-twelfth of the advance should be paid to the divers each month. He did not explain how, in Broome's secretive society, such a law was to be enforced.

On 18 January 1913 the *Nor'-West Echo* wrote:

Some pearlers have paid divers advances as high as £350, crew up to £20, and tenders up to £30. How many have thought what this means? There are 302 luggers, with a diver, tender and five crew to each boat. Place the average advance to divers at £100 (a mild estimate), that will equal £30,200; tenders at an average of £20; total £6,040; 1,510 crew at £15 each, £22,650, or a grand total of £58,890 . . . We cannot understand why pearlers allow the system of big advances to obtain. It might be considered smart business to snare another man's crack diver by bribing him with an advance of £250 or £350, but we'll be hanged if it's sound finance, and it creates a position of affairs in town which is discreditable to any place laying claims to civilisation. Could the open gambling hells, sly-groggeries, brothels, etc., flourish like a green bay tree if big advances were prohibited? Undoubtedly no.

Despite the editorialising of the *Echo*, large advances continued to be paid and the gambling tables remained busy. During the months of the lay-up the Chinese tailor in the Asiatic Quarter ran a lottery which he drew twice a day. Said the *Echo* about a visit to John Chi Lane:

> There was scarcely a building in which gambling was not being glaringly carried on. No protest was offered against our intrusion, and there appeared to be no fear of the police approaching – as if it were known they would not happen along. At one place there was upwards of £1000 showing at one time, and we have since learned that one Malay won £600 in one day and night. It goes on night and day on an appallingly large scale . . . Many of the best cooks, dhobi boys and waiters in the Nor'-West were there with hundreds of others, assisting to bleed the crews of their advances. It is said, with a degree of reason, that the coloured men should be allowed to gamble among themselves, but it has gone too far and cuts into the interests of the

pearler and business man alike, and the whole town would be better off morally and financially if the police came down on the Lane mob and scooped them all into gaol. And it would be a good thing too if every mother's son of a coloured man who has no lawful visible means of earning a living – excepting as buttoners for gambling hells – was gaoled. There are scores of them here who will not work while they are permitted to live on the advances to divers and crews.[6]

Corporal Lamb seemed to take the view that gambling was best regulated by a weekly tribute in appreciation of the police force. After all, Broome was a frontier town and no one expected the normal rules to apply. The several thousand sailors who came to town had to take their recreation somewhere, and if their misdeeds could be confined to that small area of gross licence in the Asiatic Quarter, then at least those living in the English Quarter could be left in peace. Besides, the system of advance payments had its defenders. Not all the money was blown in the gambling dens. Some was sent home to family and relatives. Given that no form of workers' compensation was paid, if a worker died or was paralysed, at least his wife and children might have something.

11 White Men are Not Suitable

Sir John Forrest – . . . but I am told that the work of diving
makes serious inroads upon the health of those engaged upon it,
and that white divers come to the surface bleeding from the ears.
Mr Mathews – That is also the experience of the black diver.
Sir John Forrest – He does not feel the strain to the same extent,
or, if he does, he does not mind the physical discomfort so much
as does the white man.

House of Representatives, *Debates*, Commonwealth of Australia,
26 October 1911, p. 1873

ON 18 APRIL 1912 Sydney Pigott had a discussion in his office
with Stanley Sanders. It was always going to be an awkward meeting.
That morning Sanders had returned to port on board the *Muriel.*
Pigott had watched him jump onto the beach and walk across to the
hotel opposite. Pigott guessed that the man was reluctant to meet
him. Pigott walked down to the dock and watched as three baskets of
shell were carried ashore. None of the baskets was full. He watched

as the shell was weighed and his chief clerk entered in the ship's journal, in his tightly crafted handwriting, the measure of shell collected. Sydney Pigott held out his hand for the book. He then sent a message over to the public bar for Sanders to join him at his earliest convenience. Pigott returned to his desk and waited.

Sanders seemed to be in no hurry to face his employer, and it was not until after lunch that he walked into Pigott's office. Pigott wasted no time on formalities. He called Sanders over to stand next to him and showed him an account book he had on his desk. Pigott ran his finger down a page of columns showing the costs of running the boat, pausing to point out the extra rations he had got in because Sanders was a white man, then across to the column showing the amount of shell collected. Pigott said he hoped Sanders understood that he would only get a commission when he collected more than 2½ tons. At the rate he was going, he would never get there. The conversation grew heated and soon the two men were shouting at each other. Suddenly Pigott was behind his desk writing furiously. He shoved the journal of the *Muriel* across his desk and asked Sanders to sign at the bottom of the page. Sanders signed. In triumph, Pigott closed the book. Sanders, barely in control of his anger, stormed out, the meeting over.

The next day the story was around Broome that Sanders had signed some sort of document saying that white men were not up to pearl-diving and that Sydney Pigott intended to publish it in the press. Noury, Hockliss and Rolland were also in town and were utterly dismayed by what they had heard. Sanders offered to retract the statement. The four men then marched down to Sydney Pigott's office and asked to see what Sanders had signed. Pigott produced the document and the men saw that Sanders had signed and dated a statement saying that white men were not suitable for pearl-diving.[1] Sanders said he had changed his mind and wanted to alter the statement. Another shouting match took place. Pigott said he wasn't going to let Sanders alter anything, claiming that the book was the working journal of the *Muriel* and he couldn't be party to tampering with an official document. As everyone became angrier, Sanders reached out, snatched the book, crumpled the offending page in his hand and tore it free. Pigott demanded he return it. Sanders refused and shoved it in his pocket. After a noisy and jubilant departure, the four men went over to the Governor Broome Hotel to celebrate.

Their triumph was short-lived. By the end of the day Sanders had been arrested by Corporal Lamb on a charge of wilfully destroying ship's property. Initially Corporal Lamb was uncertain whether the theft of a sheet of paper was a crime worth pursuing, but Sydney Pigott – who, after all, was one of the town's leading citizens and president of the Pearlers' Association – had carried on as though it was a very valuable document indeed, so Corporal Lamb thought it best to arrest the perpetrator.

Sanders was lodged in the lock-up in Carnarvon Street at the back of the police station. It was a poky little affair of half a dozen cells under a tin roof, each with a tiny window placed so high that it was impossible to see out. The intense heat inside kept the prisoners perpetually subdued. The men in the cell next door were those being held for the murder of Constable Fletcher. Outside a number of Aboriginal prisoners, chained to studs sunk into a large tree, sat quietly on the ground, dulled by resigned bafflement at white justice.

The next day Sanders had a visit from a man dressed in a neat white suit who sat on a stool outside at the cell bars. He introduced himself as Mr Clarke Hall, the solicitor for Mr Pigott. Hall said Mr Pigott would like to be as lenient as possible. Whoever was at fault, it was clear that the employment arrangement had broken down. The trust between master and servant had gone. If Mr Sanders agreed that was the position, then the employment agreement would be cancelled. Naturally Mr Sanders would also have to write an apology and pay Mr Pigott's legal expenses, which he could guarantee would not exceed £2 at that stage. Sanders sat morosely on a wooden bed in a cell two paces long and an arm's length wide and said he would have to think about it. He was reluctant to agree, especially as his employment agreement specified that if he was terminated for misconduct,

Pigott was relieved of the obligation of paying him any wages due or the fare back to England. But then the alternative did not appear to be too attractive either – the next sitting of the Broome court was not until 8 May, more than two weeks away, and Corporal Lamb showed every intention of keeping him locked up until then.

Later that day Noury, Hockliss and Rolland came to discuss the situation. Sanders asked the gaoler for a pen and paper. What he wrote is preserved among the court archives of the case stored in Perth:

Broome Jail

20/4/12

I Stanley John Sanders do hereby apologise to Mr Pigott for my action in his office on the 18th. of April 1912.

[signed] Stanley John Sanders[2]

The signatures of J. Noury, R. Hockliss and Jas Rolland appeared as witnesses.

Sydney Pigott read Sanders' apology several times before he realised that Sanders had tried to trick him. If he had attempted to use that apology, he would have been the laughing stock of the town. In a fury Pigott contacted Hall and instructed him to prepare for the criminal prosecution of Sanders with all the vigour he could muster – for what Sanders had signed was an apology for his actions on 18 April 1912. That was an apology for the day when Pigott had written in the journal that the work was unsuitable for white men.

Sanders remained in the Broome lock-up for two weeks until his case was heard in the court house on 8 May 1912. The town had two lawyers. Clarke Hall, counsel to the Pearlers' Association, had been engaged by Sydney Pigott, so Sanders sent a message for the other, Louis Coleman, to visit him in prison. Coleman had been a lawyer in Broome since 1905 and was more used to prosecuting than defending.

The master pearlers had a great deal of faith in the Broome police court. After all, as justices of the peace they frequently sat in judgement there. In a typical case such as the one heard in August 1910, the Bench was made up of Pa Norman and George Moss, both master pearlers and both owning a number of boats. Several crewmen were charged with desertion from boats belonging to a pearler named Neall.

The story emerged that a linesman had reported seeing seventeen Malays straggling along beside the telegraph line about 50 miles inland from Broome. One was wandering around naked and the rest were suffering from thirst and exhaustion. Constable Ryan from Broome, assisted by an Aboriginal tracker, went with Neall to pick them up. They were found easily enough, but were too weak to travel the miles back to Broome on foot, so Mr Flottman's bus had to be sent for. Neall told the court that the three ringleaders were still missing. He said that the seventeen brought in were mostly new men, and mostly in arrears for purchases made from his store. He said he had been put to considerable expense through their desertion and he had to pay Flottman for the bus. The bench decided to hear what two of the accused had to say:

> They declared that one bag of flour per week between five boats was not sufficient; one tin of coffee for one week between four boats was insufficient; that one boat only received one bag of water per week, which left only one pannikin per day per man; and if they wanted more they had to pay 1s per bag through the slop chest; they wanted 6 bags of water per boat per week; they had not bought any water; they only received one bag of rice per boat per week, the milk they received was the same as other stations; about two weeks ago one man came on board sick, and the master said he wasn't sick and struck him and sent him to another boat; he wanted to return, but the master refused and used bad language . . . [3]

When asked, through an interpreter, whether they would return to their boats, they one and all declined, declaring they would sooner die in gaol. They were then sentenced to ten weeks imprisonment with hard labour and ordered to pay ten shillings each in costs.

Meanwhile the hunt was on for the ringleaders. To everyone's astonishment, they walked into Broome the next day to report Neall's ill-treatment of them and demand British justice. They were charged with desertion and brought before the court. One of the defendants, Mr Ah Mat Bin Mahomet, said that the reason they had run away was insufficient food and water. The crew had become so thirsty that they had to go to Mr Percy's station to get a bag of water. On the following Saturday, they had to get a kettle full of water from Chamberlain's lugger. There was only one bottle of kerosene for two weeks. Neall had charged him ten shillings to shift to another lugger. The reason he had never complained was because he was afraid of the two whites in charge, Hans Petersen and Big Antonio.

The court asked the three men if they would return to Neall's boats. They absolutely refused. They were sentenced to ten weeks imprisonment with hard labour and the forfeiture of all wages due. The court also ordered that after their release they would have to return to Neall's boats and make up time lost on their indenture period through being in prison.

The option given to deserters of returning to employment or facing a prison term was a common method of enforcing servitude and discipline on the boats. Usually the mere appearance of two master pearlers on the bench was enough to convince runaways to return to work. The sentences handed down could be stiff, as demonstrated in another case involving A.C. Neall reported in the *Broome Chronicle*:

A series of charges at the Police Court on Friday, 5th inst., Dola Bin Mat was charged with deserting a ship at Barred creek belonging to A.C. Neall, on the 29th December, 1908. He was sentenced to 6 weeks hard labour. He was then charged by the Sub-Collector of Customs with being a prohibited immigrant, and was sentenced to 6 months imprisonment. He was also charged with stealing two rifles at Coconut Well on 20th inst., the property of Thos. Chapman, and was sentenced to 6 months hard labour, the latter sentences to be cumulative. For escaping from legal custody he was sentenced to one month hard labour.[4]

Stanley Pigott made regular appearances at the Broome police court, both as a presiding JP and as a litigant. In 1908 he took a Japanese diver and his tender to court and had them charged with refusing duty. The bench sentenced the diver to thirteen weeks gaol and the tender to eight weeks, both with hard labour. The *Broome Chronicle* applauded the decision:

> A diver and tender of Mr. Stanley Pigott's got rather an unpleasant surprise in the Police Court recently. A few more convictions of this sort will soon convince some of the flash divers that they cannot, yet awhile, dictate to their masters as to whom shall be employed opening shell. The masters will show every consideration to good and respectful divers, but the days of the waster and flash diver are numbered. No mercy should be shown, as they are a cause of discontent and trouble of every kind, and are the means of thousands of pounds being lost by the master pearlers.[5]

The resident magistrate was Major George Tuthill Wood. Born in England, he was raised in New Zealand and studied law in Christchurch. His military career was undistinguished: Timaru Cadet Corps, New Zealand Artillery, the Timaru Rocket Brigade and the Western Australian Scottish Regiment, all culminating in an appointment as extra aide-de-camp to Sir Frederic George Denham Bedford, Governor of Western Australia. From there it was a simple matter to become the resident magistrate at Broome.

When Wood arrived in Broome in January 1909, a mayoral reception was organised for him. Abraham Davis spoke on behalf of the pearl-shelling community. They had heard that Wood was a sporting man and assured him that Broome was a sporting community. In response Wood told the audience that Broome was his first choice of the various places offered to him. He said he would bring common sense to his task because he was mindful of the fact that sometimes the law became complicated in the legally trained mind.

Wood was the sportsman he promised to be. He joined the racing, cricket, rifle and shooting clubs. He became president of the Broome Turf Club, captain of the cricket team and president of the Broome Literary and Debating Society. In a small town dominated by the master pearlers, the same people met in those clubs week after week: the tennis partner one week was the rifle shoot opponent the next week, and the person seated opposite at the Empire dinner the week after.

Wood immediately stamped his authority on the court. He chastised a Chinese witness for wearing his pigtail up. He wasn't being fooled – as a mark of respect it must be unrolled. He also issued a directive that the practice of allowing witnesses to swear the oath by kissing the Bible must end.

The master pearlers expected harsh sentences for any crewman challenging their authority. Major Wood was prepared to oblige, as this case decided by him a few months after his arrival in Broome, demonstrates:

> Disobedience in the Police Court on Monday last Captain Stewart charged a Malay crew with disobeying his lawful commands on board his lugger Queenslander. After the plaintiff had stated the charge, the defendant gave as his reasons for disobeying his master that he was not sufficiently fed, that he was charged excessively for his stores, that he was not given one day a week [to rest] and generally laid an all round complaint, terminating this with a declaration that he would not go back to the lugger. The Bench sentenced him to 12 months imprisonment, intimating that should he express his willingness to go

back to his master his term of imprisonment would be reduced. He was also ordered to pay costs of £1 0s 6d.[6]

Only rarely were indentured workers adventurous enough to bring proceedings against their employers. In 1909 Mr Browne, a solicitor with a sense of justice who was new to the town, took on the prosecution in a case which seemed to him to be clear cut. Loh Chang Sung was a cook on board the schooner *Culwulla*, a vessel owned by the accused, Charles Henry Grimwood. Loh Chang Sung, with all the seamanship you might expect of a cook, had let go of a rope when he shouldn't have and Grimwood, losing his temper, had rushed up to Loh Chang Sung, hit him twice in the face, then for good measure handcuffed him and placed him in a storeroom on bread and water for twelve hours. In giving evidence Grimwood explained that he had instructed Loh Chang Sung to stand by the fender to stop the schooner rubbing against the dock but as soon as his back was turned, Loh Chang Sung had left his position and started talking to another Chinese man.

In giving judgement, Major Wood said that the defendant had no right to knock a crew member down and Grimwood would be fined £1, but no costs would be allowed as the whole trouble was brought about by Loh Chang Sung not obeying orders. The court, assisted by Mr Male and Stanley Pigott JPs, threw out a charge of false imprisonment, saying there was no detention because a master of a ship had the right, for the purposes of maintaining good order and discipline, to use such force as he believed necessary. The local press enthusiastically took to the task of reporting Browne's displeasure:

Mr. Browne: What! Do you mean to say there was not detention? We proved detention, and it is for the other side to justify. The Bench: We consider there is not sufficient evidence.

Mr. Male (chairman): You had better behave yourself, Mr Browne.

Mr. Pigott: Your old age protects you, Mr. Browne.

Mr. Browne (slamming the table again): It's a scandalous

miscarriage of justice. You can send me to gaol if you like. (Pointing to the press representative): There you are; there's something for you to report!

The Court adjourned, leaving Mr. Browne still in possession of his enraged feelings.[7]

Rarely did cases involving fights between Asian men come to court, although they must have occurred, but out of sight of the authorities and ignored by the law. One case, however, so offended fair play that Corporal Lamb took action. A Malay tender had punched his Japanese diver in the face while he was standing immobilised in his diving suit. Major Wood agreed that this was not according to Queensbury rules and sentenced the aggressor to a month in gaol.

Given the reputation of the Broome police court as a place where master pearlers were accorded their version of British justice, Sanders faced his trial with misgiving. There was a great deal of interest in his case and as Sanders was brought across from the lock-up he noticed a crowd gathered in front of the court house. At ten o'clock he was placed in the dock by Corporal Lamb. Major Wood entered the room and sat on the bench. He was accompanied by Mr J.C. Fenton JP, the man in charge of the cable office and lugger owner. A gentleman from the *Broome Chronicle* sat at a table next to the side wall with his pencil at the ready. The clerk of courts read out the charge of wilful damage and asked the accused how he pleaded. Sanders' lawyer, Louis Coleman, waved Sanders to his feet. 'Not guilty,' said Sanders.

Sydney Pigott gave evidence that on 19 April, four white divers had come into his office. While they were talking to him, the defendant had snatched a book off his table and had torn a page out. The page contained a statement made by the defendant. Pigott said he asked Sanders to return the page but he refused. The book was the working journal of his boat, the *Muriel*. Pigott said he most particularly required the entries in the journal to enable him to make his calculations with respect to the working of the white divers, which was a matter involving large sums of money.

Pigott was cross-examined by Coleman. Hadn't the defendant written an apology? Pigott produced the apology for the court and pointed out that the defendant had inserted the wrong date. See, there was no sense of remorse.

The bench retired to consider its verdict. Clear case of guilt, said Major Wood on his return. Fenton nodded. A charge of wilful damage was a serious one, said Major Wood. Fenton nodded. The defendant was liable to two years imprisonment. Fenton agreed. The police could have charged him with stealing, and then he would have been liable to three years imprisonment. Sanders shut his eyes. He couldn't believe this was happening. He heard himself sentenced to a month's imprisonment.

Coleman stood up to ask for leniency. Mr Sanders had never been in trouble with the law before. He was new to this country. Would His Worship consider the option of a fine? Major Wood conferred with Fenton. Any fine would have to be substantial. Twenty pounds; in default, one month hard labour.[8]

Sanders had to hold onto the railing of the dock. The case had taken less than an hour. Where was he going to find £20? It was the equivalent of six weeks wages. It is recorded that the fine was paid the next day. Probably Hockliss, Noury and Rolland pitched in.

Sydney Pigott had decisively demonstrated to the English divers that they challenged the rule of the master pearlers at their peril. With this lesson ringing in their ears, Hockliss, Noury and Rolland returned to sea. Sanders remained in Broome, stranded, broke and unemployable. Webber and Reid, who had left on the *Eurus* on 20 February, had not been heard from. Beasily and Freight were somewhere along Ninety Mile Beach with Hanson performing the tending duties. No one knew where Elphick, Harvey and Andrews were.

The Pigott brothers saw themselves as engaged in a battle to save their livelihood and their way of life, and they appeared to believe that almost any tactic could be justified. Had Sanders not destroyed the statement that white men were unsuitable for pearl-diving, presumably the Pigotts would have used it in the propaganda war against the government, sending copies to newspapers around Australia, dropping it off to friendly parliamentarians to make play with, and then presenting it as evidence to the Royal Commission when it eventually came to Broome.

Unfortunately for the Pigott brothers, the news reaching Broome about the Royal Commission's investigations in Queensland during April and May 1912 was a severe blow. From what they could read in the press, it appeared almost inevitable that the commission would recommend the total exclusion of Asian workers from the industry.

To the chairman Mr Frederick Bamford and his fellow commissioners it seemed clear that the master pearlers in Queensland had allowed the industry to slip through their fingers. Mr Frederick Charles Hodel, one of the leading citizens of the Thursday Island community and managing director of Hodel's Ltd, told the commission that there were no white divers left in the industry. Nor were there likely to be any in the near future. He admitted that a white diver had recently applied to him for work, but his firm had declined the offer because it was afraid 'that if we gave him a job the alien divers would go out on strike, or do what is the equivalent of a strike, pass over our shell to a boat owned by another firm'.[9]

Thomas Farquhar, a pearler on Thursday Island for nineteen years, was asked whether a Japanese diver would be prepared to teach a white man how to dive if the latter went onto one of the boats. The answer was no – the white man's life would not be worth living. Another witness, William John Graham of Thursday Island, told the commission that it would be business suicide to place white men on his boats. He explained that the Japanese 'have the big end of the wedge here'.[10]

Bernard Cohen, the secretary of the Waterside Workers Union, believed that the shellers were quite happy to have the big wedge applied to them. He told the commission:

The shellers here do not want any white men, and any white men here seeking for work as divers are always turned away with some excuse or another; and the reason is very plain, as the coloured men are ever so much more profitable to the shellers than any whites would be.

The coloured men, for instance, will and do live on rations that no white man would accept; also, the prices charged for goods from the slop chest would not be tolerated by white men . . .

We also wish to point out the fact of the shellers here saying that the industry cannot be made to pay with white labour, is, to us who know better, just a bit of bluff.[11]

Such was the ascendancy of the Japanese that it was a common arrangement for a Japanese diver, as the real master of the vessel, to provision the boat from local shops run by Japanese and then levy a charge against the master pearler in the form of increased commission. And unlike the position in Western Australia, master pearlers no longer laid claim to the pearls. The owners of the luggers never knew whether a pearl was found or not. Any pearl retrieved by the Japanese was smuggled out of the country, often by the simplest method of all: posting it back home.

Not only were the Japanese masters of the luggers, they were beginning to own them as well. Although there were laws against coloured aliens owning vessels, these were easily circumvented by having a Britisher's name on the record, while the profits were taken by a Japanese syndicate of divers and crew. It was said that the going rate for a white man acting as a dummy was £50 per annum and 5 per cent of the catch. All the white dummy had to do was to place his name on the ship's register and pretend to be a successful sheller.

The industrious Japanese were also the men who built the boats. The commission heard that shellers ordered their boats from the Japanese shipyards on Thursday Island instead of relying on builders in Sydney and Brisbane. Even the sails were run up in the Japanese compound. One disgruntled ex-boat builder gave evidence, saying he had carried on business for four years, but the Japanese undercut him, and then the Japanese bought the slip and forced him out of business. He referred to another white boat builder who drank heavily and died broke and heartbroken because the Japanese paid their countrymen five shillings a day while the white men he employed wanted fifteen shillings a day.

Many of the luggers were sailing under the Japanese flag. The commissioners were at a loss to understand how the white men, supposedly running the industry, had allowed the Japanese to gain such power. Bamford asked Thomas Farquhar, master pearler of Thursday Island:

> Q. The British flag seems to be ignored, although these boats are registered as British vessels. Should not the shellers take some action to see that the British flag is flown on every occasion? – I certainly think the British flag should be in the ascendant, and I took part on one occasion in an effort to have all the Japanese flags hauled down and the British flag flown in their stead.
>
> Q. We have been told that the Japanese divers provide their own flags, and that on the occasion of a death on board they come into port with the Japanese flag at half-mast, because they have no other flag to fly? – That is correct.
>
> Q. It would not cost the owners a great deal to provide each boat with a British flag? – No. It would be a good thing to do.
>
> Q. Are you prepared to do that? – Yes, and to notify the men that they are to fly the British flag.[12]

This was a case, if ever there was, of telling politicians what they wanted to hear in the knowledge that the following week they would be back home in the south and never likely to return. And if the master pearlers of Thursday Island were ever to be courageous enough to insist that the Japanese fly the British flag whenever the body of a diver was brought back to port, certainly a large number of flags would have to be ordered in. The manager of Burns, Philp, and Company at Thursday Island, a firm which had 24 luggers, was quizzed about the death rate on his company's vessels:

> Q. According to your figures, the percentage of mortality amongst your divers last year was 27 per cent. This year you have already lost three divers off twenty-four boats, although only one-fourth of the working time of the year has gone; so that, in other words, the mortality has been at the rate of 50 per cent per annum? – Yes.
>
> Q. Can you suggest any means of reducing that awful rate of mortality? – I do not think it would be possible to minimize the mortality. One of our divers lost his life a few weeks ago; and, on making inquiries as to the causes leading up to the fatality, I found that the boat of which he was in charge had experienced a run of ill luck, having lost a lot of time because of an inferior crew. To make up for loss of time, the diver worked too hard, and he had one dip too many. On the occasion of his last dip, he remained on the bottom for only two and a half minutes.[13]

Mr N.S. Hiramatsu, a Japanese man who had lived on Thursday Island for sixteen years and was banker and interpreter to the indentured workers, explained to the commission that the Japanese divers were very brave. They did not fear death and dived much deeper than the white man. Plenty had died during the past years, he said, but it could not be helped. Most were single men, and when they died their friends sent money home. He said he did not know how to save the divers. You could tell them not to go into deep water, but they would go.

Other witnesses spoke of the fatalistic Japanese. One pearler said that the Japanese were not better divers than the whites, but they were quite fearless. He had seen a Japanese diver get into the diving suit out of which the body of a dead man had just been taken.

Another witness explained that the 'religious belief of the Japanese and of certain other coloured men teaches them not to fear the hereafter, but the white man does'.[14]

Some of the master pearlers told the commissioners that they were not at all in favour of employing white men to dive. It was too dangerous. And what sort of white man would want to work with an Asiatic crew who, after all, 'are only one removed from the nigger'. So said Hugh John Kelly, a veteran of twelve years pearl-shell diving in Torres Strait and New Guinea, adding that 'as a rule, it is only the drunkards and ne'er-do-wells who will tackle diving'.[15]

When the Royal Commission published its interim report in 1913, among its many recommendations it wrote in favour of 'supplanting the present coloured residents of Thursday Island by a wholly white population . . . '[16] The reasoning behind this solution was that the island had become so dominated by the Japanese that a fresh start needed to be made. The commission hoped 'the industry should eventually become one undertaken by white workers only who would make their homes on the island . . . '[17]

The prejudice guiding such views, anticipating a sort of apartheid of the north, can be seen behind this insistent questioning by Bamford of a reluctant Gilbert White, Lord Bishop of Carpentaria:

> Q. It has been said that the children of coloured aliens, owing to the conditions under which they live, are more vicious than are the children of white parents. Is that your experience? – I have no reason to believe that they are more vicious. I cannot recall any particular instance of viciousness on the part of coloured children.
> Q. We are told that sometimes whole families live in one room, and that in such circumstances children often see and hear what they ought not to? – That is very probable where families live under crowded conditions, but it does not necessarily follow that overcrowding results in vice. There are overcrowded white countries, but viciousness does not necessarily follow.

Q. If it does result in children being more vicious, and hearing and seeing what they ought not to, would not those children contaminate others in the public schools? – If the children were vicious, that would be the result, but I would not like to assert that coloured children were more vicious than white.

Q. Do you visit the State school here? – Yes.

Q. Both white and coloured children attend that school. Has it been brought under your notice that the coloured children are more vicious? – No.

Q. Would you advocate a separate school for white children? – Viewed in the abstract, I do not like the principle. It seems to me to be wholly wrong. I certainly recognise that advantages would follow from separate schools, since with separate schools different systems of education and methods of training might be adopted. On that ground I should not object to separate schools, but I do not favour separate establishments solely on the grounds of colour.

Q. Do you find that coloured children are as receptive as are the whites? – I find no difference between the white and coloured children in Sunday school so far as their receptivity is concerned, nor do we find that black children are more ill-behaved than are white children. We have no trouble with them, but we have in our Sunday school only a very small proportion of the coloured children of the island.[18]

After completing their investigation in North Queensland on 20 May 1912, Bamford and the other commissioners returned to Melbourne. They had planned to then set sail to take evidence in Western Australia, but a hectic parliamentary schedule detained the group. It seemed it would be many months before a visit to the West would be possible.

12 The Fleet

*The physical depression caused by doing coolie labour in an
enervating tropical climate may easily lead to moral deterioration — hard drinking to begin with, other evils following.*

Report to the House of Representatives by Resident Magistrate
M.S.Warton Esquire, 1902[1]

THE RICHEST SHELLER OF them all was Mark Rubin. His
man in Broome had been his brother-in-law, the elegant Abraham
Davis, who lived in 'de Vahl' in Hamersley Street, but Davis had disappeared along with the *Koombana*. Ever since, a question of
considerable interest along the coast was who Rubin would appoint
in his place. It was a plum position involving the buying and selling
of pearls in Asia and Europe, and the overseeing of huge pastoral
properties along the De Grey River and in Queensland. What was on
offer was a job of prestige, immoderate remuneration and frequent
overseas travel. It was, to Sydney Pigott's mind, ideal for a man who
was well connected in commercial and government circles, was

regarded as a hard, true man, and knew everything there was to know about mother-of-pearl and pearls.

Mark Rubin's story was one of rags to riches. He had arrived in Melbourne in the 1880s as a coal lumper on a steamer. He was a refugee from the pogroms against the Jews in Poland. He spoke no English and had no money, but he could readily see this was a prosperous city, plump from the wealth pouring in from the goldfields. He picked up odd jobs and then, after a few months, he used his meagre savings to buy a wheelbarrow and a stock of haberdashery. Speaking little more than market English, he set out on his new career as a trader. Rubin was a gregarious fellow and a born salesman. He quickly graduated from a wheelbarrow to a horse and cart, and began hawking his wares further afield. He learnt that the way to big profits was to buy cheaply in the city and sell expensively to miners.

Rubin's travels took him to the opal fields of White Cliffs where he learnt the second lesson of big profits: buy gems cheaply from miners and sell expensively in the city. By combining the two principles, Rubin was, within seven years of his arrival in Australia, a very rich man. He returned to Melbourne and mixed with the Jewish community there, some of whom were, like him, traders in gems. The oft-repeated legend of Rubin is that he noticed that from time to time one of his colleagues would disappear for a couple of months and his family was always secretive about where he had gone.

One day Rubin followed the man into a shipping office where he overheard him buying a ticket to Broome. Rubin knew nothing about Broome and only a little about pearls, but he thought that if his shrewd friend was going there, money was to be made. Rubin followed him. When he arrived in Broome, Rubin found a town awash with money and men in hotels with pearls to sell. He bought up big and, following his trusted principle of selling expensively in the city, figured that the bigger the city, the bigger the profit. With a small felt bag of pearls tucked around his waist, Rubin caught the steamer to London. He was a gambler by nature and this gamble went badly awry. He had paid too much for his pearls, the market in London fell and he lost heavily.

But if markets could fall, markets could also rise. Rubin held no high opinion of the men he had met in the hotels of Broome and if they could prosper, surely he could also. He had lost money but he had learnt a lot about the valuation of pearls and, more importantly, he had made contacts among the Jewish dealers in Europe. He returned to Broome, traded in pearls and began to buy up luggers. By 1906 he had assembled the largest fleet ever seen on the coast, and put the erratic Captain Ancell Clement Gregory in charge. Then, barely two years later, Rubin began to sell his fleet and concentrate on the trade in pearls. Gregory was replaced by his brother-in-law, Abraham Davis. Rubin was now rich beyond greed.

Another Rubin legend is that he saw a great war coming and a demand for wool for uniforms and bully beef for the troops, so in 1912 he began to buy up cattle and sheep stations, huge expanses of properties along the De Grey River and beyond. Rubin was now rarely in Australia, let alone Broome. Where he actually was remained unclear to the master pearlers who watched Abraham Davis slowly sell Rubin's fleet, buy pearls (some surreptitiously from coloured crewmen) and disdain interest in the activities of the Pearlers' Association. Davis, for one, was brutally frank as to why whites should not work as divers for mother-of-pearl. In 1909 he told a newspaper: 'We lose a large number from diver's paralysis, and I suppose it is no harm to say . . . that it is preferable the black men should be sent to this deadly work than the white man should be offered up on the altar of Mammon.'[2]

Mark Rubin returned to Broome every couple of years and threw a grand party at 'de Vahl' during which he spoke to his assembled guests about the prices paid for pearls in London, New York, Paris and St Petersburg – places it seems he visited in grand style on a regular basis. After he had sailed on from Broome – in awe and with some jealousy, but never in jest – the pearlers referred to him as the 'Pearl King'.

While Broome puzzled over who Mark Rubin would favour with an appointment, the town was getting ready to welcome another visiting dignitary – Mr W.D. Johnson, the state's Minister for Public Works. Accordingly, on a hot afternoon in May 1912, at the very end of the Broome jetty, stood the mayor, Pa Norman, with his gold gorget of office hung on a chain around his neck. Next to him stood the finest dignitaries the town could muster: Resident Magistrate Wood, both Sydney and Stanley Pigott, Acting Harbour Master Captain Dalziel, lawyers Coleman and Hall, Sub-Collector of Customs Mr Huggins, Dr Blick, and Mr Green, the proprietor, editor and sole reporter of the *Broome Chronicle*. At the rear stood the town band, the members dressed in their new uniform of scarlet red coats and white trousers. There was, everyone regretfully noted, little shade at the jetty's end.

Aboard the SS *Penguin*, the man for whose benefit the welcome was being organised looked out the porthole of his stateroom to see what was happening. He stared morosely at the people on the jetty. He was sure that every one of them had a project that needed funding. A project that was important and urgent, vital to northern development and demanding precedence above all other projects.

His private secretary entered the cabin and rattled off the program: inspect the town, lunch with leading citizens, inspect the school, civic reception, discussion with resident magistrate. All to be done before seven pm when the *Penguin* was due to cast off again. So far on his voyage up the coast the minister had been asked to spend the state's treasury several times over. Silos for wheat farmers, roads for miners, police stations for policemen, court houses for lawyers, hospitals for doctors, schools for teachers, and harbours for harbour masters. Drought relief, flood relief, relief for widows, orphan relief and, most of all, relief from government taxes and charges.

He felt the SS *Penguin* bump into the dock, so he picked up his silk hat and stepped out on deck. The dazzle of sunlight stunned him and he grasped his secretary's arm to steady himself as the band began a rendition of 'Land of Hope and Glory'. Mayor Norman took the great man's hand and pumped it up and down. The minister was accompanied by six other members of Parliament, but it was Mr Johnson that Norman was most interested in. Any mayor worth his salt realised that the Minister for Public Works was the most important man in the government. The Minister for Public Works had awesome power: he could turn bays into harbours, creeks into dams, swamps into farmland and farmland into railway yards – all at public expense. Heaven knows when another Minister for Public Works would pass that way again.

Johnson was taken for a drive around the town in Norman's buggy. He saw packing sheds, the abattoirs, the hospital, the cable station, the fire station, the police station, the Customs House and the emporiums in Carnarvon Street. What struck the minister was the temporary nature of everything. It was all corrugated iron, nailed on rough-cut wood. A succession of local businessmen told him of their firm commitment to northern development, but it seemed that the only structures of substance had been built by the government. Even the large bungalows of the master pearlers were lattice and iron on timber frames. The hotels were shearing sheds divided into rooms. The packing sheds looked as if a decent wind would blow them across the mangroves and out to sea.

The Asiatic Quarter was not on Johnson's tour, but on the way to lunch at the Governor Broome Hotel, he glanced along Shiba Lane. He ordered the mayoral buggy to stop. He peered out the window, into a lane of red dust hemmed in by ramshackle, rusted buildings. Black, brown and yellow faces peered back at him. Smoke from fires hovered like a London fog between the buildings. A street vendor pushed a cart along the lane, calling out in a language the minister didn't understand. Coloured banners and flags covered with some sort of Asiatic writing he could not comprehend hung from verandah posts. He saw men with pigtails, women dressed in silk kimonos, half-naked youths in sarongs. Yellow-coloured babies played in the dust. Johnson shook his head in disbelief. Never had he thought he would see such a sight on Australian soil.

At four in the afternoon he attended a civic reception held in his honour at the Literary Institute. Pa Norman made a lengthy speech. He said that it was most gratifying to find a minister of the crown passing through the northwest, hearing and seeing their requirements first hand, when they had been so neglected by previous administrations. Although they had had numerous ministerial promises in the past, he went on, he was sorry to say that few of them were ever carried out. It was not as though the people of Broome were asking for a hand-out. They were just asking for some of their money back. The government did very well out of the pearling industry. Duty on overseas goods was £20,182 a year. Another £30,000 duty was paid on goods from Fremantle. Shipping office fees netted £240, licences £324, and landing charges £700. All that the people of Broome asked for in return was a fair share, and that their taxes not be wasted on welfare in the cities for men who were work-shy. Mayor Norman held up a list of what needed to be done. Increase of the goods shed accommodation, repairs to the jetty, upgrading of the Gantheaume lighthouse, the extension of the tram line, a small steamer to be provided by the government in case of emergency, a thorough search for the *Koombana*, a women's ward in the hospital, creation of a roads board and the upgrading of the bore water pipes to 6 inches.

Johnson thought it a hectoring, discourteous speech, but he held his peace. Then the mayor called upon Sydney Pigott to make an address on behalf of those in the pearling industry. As Pigott spoke, the minister's mood turned blacker. Johnson knew Pigott as an opponent in a previous parliament and thought him an aggressive little man. Pigott began by supporting the list of improvements proposed by their mayor, then attacked the Labor Party's decision to make the industry white. The shellers, said Pigott, would be satisfied to be left alone but they were continually being interfered with by governments.

At this Mr Johnson bristled, and when he rose he declared that he was a White Australian every time. The pearlers were being interfered with because an Australian industry should be worked by Australian people. The people of Australia had declared in favour of a White

Australia and the government had a responsibility to carry out its mandate. The day for coloured labour had gone and although it might be expensive to reorganise the industry, it must be done. It was an insult to the white race to say that it could not be so worked, and worked with great success. If Mr Pigott's opinion differed he could have his say when the pearling commission came to Broome.

The shellers had made an adversary of Johnson. When the SS *Penguin* called in at Carnarvon, on the way back to Perth, he invited several reporters aboard. He told them he had discovered in Broome that the white divers were not being shown where and how to find the shell. Johnson said that despite this, he had no doubt that the problem would be overcome and the experiment would eventually prove wholly successful. In case the point was missed, he repeated the accusations when he arrived in Perth. He added that the white diver was not yet sufficiently educated to find shell. It took the Asiatic a considerable time before he became competent enough to win a payable quantity of shell, so why shouldn't the same apply to white divers? His views were cabled to the capital cities of the eastern states and extensively reported.

It seems that during Johnson's visit to Broome, someone had told him that the master pearlers there were attempting to sabotage the English divers. It could have been anyone, of course. Sanders was still in town and had plenty of reasons to be disgruntled. There were also a few public servants in town who would have been pleased to see the pearlers taken down a peg or two, Huggins among them.

The reaction of the Pearlers' Association to Johnson's criticisms was muted. There were no protests, no denials. For once Stanley Pigott's typewriter was still. There was silence. So complete was the hush that the *Nor'-West Echo*, in two editorials in July 1912, called upon the association to abandon its 'leave us alone' mentality and to refute Mr Johnson's 'juggle of sophistry'. The association ignored the suggestion. Even in the months that followed, as the white experiment went into complete disarray, there was no comment from the association, and Stanley Pigott wrote no more letters to

Atlee Hunt. It is likely that Sydney Pigott, as the most powerful figure in the association and its president, had convinced the committee that public debate about the English divers would be counterproductive. As far as Sydney Pigott could see, the city newspapers were staunchly in support of the White Australia Policy, and any suggestion by the association that white men were not up to the task would be greeted with hostility. In Pigott's view, the less said about the white divers the better. It was a debate the association could never hope to win.

A few days after Johnson's visit, a public notice appeared in the *Broome Chronicle*:

Pearls

Mr M. Rubin desires to thank his Clients for past favours extended to his Representatives, and announces that he will be personally visiting Broome during June next.

In the meantime, Mr S.C. Pigott has been authorised by me to carry on the pearl buying business on my account in Broome, and to buy all grades of pearls, Baroque, Speculative Stone, and Blisters at highest possible prices.[3]

Sydney Pigott bathed in the congratulations of his colleagues. Since he would be travelling so often in the business of buying and selling pearls, Pigott decided he no longer required a base in Broome. He placed his house on the market and began to sell his fleet. A minor problem was that he had ongoing contracts engaging three English divers for terms running though to the next year. But, as he reflected, he had already managed to rid himself of one of these at little personal cost.

On 20 May 1912 the *Eurus* returned to Broome with Webber and Reid on board. They had been away for three months. According to testimony given to the Royal Commission by their employer, Hugh Richardson, Webber brought back 3½ hundredweight of shell. It was a ridiculously small amount. Richardson produced nothing to support his figures. Given that by the time the Royal Commission took this evidence (in 1916) Webber was no longer around to contest anything said, it is feasible that the amount of $3\frac{1}{2}$ hundredweight was a malicious fantasy.

Also, according to Richardson, Webber took on board a machine pump and sailed out on the same day. This was the behaviour of a man obsessed. Webber may not have wished to face the white population in Broome. To have had to explain why he, an Admiralty trained diver, had collected only a few baskets of shell was something he may have found too galling. Everything we know about Webber suggests a courageous, meticulous man, a man who, when set a task, would approach it with conviction and determination. His service in the navy was of steady, if not spectacular progression. His engagements with Siebe, Gorman marked him as a man who set great store on reliability. He was not one to readily accept failure. He may have regarded the machine pump, now installed on his vessel, as the answer – it would allow him to go deeper and recover shell from areas where the coloured men had never been. So, with the devotion of a zealot, he turned his vessel back to sea. He would barely have had time to take in the news of what had happened to Sanders.

Sanders was still in town. He was mentioned, as an aside in an article appearing in the *Nor'-West Echo* about Johnson's visit, as one who got into trouble and is now out of work.[4] Sanders may not have had the fare to get out of town and was probably living rough. There was a white underclass in Broome which had been attracted to the northwest by stories of its fabulous wealth but they had discovered, on their arrival, that they were incapable of sharing in it. They picked up occasional labouring work, but in this they were competing with the coloured workers. The names of some of them (and no other details) appear in court records on charges for petty offences such as being drunk and disorderly, being found on gambling premises, or the theft of trousers off a clothesline. If Webber did run into Sanders during his brief stay, one suspects that Webber would not have wanted much to do with him. Sanders had signed a document stating the very thing that Webber was devoting himself to disproving. And if Sanders was on the skids, Webber would have regarded his presence in Broome as an embarrassment.

Besides Webber had plenty to occupy his time during the hours he was in port. He had to take on stores for two months at sea, arrange maintenance of his vessel and supervise installation of the new diving pump. The pump Richardson installed on the *Eurus* would have run on either naphtha or kerosene. The air it pumped to the diver was filtered and water-cooled. Despite their apparent advantages, divers on the pearling grounds were slow to accept machine pumps. Few were convinced that smoke and spark plugs were more reliable than the honesty of a human back. The reduction in noise served only to convince some that they were not getting enough air. Divers said they missed the clack-clack-clack sound of the valves falling into place at each turn of the handle. They complained that the air being pumped down to them was much colder than from the hand-pumps. They missed the smell of coffee and the savour of the cooking. Some said there was an oily odour to the air which gave them headaches. There were also reports, more rumour than substance, that divers in Queensland had been brought up dead, asphyxiated by the exhaust smoke from the engine.

Out at sea there were days of clear blue skies and flat, calm seas. Weather ideal for bringing up bags full of shell, yet it was relayed back to the master pearlers in Broome that their white employees were having great difficulty matching the coloured divers. They took too long in staging to the surface and insisted on having a mid morning and midday break, with the result that they spent very little time in the water. And it was useless to argue with them because they insisted that such procedures were essential to protect them from the bends.

In early July 1912 James Rolland and Reginald Hockliss returned to port. Both were disillusioned men. Life on board a pearling lugger was not the sunny adventure they had been told about when they had signed their contracts in England. As far as they could see, it was a miserable, sordid existence on a substandard vessel with a job as tedious as could be imagined. And it was not as though they were making a fortune. At their present rate of collection it was unlikely they would ever recover enough shell to earn above their base salary. Moreover, when they returned to port, they discovered that the general view around town was that the sooner the Labor government gave up on attempting to foist white workers on the industry the better. Men in hotel bars told them that any white man who was prepared to spend weeks at a time in the company of a boatload of illiterate Asiatic peasants needed his head read. Couldn't they see they were being taken advantage of?

Sydney Pigott called Rolland and Hockliss in for a discussion. They had a long meeting, and the Englishmen left for Perth on the SS *Minderoo* the next day. After they had gone, the *Nor'-West Echo* reported that the 'two men expressed themselves disappointed and dissatisfied because they could not find shell, although coloured men were successful in the same water alongside them . . . The agreement was dissolved by mutual consent'.[5] The mutual consent was probably obtained by Sydney Pigott paying their fares to Perth, where they hoped to find employment. A satisfactory result, Pigott no doubt thought. Now he only had the adhesive and argumentative John Noury left on his books.

At about this time an advertisement appeared in the *Broome Chronicle*: 'A Greek diver (recent arrival) desires employment. Large experience as a Sponge Diver in the Mediterranean Sea. Apply at N. Kazako's Fish Shop, Dampier Terrace.'[6] This was an optimistic advertisement. Not surprisingly there were no takers, and the ex-sponge diver became a stevedore. A few months later, another item appeared:

> Is it true? – About a score of British workmen are at present unemployed in Broome, many of whom we know to be honest toilers, and they rightly complain that in picking lumpers for

jetty work, Greeks, who run a fish shop in town, are chosen and the British subjects passed over. By no manner of reasoning can this be claimed to be the right thing, and Capt. Dalziel would act wisely (if he wishes to avoid a 'please explain') by placing his number eights flop on it at once.[7]

Did Acting Harbour Master Dalziel respond to the tyranny of the press by stamping out the practice? Nothing more was heard of the issue, so presumably he did.

BEASILY FELL slowly through 12 fathoms of water onto a sandy bottom. The water around him was still and clear. All he could hear was the exertion of his own breath, and the far-off hum of the air pump. The shadow of clouds drifted across the floor. With the toe of his boot he scraped clear the floor to reveal sandstone. Ahead lay a plain, as smooth and flat as if it had been laid by a concreter. There was not a lot of vegetation. He saw some sponge, delicate white fans, and plants the colour of lettuce. He tugged on his lifeline for Hanson to commence a drift over the bottom.

After two hours Beasily signalled to be staged up. As his copper helmet rose amidst bubbling water, Hanson leant over the bulwark looking to see how much shell was in the netted bag. Beasily saw the satisfaction in his tender's face. He also saw Hanson glance at the crew. As Beasily climbed aboard, Hanson grabbed the bag and shook a large pile of shell onto the deck. He let it lie there for all to see what white men could do.

At first Beasily had wondered if there was any lonelier job in the world than being suspended underwater in a cocoon of silence where the only contact with another human was by yanking on a rope. Then one day it occurred to him that he was surrounded by nature, that perhaps he could find more shell by lifting his gaze from a close examination of the floor to observe the type of environment the shell liked. He began to look at sea ferns, posts of dead coral, crayfish and crabs of jagged black on white designs. He saw limy-tube worms, finger sponges and waving anemones. He watched spidery crabs, tiny shrimps and golden-coloured starfish, beaded with crimson nodules. He saw hundreds of fish of every shape and size.

One day he saw a fish of extraordinary beauty swim past his helmet. It was the size of a large plate, and coloured a deep pink. Propelled by the undulating fans of two small fins near its tail, it was as graceful as a miniature three-masted sailing ship. As it swished in and out of the bubbles rising from his helmet, Beasily watched it attempt to mouth a ball of air. It swam so close he could have stroked its belly. Suddenly there was a flash of silver, a puff of red and, when the water cleared, he could see that a predator had taken a circular piece of flesh, the size of a tennis ball, out of his fish. It swam for a moment, its fins buzzing frantically, trying to keep aloft while its innards began to trail out in pink streamers. Slowly it curved to the sand below, where hundreds of fish attacked it in a feeding frenzy. So shaken was he that he signalled to be taken to the surface. When he explained what had happened, it seemed that the only one who understood his sadness was an old ex-diver, a man from Saigon, now crippled and only fit to be a crew hand.

After weeks on a cramped boat and despite the language difficulties, he began to get to know the crew. The lingua franca on the pearling luggers was a bastardised Broome creole, composed mainly of pidgin Malay, with some Japanese, English and Aboriginal words thrown in. Beasily began to mimic the singsong, arm-waving efforts of the Malays conversing with the Japanese cook, but he found that no matter what he attempted, everyone doubled over in laughter. But then the crew found much to laugh about – at almost everything that happened on the boat, it seemed – and Beasily found their laughter infectious. After the evening meal he got them to teach him words for common items on the boat. When they tired of that, he sat against the mast with a coffee in his hand listening to them chatting and joking with each other. Some nights they invited him to make up a four playing cards, under a lamp swinging from the mast.

One Saturday in May, the fleet of Robison & Norman gathered in the waters off Cape Missiessy. Hanson stood on the cabin roof and, holding a telescope to his eye, studied each arrival as a dozen luggers appeared during the course of the afternoon. He called to Beasily and they sat together on the roof as the sun began to set. Beams of sunlight, like the Japanese flag, shone through a few wispy clouds. A line of birds, mere W-shaped silhouettes, moved across the horizon. As each boat anchored, the crew pushed a dinghy clear and rowed the distance to nearby luggers where, with hoots of joy, they greeted friends.

When the fleet awoke on Sunday morning, the schooner *Ena* was in their midst. She was a superb, three-masted vessel of over a hundred feet, built at Ford's shipyard in Sydney. Men on the luggers, emerging from their cramped cabins, wondered what it would be like to be aboard a vessel you could actually stroll around on.

After breakfast Beasily and Hanson watched the crew load the dinghy with baskets of shell. Beasily felt pleased with himself. True, he hadn't collected as many as the flash Japanese divers, but he was getting the hang of it. He was convinced it was just a matter of practice and perseverance. He believed none of that rubbish he had heard in the streets of Broome about Asiatics being able to see the shell better than the white man. He had heard others say that a man who had lost one eye had a special skill in seeing underwater – it was something to do with normal vision being distorted by the glass port of the helmet. One black eye was best, so they said, then two black eyes, and two white eyes were worst of all.

After the shell had been loaded into the dinghy, Hanson and one of the Malays rowed over to the *Ena*. They feathered oars within her shadow and waited in line as the baskets were pulled aboard in slings. One of Norman's clerks, dressed in a white linen suit and wearing a pith helmet, stood on the deck of the schooner, supervising. Hanson stood up in the rocking dinghy and nodded to him. The clerk nodded back, but was careful not to be distracted. Six baskets were lifted from Hanson's dinghy. Hanson looked for a sign of approval but saw none. Was Mr Norman on board? he asked. Indeed he was, replied the clerk. And he would be pleased if he and Mr Beasily could join him for an evening meal. Hanson said he would consult Mr Beasily, but he thought they had no other engagement. There was a smile from the clerk, who then told Hanson to come aboard and sign for the mail. Hanson climbed up a ladder and was given a package, tied up in red tape and marked for the lugger *Edgar Norman*.

Back in the dinghy, Hanson flicked through letters bearing postmarks from London, Singapore, Kuala Lumpur and Saigon. On one he recognised the disciplined handwriting of his mother. He shoved this letter in his pocket, retied the package and commenced the row back. She had written to him care of Robison & Norman's packing shed, and then added: 'On the High Seas.' He understood the disapproval implied. How could anyone whose address was care of a packing shed on the high seas be responsibly considering his future?

The crew gathered on the deck, waiting for the mail. He threw the package aboard and before he was up the ladder the red tape had been undone and the mail distributed. Letters were exchanged between the crew, and those who were illiterate had passages read out to them. Those who had received no letters said that after a while people forget you out here.

The news had gone around the fleet that the slop chest would open at ten. At quarter to ten the dinghies set off, circling the schooner until the ladders were thrown down precisely on the hour. They clambered aboard. The white gentlemen were led by the first mate down stairs amidships and along a passageway to a space built into the forward hull. The way was barred by a floor to ceiling iron grille and while the mate fitted the key into a sizeable brass lock, they peered inside. The room was lit with a golden lamp swinging from the ceiling. A delicious aroma came through the iron bars – of spices and chocolate, tobacco and coffee.

In front of the room sat a clerk with an open ledger before him.

Behind were shelves filled top to bottom with things which sailors loved after weeks at sea: wooden boxes of fruit cakes, tins of cocoa, cans of fruit, needles and thread. Bottles of spirits were lined up row upon row: Dawson's, Dogs Head, Asahi. There were jars of Doan's kidney pills, Dr Morse's Indian root and Wood's peppermint cure. There were small porcelain containers with Chinese writing on the lid and hemp packages bound by string with labels showing dragons, horses and bears. There were cigars from Manila, tea from China and tinned cheese from Gippsland.

The men lined up to make their choices, and everything they took was noted in the ledger. Back on deck, like children on Christmas morning, they stood around chatting and showing each other what they had. Some opened fresh cans of tobacco and lit their pipes while they waited as the coloured men were escorted down below to make their purchases.

On that warm Sunday, on a calm sea, the men rowed back to their boats, some taking a swig of gin as they went. Once aboard, they drank and got drunk, they gossiped, they sang, they strummed at mandolins, they laughed, they fell into the sea. Dinghies crossed the waters carrying them between vessels. In the late afternoon the cooks got together on one of the luggers to prepare an evening meal for the crews while the whites began to dress for dinner on board the *Ena*.

The term 'slop chest' was derived from its use as a place where loose clothing was stored ready for sale to sailors. It was much more than this aboard the schooners which acted as floating stations to the pearling fleet. Gustave Robert Frost, a journalist who worked for a time on a lugger, told the Royal Commission that the whole aim of the slop chest was to allow the master pearlers to sell alcohol and food to the crew at inflated prices (according to Frost, at 100 per cent mark-up), so that at the end of the season the crew would be in debt to their employer. In Frost's view:

> the biggest drunkards next to the British were the Japanese. They paid a lot for grog. The Malays were not supposed to

drink it; they were all heavy drinkers after they had been there three or four months . . . But you have to realise this, that every Saturday, the divers would come aboard the ship and buy 'slop chest' and drink gin like people drink beer, out of big enamelled pannikins. They are half mad with it. They go down in the sea on an empty stomach. Francis Alvis has gone down in the morning after having just a little bovril and nothing to eat.[8]

Those in Broome attacked Frost's evidence as fantasy. The *Nor'-West Echo* wrote that his evidence was ten years out of date, and it would be a farce if this kind of evidence was to be relied upon. In this the *Echo* was doing no more than being a hometown supporter, because a few months later it carried its own report criticising the amount of grog being sold to crews on the pearling grounds from slop chests.

Frost also claimed that in order to avoid customs duty, the goods sold from the slop chest would be marked as cash advances to the crew. Anyone in authority looking at the account books would be completely misled. It was also commonly alleged that the shellers were avoiding customs duty by rendezvousing in the open seas with schooners sailing down from Singapore. Safe in international waters, a vessel from Broome would swap baskets of best shell for alcohol, tobacco and opium for sale to the crew. According to legal advice obtained by the shellers, no law was being broken and no duty need be paid, so long as the goods did not trespass within Australia's 3-mile sea border between the time of barter and subsequent sale to the crew. In January 1909 it was alleged in the *Port Hedland Advocate* that boatloads of potato-juice gin and opium were being brought in this way and distributed at sea, at exorbitant profit, among the lugger crews.

The master pearlers denied trading in opium, or profiteering from the sale of goods in the slop chest. They admitted that there was some mark-up on the goods but they argued that it was justified because of the expense of transporting the goods, and the risks involved – a cyclone wrecking a schooner could send the whole lot to the bottom before a single sale could be made. It is also likely that some master pearlers, stung by the substantial advances they had been forced to pay their coloured crew at the beginning of the season, thought it was only reasonable that they be given an opportunity of recouping some of their money.

It was the custom of the fleet, after the shell had been collected by the schooner, for the master pearler to invite the white employees on the luggers to dine with him on Sunday night for a meal of roast meat, tinned vegetables, dumplings and gravy. The master pearler took on the role of a country squire, at the head of a table lined on each side by men in the very best clothes they could find in their kit-bags. Dinner was usually taken in the main cabin of the schooner where tall men, if they stood, had to take care to position their heads in the space between beams. After grace was said, recalling those lost at sea – not forgetting their very own *Koombana* and now, of course, the *Titanic* – they were attended by dusky waiters, barefoot and in sarongs.

13 Webber

Q. What do you consider would be the life of a diver working regularly in over 20 fathoms of water? — I can only say that he would be juggling with fate.

Evidence of Thomas J. Farquhar, sheller, to the Royal
Commission, 14 May 1912[1]

TWENTY MILES SEAWARD OF Ninety Mile Beach, William Webber hovered with his boots inches above a rock-strewn plain. Overhead the lugger followed his progress. The water was so clear and the sun so strong, he could see far into the distance. But he could see no vegetation, no seagrass, no coral. Even the fish seemed to have gone. He could have been in an open paddock on a midsummer's day. There were no proper shadows and it was difficult to judge distance; time seemed to elude him. He had to do better. As he moved across the floor, he willed himself to do better.

There was a tug on his lifeline. It was Reid, checking if he was all right. Webber sighed and signalled back: one long pull to say that he was safe. He was irritated with himself that while attending to Reid's signals, he hadn't been concentrating on the search for shell. He had to keep his mind on the job, had to do better; must do better. He saw a mound at his feet, just the right shape for a shell. He kicked it and it collapsed into sand.

The *Eurus* had been drifting now for two weeks in depths between 15 and 30 fathoms. The search for shell was supposed to be easier during the winter months when the undergrowth receded and the water was settled. At first Reid and Webber planned to move in a zigzag fashion, keeping a distance of about 25 miles from the coast, but the results had been disappointing. There was shell out there, out in the deeper water – so they had been told by men in hotels – but every day as they ate their evening meal, they could see the lights of luggers closer to Ninety Mile Beach, in waters of 10 fathoms. Theirs was the only boat out in the deeps.

After days of failure, there seemed no point in sticking to any particular plan. Webber gave no instructions to Reid. The lugger pulled Webber, half-walking, half-floating, where the tide and puffs of wind determined. Although nothing was said, Reid had begun to move the boat closer to shore and Webber had pretended not to notice.

Webber glanced around to see the hull of a large vessel approaching from his right. He watched the splash of a dinghy being launched, then oars dip into the water every few yards, as if some large water beetle was levering itself across the surface. He had seen the schooner *La Perouse* in the distance just after dawn, and supposed that Fred Gruenert, the shell opener, was being dropped off. Gruenert had come to check on how much shell he had collected. Come to smoke his stinking pipe and tell Webber that Ismel, the Koepanger, had got a haul of a hundred pairs in two weeks and was already into his bonus on the third ton.

Webber turned his head downwards, like a draughthorse, in a slow, repetitious scan of the floor. Heaven knows, he was working long enough hours, searching through the seagrass, fossicking among rubble, groping among weed, taking only 30 minutes for lunch and remaining in his dress suit in order to save time, while the sweat gathered in the rolls of his belly. He moved through a small depression, a place which, if it had been on land, would have held a pond. Here it held reddish mud which rose in billowing clouds as he passed through it. Some of it collected on the leg of his suit, and when he rubbed it, it seemed oily to his touch.

Webber bristled at the idea of facing Gruenert. Fred Gruenert was a wiry greybeard with a paralysed leg who had been a diver in the 1890s. He had rowed across to the *Eurus* a week ago and sat with Webber and Reid to slurp a mug of tea through a walrus moustache. He had the blackest of dirt under his fingernails. Gruenert had told them about the times when he used to dive off Ninety Mile Beach. He had seen a lot of men paralysed, and a few men die. It was the men who had bull necks who got into trouble. He had never seen a diver with a bull neck who was any good. As he stood up to leave, he had pointed at Webber's neck with one of those filthy fingers of his and, with an evil smile, moved the finger across his throat.

Webber saw the hull of the *La Perouse* pull away, but her dinghy remained tied to the *Eurus*. It meant that Gruenert was still aboard. Reid signalled for Webber to come up, but Webber decided not to. He signalled to Reid to slacken the lifeline and take the lugger into deeper water. He waited. For a few minutes nothing happened. He could imagine Reid in confusion. According to the Admiralty tables, it was time to stage up. Perhaps Reid was asking Gruenert what to do, but Gruenert would tell him that the tables were a load of old rubbish, and to follow the orders of the diver.

Reid signalled again. Was Webber okay? Webber signalled to be taken north, and slowly the lugger turned. Webber continued his search for shell. Every now and then Reid tugged at the lifeline. Webber ignored him. Anger and frustration gnawed at Webber. He knew he would have to come up soon. He could well be drifting over territory he had already covered. Gruenert and Reid would have thought he was staying down because he was over a good floor, that his net would be bulging with shell when they pulled him aboard. He followed a ridge of limestone. Beyond a rise he saw the ridge narrow, then, like a highway, sweep through fields of lank seagrass. Reid yanked at the line again. It was time to come up. Webber signalled to be taken to the first stage. There he waited. He had two shells in his bag. He watched the shadow of a shark pass slowly overhead before disappearing to his right. Time seemed to crawl. He counted slowly, then signalled to be taken to the surface.

According to the official accounts of that day's events,[2] Webber took only two minutes to come up to the surface after a dive of 45 minutes in 19 fathoms. If that account is correct, Webber was asking for trouble. Other, handwritten notes[3] (which although unsigned were undoubtedly written by Reid) say that Fred Gruenert then offered to take Webber to a place where he was sure there was shell. Webber agreed, and the *Eurus* sailed for twenty minutes. Webber took to the water in 19 fathoms and was immediately successful. After an hour he had collected thirteen pairs. In coming to the surface, Webber only took one stop at 4 fathoms, and then only for one minute. After he was pulled aboard he complained of a pain in his left shoulder. Reid then said to him, 'Bill, if you take my advice you won't go down no more.' Webber replied, 'I know my own business best, I ought to be underwater instead of on the deck.' He then entered the water again. Before he went down, Reid asked him what stages he was going to take. Webber said that he would please himself, and when Reid got the signals, he was to obey orders.

Webber was down an hour this time. On the way to the surface, Reid took him to 10 fathoms, but Webber signalled to be taken straight up. Reid moved him to 4 fathoms, but Webber refused to be held. By closing down the air escape valve on his suit, he floated to the surface.

Once on board, Webber, still in his canvas suit, clambered onto the cabin roof and lit a cigarette. He ordered the crew to move the boat into position to drift back along the same course. The crew had begun to work the sails when Webber, in a soft voice, said that he didn't know, he might finish for the day. He called for Reid to get him out of the suit. Then Webber grabbed his left leg and collapsed backwards onto the roof.

Reid and Gruenert undressed the stricken diver, took him into the cabin and placed him on the bunk. No amount of shaking would wake him. The two men discussed what to do. They were two days sailing time from Broome, and Webber was in a deep coma and barely breathing. They decided to make a dash for Broome where they could place Webber under the care of Dr Suzuki at the Japanese hospital.

After two hours Webber awoke, but his speech was thick and his focus of vision seemed to be in the far distance. Reid suggested he go down again in order to relieve the bends, but Webber refused, saying that he would blow himself to the surface. At about ten o'clock he started complaining about the cold in his arms and legs. He began shivering and he had lost movement in his right hand. His face was deathly white and he didn't seem to know where he was. Then he fell into a semiconscious state.

Reid wrote in his notes: 'He never spoke all night, left leg and arm went as cold as ice, remained quiet all night till morning. Asked for drink, gave him three spoons of tea, let him rest two or three hours, started to sink. About 3 pm that day turned livid. Asked: "Bill, think of me and get me out of this".'[4]

Reid also wrote that at 5.29 pm on 7 June 1912 he called Gruenert to the cabin. Gruenert knelt down and held his hand against Webber's mouth. There was no breath. The lugger was several nautical miles west of Latouche.

After another day's sailing the *Eurus* reached Broome at 12.30 pm on 8 June 1912.

This was the official version of the death of Webber. It was the version which allowed Huggins to write to Hunt that: 'It would appear from the evidence that the man himself was entirely to blame for the accident.'[5]

Webber knew the Admiralty tables better than any other diver on the pearling grounds. In the navy he had taken part in the diving experiments that had led to their creation, and he had applied them both under the discipline of the navy and during commercial operations of his own. He was also familiar with the theory that a victim of the bends can cure himself by re-entering the water and remaining at depths for an extended period. Why, then, would he follow a course almost certain to bring about his death? If the official version of Webber's death is accepted at face value, two possibilities suggest themselves.

The first is that Webber may have become convinced that the Admiralty tables were not worth following. There were those who believed that the tables, devised as they were by diving into lochs in Scotland, were not applicable to warmer waters. A report in the *Nor'-West Echo* of 17 May 1913 quoted several of the English divers (unnamed) as saying that the water around Broome 'had effects which were not consistent with established scientific reasoning'. Webber had seen around him plenty of divers – Japanese, Malays, Manilamen – who ignored the staging procedures, seemingly without ill-effects. Some men, so it was said, were immune to paralysis. Did Webber begin to think he was such a person?

The second possibility is that Webber, disorientated by continual failure, embraced a path of self-destruction. There is no doubt that he was under an enormous strain. He may have deluded himself into believing that he was doing something noble and heroic for the white races of the world. Perhaps inspired by the thought that millions of dark-skinned peoples in Asia and Africa had given way to British rule, he believed it was his duty to demonstrate that the same thing applied on the pearling grounds of Australia. He was Siebe, Gorman's man and the firm expected him to triumph. He might have hoped, on his return to England, to be hailed as the leader of the men who had expelled the last of the Asiatics from Australia. But he wasn't demonstrating anything of the superiority of his race. He was trudging to the singsong of failure, failure, failure as all around him he saw men with no training in diving hauling up bags overflowing with shell. The humiliation of defeat may have goaded him on to more humiliation.

The official version of Webber's death was written by Hugh

Richardson, Webber's employer – hardly a disinterested gatherer of the facts. The report is about three-quarters of a page long and unsigned. The heading says it was based on information supplied by William Reid (the handwritten notes) and corroborated by F. Gruenert, shell opener. Both continued to be employed by Richardson, and both had an interest in showing that their negligence did not lead to Webber's death. Huggins passed on the report, seemingly without question or further investigation, to his superiors in Melbourne. The report exonerated Richardson's firm from blame and it served to show what the Pearlers' Association had been saying all along – that this was no work for a white man.

Webber's body, wrapped in a dun-coloured blanket, was carried through the mud of the mangroves to a horse and dray waiting on Dampier Terrace. From there it was transported to the Japanese hospital where, still wrapped in the blanket from the *Eurus*, it was placed on a table in the operating room to await Dr Tamasha Suzuki, who was attending to his last patient for the day.

After completing a post-mortem Dr Suzuki wrote a brief report certifying that William Webber had died from diver's paralysis. Webber was buried in the town cemetery in the Church of England section on 10 June 1912, after a service conducted by the Reverend Needham at the Church of Annunciation. Few attended the funeral. Webber had not spent many days in Broome since his arrival in February, and hardly anyone knew him. Besides, the death of a diver on the pearling grounds was not an event of great moment, and the citizens of Broome were more concerned with the affairs of the living. The luggers were out at sea and plenty of shell was being collected.

IN MID 1912, the price for first quality shell at the London auctions reached £350 per ton. This was more than double what it had been two years earlier. Everyone said it couldn't last, but everyone acted as if it would. The master pearlers were rich beyond expectations, and they had the urge to spend. There was a craze for interior decoration. Although the ardour in Europe was for things Japanese and the catalogues showed cherry blossom fabrics, outsized calligraphy on parchment and woodcuts of golden carp, the pearlers of Broome felt uncomfortable surrounding themselves with symbols of their indentured workers. Most stayed with Sandover & Co. of Perth, or Myer of Melbourne, and ordered in marble mantelpieces, satin ottomans, stiff-backed chairs of mahogany or walnut, and tapestries of huntsmen jumping horses through the English countryside. The more adventurous went plantation style and had shipped in from Hong Kong intricately carved teak dining-room sets and camphorwood boxes. Brought in from Singapore were elaborate cane chairs – replicas of the golden thrones of the Pharaohs – with high circular backs and coloured sunbeams woven throughout. The fashion was for hallways and bathrooms to be painted mustard to shoulder level and pale green above, or some such variation, so long as the walls were divided horizontally.

But no matter how grand the interior transformation, the climate of the northwest dictated that this remain a verandah society. Broad, shady floors of jarrah, enclosed by lattice-work, encircled the master pearlers' houses. Guests were shown to cane chairs and handed cool drinks on verandahs, cards were played on red felt tables and songs were sung around pianos there. It was on the verandah that women read heart-fluttering novels during hot afternoons and took tea with friends and greeted husbands when they returned from work. In the summer months, people moved their beds out onto the verandah, and slept under netting fine enough to keep the sandflies at bay. Along the verandahs, ferns hung from baskets, tropical plants thrived in large urns on floors so highly polished you could glimpse your face in the surface, and borax in sugar paste was placed discreetly in bottle tops for the cockroaches.

Meals were usually taken on the verandah. Fresh fruit and vegetables were difficult to obtain. They were shipped from Victoria or

Tasmania and, after a journey of three to four weeks, showed their age. When the steamer from Singapore docked, people would carry away mangoes, pawpaws and hands of bananas. It was cheaper to bring San Francisco flour through Singapore than from Perth. Citizens still spoke of the great flour famine of 1909, when because of a mistake in the shipping office, none was to be had in the town for three weeks. Oranges came from Italy or California. And although there were several dairies, supply was irregular and often families had to make do with condensed milk and ghastly tinned butter which looked like fat swimming in oil.

Houses were raised several feet above the ground on concrete stumps with ant caps secured on as protection against the termites. A prudent house-owner would install flat iron shutters on the windows which could be pulled down and bolted if the barometer suggested a cyclone. For the same reason, chains crisscrossing the roof could be tied to capstans sunk into the lawn. Many houses had no connecting doors between the rooms, each opening onto the verandah which looked out to a garden of bougainvillea, frangipani, tulip trees and ferns. Paths of crushed pearl-shell curved around spreading palms. Along the back fence, discreetly covered by creepers, was the wash house, wood shed, chicken run and an iron-clad 'boy-house' for the Aboriginal servants.

In 1910 the white women of Broome organised a public meeting which decided to petition the Federal Government for 'permission to indent Asiatic servants for domestic purposes'.[6] Mrs Hugh Norman, the Lady Mayoress, Mrs G.T. Wood and Mrs Stan Pigott were elected to the committee. Of course it came to nothing. Viewed as an indication of how deeply deficient was the master pearlers' understanding of the White Australia Policy, it would have been greeted with scorn, if not indignation, by the government.

DURING JUNE of 1912, Judge Burnside arrived from Perth to conduct the Quarter Sessions. He presided over five trials – four for murder, including the trial of those accused of the murder of Constable Fletcher, and one for 'an abominable offence' (buggery). Hall prosecuted in two and defended in two, neatly opposed by Coleman, who defended in two and prosecuted in two; those charged with the abominable offence were unrepresented. In the first trial, three Aboriginal men were found guilty of the murder of a member of their tribe and sentenced to death. In the second, Bengu, an Aboriginal man, was found guilty of the murder of a native named Dicky and sentenced to death. In the third, a Japanese diver named Mayamoto was charged with the murder of his tender: during an argument the tender had first struck Mayamoto with a marling spike and Mayamoto had stabbed his attacker though the heart with a long-bladed knife. The verdict was manslaughter and Mayamoto was sentenced to three years hard labour.

On Friday, in the final case for the week, a native of Chile and an Aborigine were found guilty of the charge of committing an abominable offence and sentenced to five and three years imprisonment respectively.

The trial of the four accused of the murder of Constable Fletcher took up the whole day, and the jury had to be locked up overnight in order to get a verdict out of them. The evidence they heard was markedly different from that presented at the inquest. No longer was Fletcher an innocent bystander interrupted while carrying goods from the hotel to the Presbyterian mission boat. In fact he was meeting Freeman and Fimister to go on a picnic that night. When Freeman got into a fight with Thomas Bilheeba, Fletcher joined the brawl and floored two of the men. It seemed clear enough to the jury that Bilheeba had risen from the verandah and stabbed Fletcher in the neck, but what was the involvement of the others? Were they merely participants in a pub brawl, or should they be held responsible for Bilheeba's actions in knifing the policeman? On Thursday morning, the jury returned a verdict of murder against Bilheeba and one other named Candido Colestrom, and acquitted the other two.

Judge Burnside sentenced Bilheeba and Candido Colestrom to death, and they were taken to the Fremantle gaol to be hanged.

It was the practice in Western Australia for the Attorney-General to seek the views of the trial judge on whether the death penalty should be carried out. Judge Burnside had been troubled by the verdict of the jury and the sentence of death he was obliged to impose. He wrote to the Attorney-General, Mr T. Walker, recommending that the sentences be commuted to terms of imprisonment:

> The evidence showed that Thomas Bilheeba had been drinking and was intoxicated . . . Fletcher, the murdered man, hearing the row had come out of the bar and instead of using his efforts to put an end to the row he 'sailed in' as the witness expressed it, and gave the man Thomas Bilheeba a severe handling. In the meantime the barman Freeman was treating Candido similarly. During the fight Bilheeba drew a pocket-knife and stabbed Fletcher. Upon Fletcher calling out he was stabbed the fight stopped and the accused and all other Malays or coloured men nearby were arrested. The white men were clearly the aggressors. They were sober and the deceased was a policeman whose duty it was to put a stop to fights and not to 'sail in' as he did. Candido is in law liable to the death sentence because of the view the jury took of the facts. He, however, took no further part in the row than the fight with Freeman. Had Bilheeba been found guilty of manslaughter Candido must have been acquitted.[7]

Attorney-General Walker considered the judge's report carefully. Although there was a sizeable lobby in the Labor Party in favour of abolishing capital punishment, he knew that this was not the feeling of the public at large. The murder of a policeman by two Asiatics was hardly the stuff of which test cases were made. There would be considerable opposition, especially in the northwest, to any action seen as going soft on the coloureds.

A few days later Attorney-General Walker took Judge Burnside's letter to the Executive Council. It commuted Bilheeba's sentence to life, and that of Colestrom to ten years. For this action the government was heartily condemned by the Perth *Sunday Truth*:

> The assassins of Constable Fletcher are to cheat the gallows . . . Bilheeba, the actual stabber, is to be imprisoned for 'life', which means, in plain English, twenty years. Colestom, his accomplice in crime, will nominally serve a ten year sentence, but allowing for the usual 'good conduct' remission it will really amount to seven and a half . . . Meanwhile, the mutilated body of the man they murdered will lie mouldering in the grave; his widow, perhaps, will experience want as well as sorrow . . .
>
> Nor was there any appeal for clemency from the public of Broome. The only petition that came from Broome was an earnest petition that the murderers might be hanged at Broome gaol, as a warning to the 'silent, sullen people' who swarm in that part of the Commonwealth. Why, then, has the prerogative of mercy been exercised? Simply because the majority of the Executive Council are soft-hearted (and soft-headed) old women who aim at being considered humane and only succeed in being unutterably foolish.[8]

DR SUZUKI held a three-year permit to remain in Australia, and at the end of 1912 it came up for renewal. Atlee Hunt, somewhat chastened by the storm of protest that had met his earlier decision to let Dr Suzuki in, asked the Broome council to advise him of the feelings of the town towards the doctor staying for another term. The councillors immediately discovered that this was an issue likely to split the white community (the views of the non-whites not being sought). Some, much impressed with Dr Suzuki's attention to their medical problems, argued that he should be allowed to stay. Others, relying on a principled adherence to a White Australia, argued that no Asiatics (apart from those in the pearl-shelling industry where they were irreplaceable) should be allowed entry to Australia. Some called for a referendum. Instead the council announced its intention to set the matter down for a debate to take place on 25 June 1912 at the Broome council chambers.

Notes of the debate subsequently appeared in the *Nor'-West Echo*:

> The Mayor: I do not consider it is a question the council should be asked to decide – it is purely a question for the Department of External Affairs. At the same time, I do not think there would be two opinions in town if the question were: if Dr Suzuki should leave, would we have another Japanese doctor – it would be no.
>
> Cr Capes: Well I signed the requisition in favour of the retention of Dr Suzuki, and am prepared to back my opinion. Two doctors are needed here, and I cannot see why the coloured people should not be allowed a doctor of their own. I and many others can speak highly of Suzuki's actions, instance the time when (to the neglect of his own practice) he went all the way to LaGrange in an open launch to save a white lady's life. He is a gentleman, and Broome will suffer no harm by retaining him.
>
> The Mayor: Are you in favour of another white man replacing Dr Suzuki?
>
> Cr Capes: We are not here to discuss that.
>
> The Mayor: Not if we had a guarantee of another white doctor? It's the policy of Australia.
>
> Cr McDonald: Let them start with their policy on the cooks and gardeners in the cities.
>
> Cr Capes: If we go on the policy of Australia, let us put the coloured labour out.
>
> Cr Grimwood: Two white doctors are much better than one

white and one coloured. Coloured men get as fair a deal from the white doctor as they do from their own. If they are going to enforce white divers, let us go the whole hog and have white doctors, too . . .

Cr Dyson: I am not prejudiced in favour of the coloured man, but I endorse Councillor Capes's remarks.

Cr McKenna: So long as we have coloured crews here I see no objection to Dr Suzuki remaining. In the event of him leaving, I would not like to see another foreigner allowed in.

Cr Rogers: I have no personal feeling in the matter, but if put to vote I'll vote for the retention of Dr Suzuki.

Cr Capes: In my opinion a majority of the people favour the retention of Dr Suzuki, but will not listen to another Japanese doctor being admitted.[9]

The debate went around in circles, until finally the council, being quite divided on the question, resolved not to express an opinion. A few months later Hunt extended Dr Suzuki's permit for another term of three years.

14 Noury

Next morning I paid a visit to the Asiatic Quarter and had to rub my eyes to make sure that I was not in Asia instead of 'White Australia'.

Senator Staniforth Smith, 1902[1]

NOURY FELT THE TIDE turning. It was now July and he had been working on Sydney Pigott's boat for five months. He had experienced five months of frustration and failure. As much as he tried, he was still not matching the indentured divers in shell collection. But, as he told himself, he was competing against men who had been diving for years. They were younger than he was, with keen eyesight and absolutely no regard for their own safety. Nor were they professional divers like him. As far as he could see their sole aim was to make as much money as possible, go home rich, and never dive again.

The tide was so strong that the lugger appeared to be getting ahead of him. He drifted over a hillock and found himself among weed as thick and leathery as kelp, and kept perpetually restless by the flow of water. Then to his delight he began to find shell – lots of shell – on rocks, among the weed and attached to boulders. He picked up four clustered together, then two more a yard away. He knew it was time to ascend, but this was the best patch he had struck for weeks. He signalled for the tender to keep him down.

For the next half hour Noury moved through the seagrass until finally, with a sense of achievement, he crammed the last shell into his bag. He ordered the tender to haul him up. About a third of the way to the surface, Noury was held steady. He knew the wait would be for five minutes and he counted through the seconds, keeping time with the turn of the pump as it whistled air into his helmet. He began to feel cold, yet he was perspiring. His undergarments felt moist, caused, he supposed, by the humid air pumped to him from the surface.

He was taken to the next stage. The seconds dragged into a minute, then he counted through the next. The marks painted on the lifeline indicated he was in about 5 fathoms. By his reckoning, the tender seemed to be calculating by a slow watch, but Noury waited. He played it by the book; he remembered Webber. The tender took him to the final stage. Here he would stay for 25 minutes.

High above him he saw a spear of silver bubbles, indicating that one of the crew had dived off the lugger. Another jumped in, kicking and swimming down deeper but then, running out of breath, he did a duck turn and trod water for an instant. Noury recognised him as one of the pump hands, a boy of about sixteen. He waved. The boy waved back before shooting to the surface. A third dived in. It was a game to see what the funny white man was doing down there.

The boys disappeared around the other side of the lugger, and Noury was alone again. He counted off the minutes. Just as the tender began to pull him up, he felt a sharp pain in his knee joints. He signalled a halt. The lifeline went slack and he held his position, taking deep breaths as he jiggled his legs up and down. He counted slowly to a thousand and the pain receded, but before giving the sign to come up, he counted to another thousand. When he broke surface, the fierceness of the sun startled him. The flag on the mast of the lugger hung limp. Noury clambered aboard and leant against the rail. He said he didn't feel well. The sun was beating down on his head, so he placed a towel around the top of his corselet to prevent the escape of the cold air from inside his suit.

He was holding a mug of coffee to his lips when it fell. The coffee splashed down the canvas and the mug rolled across the deck. He examined his fingers in shock. The crew was looking at him. He opened his mouth to explain that it was nothing, that he felt fine, but no words came out. As he was puzzling over this, there came a pain in his legs. It was shooting, surging, burning, tearing, deep within his knee joints. Never had he experienced such torment. He gasped in horror at it. He couldn't believe pain could be so bad. He felt a deep chill move through the walls of his chest. It seemed to grow dark and he wondered if a cloud had passed overhead. He looked up and saw that the sun had turned a bluish-black, like the colour of a bruise. The pain was no longer with him. Then in the strangest of sensations, he felt areas of his brain close down, one after another.

When he recovered consciousness, he was lying on his back on the deck. He was no longer in his diving suit. He could feel the bones in his lower back grinding against each other. He was aware that time had passed, was still passing, and he was floating above and around himself, free of his body. He tried to speak but his tongue lolled lazily behind his teeth, unwilling to form words. It was strange, but he didn't feel worried. All he wanted to do was sleep. He wished people would stop shaking him and trying to pour liquid into his mouth. He struggled. He was pulled to his feet, and he was pushed and shoved by malign hands into a diving suit. He tried to touch a brown face he saw in front of him, but his arms wouldn't move. He called out, but no one replied. He heard a splash, then felt himself spiralling like an autumn leaf into a deep, black void. The water was alive with ebony bubbles and it was cold. He could hear the hiss of air in his helmet. He saw the phosphorescent dart of some sea creature.

He awoke in water as black as printer's ink. Gradually, as he recovered his senses, he worked out that the crew had put him over the side in an attempt to cure him of the bends. He wondered how long he had been down. All he knew was that he was in darkness. He tugged at the lifeline and immediately there was a jerk back to him. He tried to look upwards, but was struck by a sharp spasm in his neck. The pain became intense so he jerked the lifeline, telling them to take him down further. There was a long pause. Perhaps they were discussing what to do. He jerked the rope again, and they dropped him lower. As he twirled down, the pain subsided. He stayed there, lonely, cold and frightened. Time seemed to move slowly but oddly, when next he looked up, he could see sunlight angling in through the water. Waves ruffled the surface above. He had urinated and there was a yeasty odour in the suit. Slowly, one by one, he tried out his limbs – his arms, his hands, his right and left leg. One of his legs was paralysed. He waited another hour, then attempted again to force his leg to move, but it was no longer his to command.

Above him, dancing like butterflies, were several fish which had been caught on lines thrown over for the night. He watched their persistent tugging and jerking as they tried to throw themselves clear of the hooks in their mouths. As the sun rose higher, the fish, one by one, ceased the fight. A feeling of desperate sadness enveloped him. He was about to signal to be taken up when overhead he saw the largest of the fish, in a final jiggling struggle for life, attempt to tear itself free. Its thrashing caused the others, one after another, to join in. Suddenly the largest fish broke free, and then another, and he watched the two dart away into the depths. Noury signalled to be taken lower, this time determined to count to ten thousand.

TWO ORDERLIES carried Noury on a stretcher through the streets to the government hospital. He was conscious and free from pain, but seemingly he had lost the use of his right leg. He was laid on a bed in a corridor for several hours while waiting for attention from Dr Blick.

Dr Blick, in a note for *The British Medical Journal* in 1909, described his therapy for paralysis caused by the bends:

> The treatment . . . is that of all organic nervous diseases – one can only wait on Nature's efforts, though in this disease Nature is kinder than usual. General hygiene, massage, and electricity, all are useful to some extent, and, of course, any complications which arise must be treated. I have been often astonished at the way apparently hopeless paraplegics have recovered in the course of many months.[2]

Noury's recovery followed the course anticipated by Dr Blick. Although at times he felt as though his muscles were wasting away, gradually, over the weeks, movement returned to his leg. Sydney Pigott visited his employee's bedside several times and when it became clear that Noury would need a considerable period of convalescence, he invited him to stay at his house. Noury accepted, and the same two orderlies carried him the several blocks to Pigott's house and settled him in a bunk on the verandah overlooking the bay.

Noury didn't see Pigott for a week. He was looked after by an elderly Japanese servant who told him that Mr Pigott was away on business. There did not seem to be anyone else in the house. The man said he had worked for Mr Pigott for fifteen years. Mr Pigott was a very good man, kind and generous. Mr Pigott had employed him ever since he had been injured at sea. But it was a sad house now, since Mr Pigott had lost his wife and the children. The Japanese servant massaged Noury's leg with warm rosewater every day. He said that he too had been paralysed diving. Many times, but after a while it goes.

Then after dinner one evening, while Noury lay reading in bed under the light of an oil lamp, Sydney Pigott opened the French doors further along the verandah and stood there, looking into the garden.

Pigott turned and wished Noury good evening. Noury nodded in return and put down his book. He called to Pigott, thanking him for allowing him to stay in his home. Pigott said it was nothing. He walked down the verandah and sat in a rocking chair at the end of the bed. He said he had been away for a few days, down to Onslow by the steamer buying pearls for Rubin. He offered Noury a Monopole, and lit one for himself. Pigott said he supposed that Noury would be giving diving away now. Noury shook his head. He knew nothing else. He loved diving. He had never wanted to do anything else.

CHARLES ANDREWS was the tender employed by Stanley Pigott to work with Elphick and Harvey. According to Stanley Pigott's evidence to the Royal Commission, Andrews had no notion of how to sail a lugger over the shell banks. Indeed, said Pigott, Andrews was such an incompetent seaman that he was forced to put on extra coloured crew to take over until Andrews could handle the work himself. By then, Elphick and Harvey preferred to work with the coloured tenders and Andrews was left with nothing to do.

Andrews, no longer wanted on Pigott's boats, asked for his discharge. According to Stanley Pigott, Andrews told him that 'he could not learn and was not suitable for this work'. This was understandable: Andrews was an engineer, not a sailor. Pigott then offered him a job as a shell opener. The going rate for a shell opener was £7 a month and 10 to 15 per cent on the value of pearls, which was more than Andrews could earn as a tender at £6 per month and 5 per cent on pearls.

It was also understandable that Elphick and Harvey wanted a tender they had confidence in. On the pearling grounds, even on those boats where the master pearlers still claimed to be in control, it was the diver who picked the tender and could insist on his being sacked. But the relationship was much more complex than that of a boss and a subordinate. The diver's life depended on the skill of the tender. On the luggers with Asian crews, the tender was usually the older of the two, often a retired diver himself, and he fussed over the younger man like a mother hen. He was responsible for the diver from the preparation for the descent until he hauled him back on board. He spent hours holding a lifeline and air-hose in his hands, peering into water shimmering with the reflection of the sun. It was hard on the eyes and stressful if he was uncertain about what was happening below. A moment's inattention could end disastrously for the diver.

After interpreting the diver's orders he had to direct the crew to sail at a pace just above walking. Usually the boat drifted under bare poles, or with just a triangle of canvas on the jib. The lifeline and air-pipe had to be kept taut so the tender could keep the diver supported by the tension in the rope, but not so taut as to tug the diver's head upwards, or to hinder him when he reached for shell. After months of working as a team, a capable tender would know exactly what the diver was doing below. Through the movements of the coir lifeline he could tell each time a diver paused, bent over and placed a shell in his bag. He could check the depths by noting the marks at 10-feet intervals painted on the lifeline. By following the line of bubbles rising from the bottom he could judge the direction the diver was moving, the strength of the tide and when the diver adjusted the escape valve. A sudden pulling of the air-pipe may have meant that the pipe had become entangled in a coral growth or a serrated rock. If this happened, the tender had to quickly send the lugger back on her course, to free the line before it severed.

When the diver came to the surface for a break, there usually wasn't time to get him out of the canvas, so he sat on a stool as the tender took off his helmet and handed him his pipe or a cup of tea. In 1911 off Port Darwin, a diver was sitting in his diving suit when a sudden gust caused the boom to jibe and the diver was pitched overboard. Weighed down by leaden boots, water flooded into his suit and he sank to his death on the sea floor.

Before they left port, the tender and the diver would sit either side of the hold and pull all 40 fathoms of the air-pipe through their fingers, twisting each segment, looking carefully for weaknesses or small cracks, feeling for the wire reinforcement spooled through the length of the rubber. It was just possible that during manufacture the wire had been left out for a couple of inches and at that spot there would be a weakness. The hose was made in 60-feet lengths and the bronze couplings had to be carefully checked. Paradoxically, any weakness in an air-hose, or in the dress for that matter, was likely to be revealed not at great depths, but as the diver came towards the surface. This was because at depth, the water pressure compressed the rubber and sealed off cracks, but on the way up or down, in shallower water, a weakness would be tested by the air pumped from above, and any air bubbling free would instantly rend the hose apart. For the same reason, the domed diver's helmet was not equipped to withstand great pressure. After years of use some helmets became leaf thin but remained rigid at the bottom because the pressure inside them roughly matched that of the surrounding water.

Long as the diver's hours were, those of the tender were longer. While the diver ate breakfast, the tender greased the air pump, dropped oil on the thread of the air escape valve of the helmet, washed the face glass in soapy water and polished it clean. Tenders wore a canvas bag around their waists containing spanners, spare helmet nuts, valves and springs, hose couplings, butterfly nuts, screwdrivers, washers, pliers, oil, pieces of canvas cut to size for patches, and rubber cement of gutta-percha and gum turpentine.

Before the first dive of the day, the tender should have dropped a lead line, with putty fixed at the end, over the side, and brought up fragments of the deep – sand, small shells, seagrass and stone – to tell him whether they were over decent pearling grounds. When the tender came to dress the diver, he had to ensure he did not have food on his hands in case the smell attracted sharks. While the rest of the crew were relaxing on the deck after the evening meal, the tender sluiced the canvas suit inside and out with saltwater and placed it on the hatch to dry overnight.

Every few days, a conscientious tender would kneel on all fours and carefully examine the canvas of the dress and flex the seams. Patches in diving suits had to be glued from the inside. Naphtha was generally used to lift off the canvas to expose the rubber lining which lay between the inner and outer cloth. If necessary a patch would be glued onto the rubber, the canvas glued back into place and a second patch glued onto the interior of the suit.

WITH THE death of Webber, Richardson had the problem of what to do with Reid. Shell was fetching a fortune, so Richardson was anxious to get his boat turned around and out to sea as soon as possible. Getting a replacement diver would not be difficult – he might even be able to re-employ the Japanese diver whom he had sacked to take on Webber or, failing that, he could get a young try-diver from among the crew of his fleet. The problem was that no coloured diver would ever accept Reid as a tender. The only solution was to talk Reid into becoming a shell opener.

The job of shell opening was not highly regarded. The view on the pearling grounds was that the main qualifications of a shell opener, apart from being white, were that he be a drunkard, have an ability to get on with the coloureds and have no idea of sailing. Said the *Nor'-West Echo*: 'These men have been attacked as limpets on the industry, but manfully defended by others . . . It is a monotonous, lazy life, likely to render a man useless in other walks of life.'[3]

The only reason the master pearlers tolerated 'white limpets' on their vessels was because they hoped to stop the pilfering of pearls. The master pearlers were convinced that if they let the coloured crew open the shell, not a single pearl would ever be handed in. In this they may have been correct. A man on a lugger who found a sizeable pearl was set for life. A pearl could be worth more than a lifetime of earnings, enough to buy a house, a wife and even respect. And it was theft without a victim. No one was hurt. There was no sense of loss. No hue and cry. No one ever knew.

The Bamford Royal Commission had heard that the shellers of Thursday Island no longer claimed ownership of pearls. In Western Australia, the battle was still being waged. At the turn of the century most of the boats sailing from Broome were manned entirely by a coloured crew, but in subsequent seasons there was a concerted effort by the master pearlers to regain their pearls, and by 1912 the majority of the luggers carried a white shell opener.[4]

It might seem touching that the master pearlers had such faith in the morality of the white men they allocated to the boats. The answer was not that the white shell openers were remarkably honest, but they knew the game was to hand in a pearl every now and then, more than enough to cover the cost of their wages. In an earlier chapter of this book it was related that in 1908 Stanley Pigott had taken one of his Japanese divers to the Broome police court and had him sentenced to thirteen weeks imprisonment with hard labour because the diver had refused duty (that is, he had gone on strike) in an attempt to dictate to Pigott whom he should have as a shell opener. Pigott was much applauded by the white community for this action because it was understood that if a shell opener congenial to the crew were placed on board, few if any pearls would be handed in.

The shell opener's work took about an hour a day, although a slow, careful search over a cup of coffee and a puff of opium might stretch the job out to an hour and a half. There was no need to rise early – there was simply nothing to do until sunset. As the diver brought up each shell, it was set on its heel in the sun, slowly cooking to death. The shell opener idled away the day, waiting, until finally, as it got cooler, the shell opened its mouth to breathe.

The master pearlers gave hopeful instructions to their shell openers: never let the shell out of your sight, never open it in front of the crew, never leave the task until the next morning, confiscate all wire from the crew because they will use it to fish in the flesh of the shell before you have got there, control jubilation if you find a pearl and never, never show a pearl to the crew.

A secretive spot to open the shell might be aft of the cabin, but the crew, battling boredom, would listen to the activity or, as a tease, peer over the roof at what was going on. Seated on a wooden box, the shell opener placed the shell on a hardwood chopping block. The first job was to get rid of the growth of barnacles or sponges adhering to the outside. These were hacked off with a tomahawk or a cut-down cane knife. If the shell was closed, the shell opener would hold it on the deck with his feet and slip a short, flat blade – no more than a bread and butter knife with a rubber hose rammed onto the end – between the lips of the shell, sever the adductor muscle and twist.

Larger pearls were more likely to be found in the beard running around the outer edge of the shell and were instantly visible against the dull grey of the flesh. But it was rare to find one. World-weary shell openers went for months without finding a pearl; some the entire season. But like addicted gamblers, they retained the illogical insistence, as they reached out for the next shell, that this was the one, the one containing a perfect teardrop which would sell for a fortune. After searching the beard the shell opener, with his eyes shut as if deep in meditation, would plunge his hand up to the wrist in warm slime, probing and pushing in the flesh. He may have made a fist and felt the mush through his fingers, and then run the tips of his fingers across the shell's surface, hoping to feel a nodule. The more conscientious opener would slosh the flesh in a bucket of sea water in the search for seed pearls. By this time several seagulls would have appeared, watching with a cocked eye for the shell's innards to be flicked over the side.

The shell opener's battle was with boredom. Some may have read books they brought with them, swapped these at sea for other books, dictionaries or mail-order catalogues. They may have fished until they became bored with pulling up fish. More fish than could ever be eaten, they were lined up on the deck then thrown back, until the diver complained that they were attracting sharks. The shell openers smoked cigarette after cigarette. It was a sea-bound prison relieved by scrimshawing shells.

If a pearl was found, the strict rule was that it should be dropped directly into the pearl box. Pat Percy, a Broome policeman turned pearler and publican, claimed to have invented the pearl box in 1911. He even went so far as to run a series of belligerent notices in the *Broome Chronicle* threatening to prosecute anyone who made one without his authorisation. Percy was correct to be concerned about copyists because it was a simple thing to make – it was no more than a locked wooden box with a metal tube leading into it with a flap at one end, so that once inside, no amount of jiggling could get the pearl out. The only key was held back in port. The pearl box was designed to protect the shell opener from himself. Master pearlers knew that crew members on a lugger at night got bored with looking at the stars, so they started drinking. If a pearl wasn't locked away, it might be taken out and run through fingers and shown to the crew, and the next thing, no one knew who had had it last. Someone may have swallowed it, or secreted it in their clothing. The master pearlers believed that Percy's box served to take temptation away from weak souls.

On the ship's papers it was likely that the white shell opener would be nominated, as a matter of form, as the captain, but everyone knew that it was the diver who controlled the boat. Despite this some shell openers got an inflated view of their position. One wrote to the newspaper:

> there is a factor in the game . . . which humiliates the Britisher to such depths of shame that he feels himself an infinitesimally small atom in the presence of five or six Asiatic coolies . . . Steps should have been taken long ago to have compelled the master pearler to give the white man stipulated authority over his coloured companions on the luggers . . . There are fleets where Japanese divers rule supreme, and at a word from the diver the shell-opener is dismissed. This is bringing ignominy upon the

whole industry, and those pearlers who are using every endeavour to avoid complications will suffer equally with those who are buying the trouble. It is asserted by some that they are unable to alter their position, an admission of incapacity and impotency which suggests that the industry's interests would be better served if they got out of it. The several very recent instances of divers getting shell-openers the 'sack' should be made the subject of searching inquiry by the Association before the Pearling Commission does it for them.[5]

Not all master pearlers thought that putting a white man on board their luggers was the cure for pearl thieving. It meant another body on an already crowded boat, and some were realistic enough to realise that an idle white man was likely to upset the coloured crew. The shell opener usually insisted on taking the bunk in the aft cabin which he shared with the diver, while displacing the tender, who had to sleep wherever he could, or squeeze in with five others in the forward cabin. Some of the bigger fleet owners, instead of hiring a shell opener, purchased a steam launch to go around the luggers and take the shell back to the schooner to be opened there. Still, it must have been tempting for the crew to poke around inside the shell awaiting collection, and no doubt they did.

Despite the use of shell openers and the pearl box, most master pearlers were convinced that they were being robbed blind. There was a ready market for snide pearls in Broome, and the master pearlers were as much involved as anyone else. Trading took place in the public bars, the gambling joints, the shellers' packing sheds and in the pearl cleaners' shops in the Asiatic Quarter. If a pearl was offered at a good price, one never expected an honest explanation of where it had come from. It was said that the only people in Broome who didn't buy snide pearls were those who had no money and those who couldn't find a pearl to buy. Pearls regularly went through several hands, gaining in price and respectability as they were traded up the social structure, eventually reaching the buyers who came from overseas every few months – buyers such as Liebglib, Rosenthal, Tchernousky, Sussman and Frere from Europe. From Singapore came Thom Fong, Fong Joe, Fong Hang, Jack Sam and Lew Tack. T.B. Ellies bought and sold pearls, as did Abraham Davis and later Sydney Pigott, on behalf of Mark Rubin.

The Pearlers' Association continually made proposals to stamp out the trade in stolen pearls. The pearl cleaners were thought to be the main culprits. With a few scrapes of their files, the shape and size of a pearl could be altered beyond recognition. It was urged that legislation similar to the Illicit Diamonds Act of South Africa be passed making it illegal for a person to hold a pearl for which he could not account. Arthur Male, the state member of Parliament, proposed that all pearl buyers and pearl cleaners be obliged to keep a register, like the one required for ships, of each pearl that came into their possession. Male wrote to the premier about another good idea of his:

> There is no doubt a lot of illicit pearl dealing exists on the Grounds. I have given the question some attention, and I would suggest the Department engage the services of a trustworthy man who should be sent to Broome and the Pearling Grounds to investigate the matter. He should be sent up unbeknown to anyone but his superiors. He should go up as an ordinary individual and obtain a position as Shell Opener on someone's fleet. If he is a capable man he should have no difficulty in obtaining sufficient evidence to make specific charges if illicit dealing is found to exist.
>
> While I was in Broome, the Pearlers held their Annual General Meeting, and to show their earnestness in connection with this question they passed a resolution agreeing to substantially assist the Government financially in this matter if required.[6]

Male's proposal for an undercover shell opener was not picked up by the government, perhaps taking the view that every master pearler who attended the annual general meeting of the Pearlers' Association had been alerted to the plan.

THE EVIDENCE to the Royal Commission was that every one of the English divers contracted the bends, some several times. Ernest Freight, working on Robison & Norman's boats, was paralysed in both legs.[7] He ordered the lugger to return to Broome and spent the next fortnight in bed worried sick as movement slowly returned to his limbs. Among Hugh Richardson's notes preserved in the Battye Library in Perth is an entry recording that on 22 September 1912, two of Stanley Pigott's divers, Elphick and Harvey, were paralysed. The notes go on to say that nearby a Japanese diver on the *Lawrence* was paralysed in 22 fathoms. All three were decompressed and recovered.

The decompression Richardson referred to was not undertaken in a specially built chamber, but by dropping the diver back over the side of the lugger into roughly the same depth of water as he had just come up from. In reading the reminiscences of old pearlers, it is remarkable how many of them claimed to have invented decompression (or recompression as it was sometimes, quite logically, called). The usual story is that, out at sea one day, a diver came up blue in the face, and the white man had a brainwave and, to the crew's amazement, ordered the diver back down again. After a couple of hours, to the cheers of everyone, the diver was hauled up, fully recovered.

In fact decompression as a cure for the bends had been in use since the turn of the century. It was a terrifying experience for the diver: hanging between life and death in a dim void, feeling ill and moving in and out of consciousness, his anxiety often exacerbated by oxygen drunkenness as the crew overpushed air into his helmet. Nor was it a miracle cure – sometimes the patient was brought up showing no improvement, and occasionally he was dead.

Getting the bends would have mystified the Englishmen. They had all dived for years without suffering ill consequences. They had an almost religious faith in the Admiralty tables and believed that if they followed them, damaging nitrogen would escape harmlessly from their blood. What they didn't take into account was that in England they were diving for short periods – perhaps a few days on salvage and underwater repairs, but then with no further engagement for weeks. But in the seas of the northwest of Australia, they were diving from dawn to dusk, six days a week, month after month and the nitrogen was gradually building up in their bloodstreams. Temporary loss of movement and joint pains were accepted by the Japanese and Malays as part of the job. Paralysis of the bladder was so common that, according to Dr Blick, 'no diver would consider his outfit complete without a soft catheter'.[8] At the government hospital Dr Blick frequently had to treat complications 'set up by imperfectly cleaned catheters used by the diver's friends, often over several days, as they brought the stricken man back to port'.[9]

In the hotels of Broome, the Englishmen heard scoffers say that the paralysis was not caused by the release of nitrogen at all. Other explanations were offered. One was that air pressure, squeezing the arteries in the hands and legs, backed blood up to the heart valve causing it to stutter. For that reason men susceptible to heart attack – those with florid complexions, broken veins on their cheeks and bloodshot eyes – should never dive. Another theory was that pressure caused a breakdown of the nervous system and messages to the legs and arms failed. Others attributed the bends to the chest wall becoming unduly compressed. This explained why divers should not go down while suffering from bronchitis, catarrh or whooping cough. Via South Africa came the report that in the depths of the diamond mines, men who had collapsed were cured by making them crunch on raw salt. And if a diver's ears began to ring (a sure sign of the approach of the bends) a trusted cure was to block off the nostrils by pressing up against the face glass, and giving a good snort.

Along with these offerings came other gems: the bowel should be regularly opened because if unduly gorged it would press on the diaphragm and obstruct the action of the heart and lungs; it was a good idea to do gymnastics underwater as the activity released the bubbles all the quicker; heat was the cure for the bends, heat provided by rubbing in horse liniment or alcohol mixed with chilli (either would do), or the lighting of pith balls on the chest, a good camphor rub, or by the application of warm oil trickled into the patient's ear holes. The Japanese believed wholeheartedly in dunking bends victims in hot baths in an effort to restore movement to their limbs. Dr Blick wrote that he had seen cases where divers had been parboiled to such an extent that they died as a result of the intended cure as much as anything else.

Elphick and Harvey recovered from the paralysis soon enough, but with recovery came the realisation that they were expected to return to the pearling grounds. Instead they decided to give notice. They spoke to Stanley Pigott, who saw it as his duty to get them to sign a statement which he could use at the Royal Commission. The men baulked. They had no wish to repeat the experiences of Sanders, but then, if they attempted to board a steamer without a release from Pigott, they were only too aware that he could have them charged with desertion. Eventually a compromise was reached. They signed a document praising the pump Pigott had supplied, stating that it gave a plentiful supply of air, it was more easily worked than any other pump, and was very satisfactory to them. It wasn't much, but it was the best Pigott could get, and he produced it to the Royal Commission when it eventually came to Broome to show he had provided the men with the very best of equipment.

There is no record in the local press of a farewell dinner held to honour Elphick and Harvey. Their failure to match the Asiatic divers was no occasion for celebration, so they probably packed their bags, boarded the steamer and simply sailed away. Noury was still recovering on the verandah of Sydney Pigott's bungalow. Andrews and Reid were now shell openers on the high seas, and Beasily and Freight were working on Robison & Norman's boats, with Hanson as the tender. Meanwhile, Sanders was about to return to diving. In the bar of the Pearlers' Rest Hotel, he had become friendly with Charles Alexander, a struggling master pearler with only two luggers. The two had agreed that, commencing in the new year, Sanders would be the captain of one of the boats, do the diving himself, and be paid a share of the profits.

In August the price for the highest grade of sound and bold mother-of-pearl reached £530 a ton at the London auctions.[10] It was a record. Although those celebrating in Broome didn't know it, it was also the highest price that would ever be paid. On 27 July 1912 another record was set: the SS *Charon* left port with 883 cases of mother-of-pearl valued at £32,927.

ALL ALONG the coast as the news spread from boat to boat, the Japanese flag was lowered to half-mast and luggers set their sails and quit the field to return to Broome. The shellers watched in resignation as over half the fleet slid into the trenches of Roebuck Bay. A week of diving would be lost and there was nothing they could do about it. His Majesty, the Emperor of Japan, had died. The 121st Emperor had been on the throne since 1860, and few Japanese could remember any other Emperor. The Japanese Club held a solemn ceremony and all the Japanese of the town, accompanied by drums and bells, marched to the water's edge. Then the procession wound back along the dusty streets to the town. As soon as the observances were over, a thousand Japanese crewmen broke ranks and descended on the brothels and gambling dens of the Asiatic Quarter for several days and nights of whoop-de-do before returning to sea.

Over the years Sub-Collector Huggins' annual reports written to

Hunt had shown a steady increase in the number of Japanese indentured workers in Broome and a corresponding decrease in the numbers
of other nationalities. By 1912 there were twice as many Japanese as the
other races combined. The Federal Government saw this as undesirable
and periodically wrote to the Pearlers' Association suggesting that some
action be taken to reduce its reliance on the Japanese. If the industry
must have coloured labour, the government indicated it would prefer
to see an increase in the number of Malays. The government held the
view that, unlike the Japanese, the Malays were a tractable people who
readily accepted the superiority of the white man. In this the government was merely reflecting commonly held racial stereotypes. In the
popular mind Malays were seen as a happy-go-lucky people who, if
they were treated with respect and consideration by the Britisher,
would show deep loyalty and affection in return. Their biggest disad-
vantage was that they were unpredictable and, for quite unaccountable
reasons, might run amok with a knife. When whites murdered you
might look for a motive, but not so for Malays.

Thanks largely to Gilbert and Sullivan, the Japanese had been
regarded as neat, doll-like people in colourful costumes, with quaint
if slightly barbaric customs. That perception changed in 1904–5,
when Russia was completely humiliated in a war with Japan. It was a
revelation to the world that a country of small Asian men could
defeat a European power, albeit a very sick one. Thereafter the image
took on a more sinister edge and the Japanese became determined,
ambitious and militaristic.

Not that the racial stereotypes ended there. The natives of
Koepang were seen as similar in temperament to the Malays, but they
tended to suffer from loss of heart and if they made up their minds
to die, whether ill or not, they would die. The Chinese were considered to be a bit like the Japanese, but less proud. Their children were
pretty, but the adults grew up short-sighted and bucktoothed. They
were also less fatalistic. And they showed no interest in diving. That
was their character. If you thought of Chinese you thought of laundries or mining, but never diving. Papuans or Aborigines would

never agree to get into diving dress. Nor would an Indian. A Torres Strait Islander might. White men would, of course, and they would be good at it, but the pay and conditions were bad, so they tended not to.

In August the Japanese fleet returned to Broome, as it did every year, for the solemn feast of the *O-Bon marsuri* in honour of those who had died. Under a full moon, a candlelight procession wound its way to the Japanese cemetery, accompanied by the tinkling of bells and the soft beat of drums. Small lanterns of intricate and fantastic shapes were placed on each grave, along with provisions for the longest of all journeys: rice, quails' eggs, noodles, nuts, dried peas, and a half-bottle of rice wine (the other half having been drunk by those who knew the deceased best). Later that night, to the accompaniment of lutes and drums, miniature hand-carved boats, rigged with tiny sails, lit by candles and laden with packages of food, were set to glide on the dusky waters of Roebuck Bay. The Japanese believed that each little vessel carried the spirits of the dead for a leaving of the earth. Dressed in kimonos, the ladies from the brothels, so rarely seen in public, stood as silent shadows behind smoking joss sticks.

DR BLICK'S health did not improve. He continued to suffer from some vague stomach growth which left him wasted and continually ill. He was unable to see patients for days on end. Then one day he gave notice to the government hospital that he was leaving to seek medical treatment in England. The voyage would take eight weeks.

Now Dr Suzuki was the only medical man within hundreds of miles. The town blessed its wisdom in allowing the Japanese hospital to continue in its midst.

After a couple of months, a locum, Dr Paton, arrived from Perth to work in the government hospital, but just as the citizens of the town were getting used to him, he left and was replaced by Dr Shaw. Finally a permanent doctor, Dr Goldstein, was found for the government hospital. In the meantime, most continued to consult Dr Suzuki.

In November 1912 a cable arrived from London with the news that Dr Blick had died after undergoing an operation for a malignant growth. His widow was still in Broome and people dropped around to say how sorry they were. Before proceedings commenced at the police court on the day the cable was received, Major Wood praised Dr Blick's period as acting resident magistrate, his contribution to the town and his keen involvement in the town's sporting life. His remarks were supported by Corporal Lamb on behalf of the police, and by Mr Coleman on behalf of the Bar. A few days later, the executor of Dr Blick's will called on the citizens of the town to do the right thing and pay all outstanding accounts – after all, Dr Blick had left a wife and several young children.

15 Barker, Leprosy and Rape

The percentage of casualties amongst whites is nothing compared with that amongst Asiatics. Unfortunately when a white diver meets with a mishap, it is published throughout the world, but when an Asiatic is killed or crippled nothing is heard about it.

Mr Gardiner to the House of Assembly, Western Australia, *Debates*, 27 June 1912, p. 22

IN AUGUST 1912 THE Bamford Royal Commission was back in Melbourne. The commissioners called in Atlee Hunt and confronted him with the news that the fatality rate among divers on Thursday Island was 11 per cent per annum. In Western Australia it appeared that the situation was even worse: 'It would be 20 per cent,' said Senator Givens to Hunt. 'In five years everybody engaged in the industry would be dead, if the supply of divers was not being continually renewed.'[1]

Hunt readily agreed that the situation was appalling, but insisted that it was not a matter for the Commonwealth Government. Safety

was a matter for the states, or private enterprise, or individual morality, but not for his department. He had no idea of the number of
fatalities and it was not his department's duty to keep records. All his
department did was regulate the introduction of aliens for work on
the pearling fleet. Senator Givens bristled at that answer:

> Q. If I induce somebody to come here under my authority, I
> should say it was my duty to keep such a record? – That might
> be the case if we held out any inducement for them to come
> here, but we do not.
> Q. They come out with the permission of your Department? –
> Yes.
> Q. Do you not think that entails some responsibility on the
> Department? – No. Strictly speaking, I cannot see that it does.
> Q. Then you and I read our duty rather differently in that
> direction? – I am speaking not as a citizen, but as a departmen-
> tal officer.[2]

An answer which seemed to stump Senator Givens who, after a
moment of reflection, moved on to other matters.

Not only did Hunt shun responsibility for the high death rate
among divers, but no one else accepted responsibility either. It was an
industry devoid of regulation. Rarely were checks made by the shipping master to see if a vessel was overloaded, carrying more crew than
her articles allowed, or provisioned with inadequate stores. One
sheller, a witness to the Roth Royal Commission in 1905, said the
last time any of his boats had been inspected was 1886.

In 1911 Harbour Master Gregory, in a brave attempt to enforce
safety standards, brought a charge against Captain Frederick Everett
for the death of two of his crew. When a willy-willy had struck one
of Everett's boats, two had drowned and three had been forced to
swim to land because there were no lifebelts aboard. The charge was
thrown out by Magistrate Wood. Captain Gregory was mistaken.
There was no requirement to carry such equipment – that only

applied to trading vessels going to sea under the Navigation Act and not to pearling luggers. Soon after, Arthur Male, the local member of Parliament, conducted a survey and found that only ten boats sailing out of Broome carried lifebelts.

Nor was there any form of compensation for the family of deceased workers. If a crewman was permanently paralysed or crippled with diver's rheumatism, he was shipped back home to a life of dependency on his relatives or, failing that, begging and destitution.

The master pearlers asserted that they did care about the welfare of the men on the boats and they issued frequent instructions to their crew about safe diving. Critics had to understand that they had no control over what the crews did when they were out at sea. Besides, argued the shellers, apart from the natural concern they felt for their workers' lives, there was a forceful financial incentive to maintain safety. It was a time-honoured custom (or a provision of the Merchant Seaman's Act – no one was sure which) that a master had to pay for the burial of the dead on his boats, and a reasonable funeral in Broome cost at least £5. If the crew insisted on bringing the body back to town, several hundredweight of shell was lost. There was also the cost of engaging another crewman.

Despite these protestations, there is nothing to show that the master pearlers ever did anything concrete about the loss of life. A medical kit was almost never supplied. No lessons were given to divers in safe diving practices, and diving skills were picked up on the job. The master pearlers accepted as a natural consequence of diving that some first-time divers would suffer from intense pain in their ears (even discharging blood), but for most it only went on for a few weeks, and as for the others – it was a way of weeding out the unsuitable.

Tenders were not instructed in the use of equipment, or safe ascending stages. Limits on diving depths were not enforced. Decent food, readily and cheaply available to avoid death from beri beri, was never provided. If a diver got into difficulties on the seabed, there was no possibility of another diver going down to rescue him, because although there may have been an extra suit, there was never an additional pump. And although by 1910 the life-saving potential of decompression chambers was well understood, one was not installed in Broome until the start of the pearling season in 1915, and even then it was not through the generosity of the shellers but because it was donated by C.E. Heinke & Co. The general approach to the welfare of the crew might be gauged by this item published to amuse the readers of the local newspaper:

> It appears that two or three of the recently imported Malay divers were meretriciously mendacious, and had never been in a diver's dress until after landing in Broome. One paid dearly for his mendacity last week; on his first dip he commenced his descent heels up, and on being righted went down like a stone. He knew nothing about the game, and on being hauled aboard, from ten fathoms of water he was a much blacker man than when entering the dress.[3]

THE *BROOME CHRONICLE* was a weekly of four broadsheets. The editor and sole proprietor (titles he placed, along with his name, at the bottom of column six on the last page of each edition) was Edward Lewin Green. The front page of the *Chronicle* was set aside for advertisements – and most of the second page if it was a good week – so Green only had to worry about filling two and a half pages to give the customer value for the purchase price of sixpence. The rest of page two was taken up with columns of telegrams about the goings-on in the state capitals and cables from London.

On the third page Green wrote a column headed 'News and Notes', containing quirky little items he lifted from the periodicals and papers delivered on the last journey of the steamer – items such as the sensational luck of Captain de Courey Bowers at Monte Carlo in winning £220,000 ('He employed five players and his method consists of staking 1000 francs on the red and letting it run'), the uproar at a murder trial in Adelaide ('Harris was seized by a detective and forced back shouting, "You destroyed my daughter, you devil"'), and how much Signor Caruso was paid ('He signed a fresh engagement for three years, making five years altogether, with the management of the Manhattan Opera in New York, and will be paid at the rate of £500 a night').

The back page was devoted to local activities: the times of church services, the latest meeting of the Broome Turf Club, proceedings at the police court, the health board and the municipal council, a column about doings on the pearling grounds, and Green's own turgid editorial comment. His printing press was fairly rudimentary (when a fire burnt down his premises in 1908, he valued his plant, stock and fittings at a modest £200) and any elaborate work had to be ordered from a larger centre. In his paper of 10 February 1912, Mr Green, after acknowledging that the Christmas supplement was to be found in the current issue, apologised to his readers – although he had placed the order in October of the previous year, the supplement was delayed by a wharf strike in Sydney, another in Fremantle, and then his agent had negligently missed two sailings of steamers for Broome.

On 8 June 1912 Edward Lewin Green sold out to Mr W.H. Barker. The new owner promptly got to work and in the space of one edition, rechristened the *Broome Chronicle*, the *Nor'-West Echo*, redesigned the masthead and thought up a new credo:

> The largest newspaper published in the Far Nor'-West, containing the greatest amount of diversified news of any paper published in these parts (news for the squatter, the pearler, the farmer, the business man, the artisan, the poulterer, the scientist, the humorist, the moralist, the housewife, etc, etc) and circulating extensively in every town on the coast from Wyndham to Onslow, among the squatters inland from Derby,

inland from Hedland and elsewhere. Its fearless policy makes it welcome everywhere, therefore as an advertising medium it has no equal. Job printing at Perth rates, plus 10 percent.[4]

On an inside page Barker immediately showed just how fearless the *Echo* would be with a thumping attack on the Broome Aborigines:

> Idle Natives: The police would be conferring a favour on the town and a blessing on the poor, doomed natives if they got a move on and cleared the town of the horde of hungry, drunken natives who won't work. From every part of the town complaints are made to the effect that the unemployed native is a nuisance and a menace.

It seems the police didn't act as Barker thought they should have. He rallied a few weeks later:

> The Natives – The system which permits so many aboriginals to wander about Broome is exercising the minds of most well wishers of the community. We could make the oldest inhabitants blush with shame were we to put into cold type the bare facts without any paint. In the name of morality and humanity we appeal to the authorities to do their duty, otherwise we will be compelled to make such disclosures as will justify the Government clearing every aboriginal out of town. Make no mistake, we mean business, and will speak with no uncertain sound when we start.[5]

And start he did, two editions later:

> The natives – This week's court proceedings quite justify our published comments on the deplorable state of affairs. During the past fortnight one white lady was threatened by a nigger

with a tomahawk, while another had to defend herself with a chair, which she broke over a nigger's head before assistance arrived. This week's court:

Wannare, alias Louie – 1. disorderly conduct, cautioned; 2. assaulting a gin, 1 month; 3. supplying natives with liquor, three months.

Annie Mariano (ex-mission girl, married to a coloured man) – 1. habitual drunkard, 2 months; 2. obscene language (air blue for half a mile round, beat any pearler), 1 month.

Warrabul – drunk, fine of 10s promptly paid.

Tomy Hong (half caste), supplying liquor to natives, £20 or five weeks.

Jacob Baker (half caste), liquor to natives, £20 or five weeks.

Judina, alias Lena, drunk, cautioned.

Warrawarra, alias Kennedy (ordered out of town long ago) – 1. drunk, 21 days; 2. bad language (sample submitted beat Pilbarra's 'Bullocky Jack' easily), 1 month; 3. resisting the police (who are prepared to back him for a round or two with coon Johnson), 1 month.

Arthur Royal (white) supplying natives with grog, £20 or 5 weeks.

Jacob Sencren, supplying natives with grog, six months.[6]

Mr Barker discovered he had tapped a vein close to the heart of his readers, and the words of hate became more extreme:

Some of our leading residents maintain that we cannot do without the binghis. Many others who have been in Broome some time consistently refused to have them about their premises. Fancy having your meals cooked, your dishes washed, and your back premises used by a diseased gin. Faugh! Have the people of Broome lived so long amidst these horrors as to be callused? See yonder. There is wee Willy being nursed by a dusky Lucy, who is such a good nurse, and so fond of your little one. See her take her black cuddy out of her mouth and kiss the little chap. No fancy picture, my lady, for we have seen it done. See that bunch of flies on the bleary eyes of yonder buck, reeking of disease. Where will they alight next? In your eyes, in mine? Bah! Many will doubtless maintain these are extreme pictures. Perhaps so; but the last picture is of possible every day occurrence.[7]

Reading these words almost a century later, it is difficult to accept that Barker could have held such viciously racist views and felt justified in printing them in his newspaper. It is tempting to hope that he was an extremist whose opinions were not shared by the local community. Unfortunately all that we know about Barker and the northwest suggest that this was not the case. He was an experienced newspaper man. He owned several publications in Western Australia and he knew his audience well. Certainly the *Nor'-West Echo* did not suffer because of his outbursts. The familiar advertisement from corporate bodies such as the W.A. Government Steamship Service and the Commonwealth Bank continued to appear in its pages, along with those from the pearling houses of Robison & Norman and Moss & Richardson and the Japanese store holders Nishioka and Toku-maru. There were no letters to the editor in protest, and as will be seen in the following pages, his suggestion of expelling Aboriginal workers from the town received support from Mayor Norman. Without restraint his crusade against the Indigenous people continued.

Then occurred two incidents which gave Mr Barker's campaign further impetus. In normal times they may not have caused much of a fuss, but Barker seized upon them. The first was a leprosy scare. The second was a rape of a young white girl by an Aborigine.

In the first week of October 1912, the town was abuzz with the news that two cases of suspected leprosy had been detected by the resident medical officer. One supposed carrier was an Aboriginal man who, after a preliminary examination by Dr Goldstein, escaped from the hospital and was at large somewhere. The second was Cecilia Antonio, a half-caste woman who sold vegetables in the

Asiatic Quarter. She was brought in by the police and locked up. Dr Goldstein sent samples which had fallen from Cecilia Antonio's fingers, and tissue from the long since decamped Aboriginal man to the government pathologist in Perth. The results, telegraphed back, were announced by Mayor Norman to the townsfolk. The diagnosis was *ulsus tropicum* in the case of the man, and in the case of the woman – well, Pa Norman was too much of a gentleman to reveal what it was, so he confined himself to saying that it wasn't leprosy. Barker wrote in his newspaper:

> It is a relief for all in Broome to learn that the 'Leprosy Scare' has petered out . . . In the second case no mention is made of the correct diagnosis of the woman's illness; the public are left to wonder, and can only conclude that it is a dreadful venereal disease for which the woman has been treated for years past. It is well, if such be true, that she remain where she is isolated and quarantined, as up to last week she used to handle fruit and vegetables in hawkers' baskets and her washing was always done at a certain public laundry, the consequences from which can be better imagined than printed.[8]

So Cecilia Antonio remained locked up in the hospital. But was the scare really over? Barker kicked it along in the next issue:

> Leprosy Scare – It transpires that the wires sent to the Broome authorities re the pathological examination of tissue from the half-caste Manila woman were misleading. Negative results were obtained from the dead fingers sent to Perth, but the authorities requested 'better specimens' to be sent in a manner minutely described . . . The Government Pathologist was not satisfied that the woman's hand would be bloodless and dead and bones crumbling without something seriously being the matter. However, the local Health Board intend to keep the woman and the house in quarantine until 'live' tissues are sent to Perth.[9]

Dr Goldstein despatched more pieces of Cecilia Antonio's fingers to Perth, but again the samples were inadequate for conclusive analysis and more were called for. Dr Goldstein obliged. As the days passed, the *Echo* speculated about the result. Said the paper on 11 January 1913: 'A resident of Broome who has seen leprosy in various stages in several places was shown this poor creature, and unhesitatingly declares it is leprosy.'

Finally, in February, a telegram arrived from the department clearing Cecilia Antonio of leprosy. After four months in detention she was set free – an action which drew a protest from the *Echo*:

> Alleged Leper – By order from the fossilised medical department in Perth, the frightfully diseased half-caste woman, so long quarantined between the two Broome schools, has been released, and may frequently be seen exhibiting the rotting stump of her hand to passers by. Nearly every day some piece of bone or decayed flesh falls from this poor creature's arm, and, as the yard surrounding the house is full of fowls, whose eggs and carcases are vended in town, the possible consequences of the disease (syphilis, chronic, specific, and infectious) spreading can easily be imagined. Her husband, who is living with her, catches and sells fish. We make no apology for charging the Local Authority with wanton neglect of a public duty in permitting this state of affairs to exist any longer, when, as the mouth-piece of the community they could, with but little effort, have the woman removed to the lock-hospital island.[10]

The 'lock-up hospital island' referred to by Barker was on Bernier and Dorre Islands, 30 miles off the coast at Carnarvon. Daisy Bates called the islands the 'tombs of the living dead'.[11] Aborigines and half-castes were confined there: the men on Bernier Island and the women on Dorre Island. Both islands were waterless and windswept. They were places of heat, isolation and chains. There, the cure for leprosy was death.

Leprosy was unknown among the Aboriginal people prior to European settlement, but they were to suffer from it most. The first reported case was of a Chinese miner who in 1908 walked in from the goldfields to Broome. Then leprosy began to appear among Aboriginal communities clear across the Kimberleys. How it spread so rapidly is not known, but the whites blamed the Asiatic crews of the pearling luggers venturing inland in search of women. Following a public meeting, the mayor of Broome asked the government in Perth for assistance, saying that as a temporary measure the council intended to expel diseased Aborigines to beyond the town borders.

There was an immediate reply from the premier: 'Leprosy matter receiving close attention by Government.'[12] Then nothing. Nothing for days, for weeks, for years. The temporary solution became the final solution. Diseased Aborigines knew that if they came into Broome they would be taken to the lock-up hospital, so they kept out of the town, off the boats, away from the homesteads, and confined themselves to the isolation of the dry interior where they infected those they met there.

Cecilia Antonio was not taken to the lock-up hospital. She was allowed to remain with her husband. They struggled on to make a living as slowly her health declined. She seems to have been a remarkably brave woman – probably she was illiterate, so she may have been spared the hateful words written about her by Barker. Hopefully no one felt it was their business to read them to her. She only had a few weeks to live. Her death from chronic sepsis, the result of syphilitic ulceration, appeared in Dr Goldstein's report to the Broome council of 4 March 1913.

Meanwhile, Mr Barker reported a rape to his readers in this item:

> On Saturday morning, a little before 8 o'clock, Mrs Barker . . . let a young girl (12) in her charge take a girl (7) and boy (4) for a walk, with strict instructions not to go inside the common, but to walk along the cleared roadway towards the race course.

The order was disobeyed, for the children went through the common gate and along a pathway to a spot about 300 yards from their home. They then turned for home and confronted a nigger, known as 'Jacky Taylor'. They took no notice of the nigger, who passed but immediately turned and grabbed the eldest girl and commenced dragging her further into the bush. The three children screamed, the little boy attacking the nigger with his cap, succeeding in knocking the nigger's hat off . . .

The police and the doctor were soon on the scene and Con. Pollett quickly discovered the 'wanted' man leaving his master's house and arrested him. The brute had been home and changed his pants, and was probably making for his own country beyond Derby. The children had no doubt about the wretch, who denied his guilt.

He was taken to the scene of the outrage, where he identified the hat as his, and then confessed his guilt, adding that he went 'a bit mad' . . .

The case will be heard before the court on Monday but will be heard with closed doors. The Aborigines' Department has engaged counsel to defend the man.[13]

In his editorial remarks, Barker linked the assault with the leprosy scare:

It is well known that the whole race suffer more or less from a loathsome disease, a disease whose ravages may be checked, certainly, but one also that is never cured, and is also hereditary . . .

Let the men of this place awaken to a sense of their responsibilities to womanhood. All must agree, after last Saturday's disgraceful outrage, that the time has arrived for every man amongst us to realise that the essential womanhood of the attacked babe is identical with that of our mothers, our daughters and our wives, and for the sake of our mothers' love we dare not permit a continuance of the present state of affairs. As men, everyone of us must make what effort we can to rid the town of the rambling natives, and save our innocent girls from the possibility of being tampered with. Nothing short of pushing the niggers out of the town will provide an adequate defence for the honour of our children and womenfolk. Is virtue and honour to be sacrificed to the whim of a few who want household slaves for nothing? – No! A thousand times no![14]

From 12 October 1912:

The binghi, charged last Monday with outraging a little white girl the previous week, admitted his guilt and was committed for trial. The Mayor, Mr Norman, J.P. who (with Mr Russell J.P.) was on the Bench, was so affected by the proceedings, that he has dispensed with the services of all binghis, and declares he will not have another about his place. For this action he is to be commended by all men and women of the town – it is an action which should be followed by every resident. The day after the trial, not far from the scene of the outrage, another nigger entered a lady's bedroom while she was dressing. Women, old and young, cannot now feel safe, day or night, until every binghi is hunted out of Broome, and unless our wives and families live with us here, life will be unbearable to mere white men, and the place must recede.

It soon became clear that Mr Barker was facing an uphill battle in asking the householders of Broome to do without their servants. Citizens might have agreed, as a general principle, that Aborigines should be expelled from the town, but this could not possibly apply to their own faithful servants who had been with them for years and simply adored their children.

It was rare for the house of a sheller to be without a mission-trained girl dressed in a mother hubbard working inside, and a boy in britches tending the garden. This was no climate for a white woman to be toiling at housework, and who else would polish the expanse of verandah flooring around the house? Silver cutlery became tarnished in a trice in the tropics, teak furniture became dulled and gentlemen's shoes needed to be blancoed daily. Pa Norman issued a clarification: he had not said he would get rid of all Binghis in his employ, only that he would get rid of all male Binghis.

For the next couple of months the police attempted to clear the town of the Aborigines who had neither work nor proper reason to be sitting around in the parks of the town. It was a hopeless task and the constables quickly realised the futility of it. Broome was a town bordered by sandhills and flat scrublands. There were no fences to keep the fringe dwellers out, and no sooner were they pushed out on one side than they passed silently and persistently back again on the other. Corporal Lamb gave up, and Barker retreated into sarcasm:

> The Niggers – There was an awful lament in Broome on Monday morning. Rachel in the wilderness was a fool to it! A score of binghi servants had during the previous 24 hours 'gone into recess' and there was so much work to do. Our scribe . . . met strong men, reduced to tears, on their cabin door steps. Their grief was indescribable. 'My xxxx binghi have cleared out, and I have so much work to do, what am I to do.' We understand that several employers have issued warrants for the arrest of their deserters and, as taxpayers, we unhesitatingly protest against the public funds being used to bring back unpaid binghis to be a menace to our womenfolk. They are children of the bush, and should be left in the bush.[15]

Jacky Taylor's trial for rape took place in the Broome court house. The *Nor'-West Echo* of 21 December reported that: 'The jury did not take one minute to consider their verdict of guilty. Prisoner was sentenced to 10 years' imprisonment and received 12 cuts from the cat. (They hang carrion of this kind in other States.)'

The *Echo* really had no need to trouble itself about whether Taylor should have been hanged. He had been chained around the neck since his arrest in September and the chains were likely to remain there for the rest of his sentence. He would soon be taken to a white man's prison, from which there was little chance he would leave alive.

16 The Blind Rider

> *There appears to be an idea in the public mind . . . that the Nor'-West – and Broome particularly – is one of the God-forgotten corners of the Commonwealth; that the pearlers are a kind of slave-driving Legrees, and the divers and deck hands on the boats are treated as the slaves were in the days prior to abolition. Which is just so much plain bunkum.*

Abraham Davis to the Perth *Truth*, 20 February 1909[1]

IN OCTOBER 1912 TWO men took the train to the end of the Broome jetty. One caught the steamer headed north to Singapore; the other took the steamer headed south for Perth. The man heading north was Sydney Pigott, travelling first class with an attaché case containing the finest pearls. The other man was John Noury, travelling third class, embittered, broke and facing an uncertain future.

Noury was cured of the paralysis. He could walk without difficulty and seemingly he had suffered no after-effects. He had decided not to return to England. He had been told that there was a shortage of experienced divers in Sydney and Melbourne. He had heard that employers were paying good money for divers to work in port construction.

Before Noury boarded the steamer, Barker of the *Echo* had bailed him up and asked him if he had any comments to make now that he was leaving. Noury put the best polish on things. He was quoted as saying that 'he had a few "spasms" in deep water, but had recovered. While he was satisfied white men might learn to find shell after 12 months' practice, the risk was great, the work arduous, and "not worth the candle".'[2]

With Noury's departure Sydney Pigott had gotten rid of the last of his English divers. He felt well satisfied at the way things had turned out. He looked forward to making a substantial profit selling his pearls in Singapore, thus establishing himself in Rubin's eyes as a worthy replacement for Abraham Davis. From Singapore he planned to catch a boat to the Torres Strait and then to the Dutch East Indies, purchasing pearls, and be back in Broome for Christmas. He looked forward to making a series of journeys to ports in Asia and Europe over the following year, carrying just a few bags of luggage and a small attaché case to secure the pearls. His house and fleet of luggers were up for sale. He had let it be known that the asking price for his house and two adjacent blocks of land was £900, although he also let it be known that he would accept £800 for a cash sale. His favourite boat, the *Nollie*, could be bought for £800, the rest for a little less. The consensus around town, though, was that Pigott had overpriced himself. He was leaving Broome for good, everyone knew that, so the canny decided to wait. There was plenty of time yet to make an offer.

Two weeks later, another Englishman followed in Noury's wake. This time it was Ernest Freight. He had arranged for his wife and children to emigrate and had decided that Broome was no place to bring up a family while he was at sea for weeks at a time, particularly on the wages he would earn from Pa Norman. He arranged work for himself with the Fremantle Harbour Trust on a much higher wage than he could ever get diving in the northwest.

YASUKICHI MURAKAMI decided to buy a motor car. No other Asian in Broome owned a car and he liked the idea that he would be the first. In the past few years he had watched in envy as a succession of master pearlers had taken delivery of brand new automobiles, winched off the steamer from Perth. The store he ran in John Chi Lane was bringing him wealth, as was his role as banker to the Japanese crewmen, so he felt he could certainly afford a car. He may have had to resort to trickery and a white dummy to buy a pearling lugger, but he assumed he could be straightforward about owning a motor vehicle. He ordered a Sunbeam to be delivered by steamer from Perth. It then occurred to him that rather than have his car standing idly by when he wasn't using it, he could employ someone to drive it as a taxi. As he warmed to this idea, he realised that a goodly number of his passengers would be coloured seamen, most of whom had never been a passenger in a motor car before, going backwards and forwards from the hotels to the brothels and gambling joints in the Asiatic Quarter. He struck on the audacious touch of putting a white man in the driving cabin, perhaps dressed in a cream coat and black cap. He contacted agents in Perth, and soon had a man named Hubert Haustead accompanying the car from Perth. All that remained was for him to make an application to the Broome council for a licence. Normally such applications would be stamped by the clerk over the counter, but this one was a little out of the ordinary, so it was placed on the agenda of the full council.

Council's deliberations were held on 5 November 1912. Most councillors doubted that an Asiatic should be given a driving licence, however there was uncertainty about whether the council had the power to block the application. Mayor Norman thought the legal position may have depended on whether the man was naturalised. Councillor Capes said it was unfair to the other cab drivers who had their horses to feed. Councillor Coleman spoke in favour of the application. The application was deferred pending the receipt of legal advice.

Murakami was furious. This was exactly the same trick the councillors had used to delay the approval of Dr Suzuki's hospital for a year, and he was determined not to let them do it to him. He wrote to the *Nor'-West Echo*:

> I landed the car fully believing that British Justice, of world wide renown, would be meted out to me by the Councillors and a licence be issued as soon as the car arrived. Contrary to the first tenets of British based Justice, and all my pre-conceived ideas of its grandeur, I now find my application hung up 'pending further advice', a clear attempt to delay the application until a by-law can be put through to enable councillors to differentiate between races. Nowhere in the British Empire are Parliament or subordinate bodies permitted to make laws apply with a distinction between any race of people.[3]

Surely a letter written in jest. Murakami would have known that no end of laws were passed by Australian parliaments designed to discriminate against free Asiatics, deny them voting rights or the ability to work in specified industries. He had suffered under such laws for years. So strict were the rules against persons with any Asiatic blood owning boats that in a case in 1913 'the State Government clearly indicated that a pearling lugger licence would not be issued to any half-caste Aboriginals'.[4]

A few days later the council received a wire back from Mr Northmore KC in Perth, stating that the council had no power to refuse a licence simply because the applicant was an Asiatic alien. For that advice he charged seven guineas. Mayor Norman buckled, and

Murakami was granted his licence. That night a white driver in the new Sunbeam waited at the cabbies' rank. He did a roaring trade. Not that he would have been offering a speedy journey – council bylaws prohibited a motor vehicle from being driven at more than walking pace at any street intersection, but that probably suited most passengers, who thought the longer the journey took, the greater the fun.

As the year drew to a close it began to get hotter, and the towns-folk searched the horizon for signs of rain. They watched clouds build up in the morning, saw them finger across the sky, only to wisp away to nothing, and by noon the sun would blaze down again. The grass in Bedford Park turned brown, the gardens wilted and horses trotting along the streets left behind a pall of red dust. In most houses the tanks were empty and people had to rely on the despised bore water. It was smelly, and flowed orange from the taps. A hose left run-ning overnight would turn the lawns ochre by breakfast.

As December approached, the clouds became more threatening, dropping an occasional shower before moving on to leave the town trapped under stifling skies. People found it difficult to sleep at night. At dusk families gathered on the foreshore, hoping to catch some air while the youngsters splashed about in the bay and the hotels sent Aboriginal boys across the road bearing trays of iced lemonade. The children paused when they heard the sound of thunder, and far away, out to sea, everyone looked up to see threads of lightning jumping between the water and the dark clouds.

Then one morning the town awoke to see that the sun was cov-ered by tumbling black clouds. It was still dark at nine. Just before lunchtime, plump, warm drops, as if squeezed through a colander, landed in the dust of the streets. An indescribable smell a bit like moist compost rose in the air, and suddenly there was a drumming on the roofs. The rain fell the rest of the day, all that night and all the next day. The roads ran in red waves, children splashed naked through torrents of water and slithered in mud, and when the people next peered outside, the grass had turned green.

From early December, the luggers began to scurry home to Broome for the lay-up. Beasily and Hanson on the *Ena* rounded Channel Rock and headed into Dampier Creek as dawn began to break. Beasily stood on the deck of the *Ena* looking out for a glimpse of the tin roofs of the town. He was feeling pleased with himself. The hold under his feet was full of baskets of shell and he felt that at last he was understanding the pearling grounds with its moods and subtle signs of where the shell might be found.

In fact Beasily had decided to dive for another season and approached Pa Norman for a renewal of his contract. He received a cautious reply. Norman was now president of the Pearlers' Association and he could hardly be seen to be refusing to take on a white diver. But then Beasily had to understand that the white experiment was over. The scheme had been a failure and any favours for the white man were finished. If he wanted to take up an engagement on one of the boats of Robison & Norman, he would have to work under the same conditions as the coloured divers. That would mean working with a coloured crew and tender for a wage of a £3 a month and £30 for each ton of shell collected. Beasily accepted. And, said Norman, there would be no place for a white tender on a coloured boat; Hanson would have to go. This presented no problem for Hanson, who was intending to leave anyway. There was more to life, he thought, than spending months at sea in a repetitious search for a mollusc fathoms below.

Reid, on one of the Moss & Richardson boats, returned to Broome two weeks before Christmas. He was tanned to a honey colour. He told everyone in the hotels that he liked shell opening. It was an easy, relaxed life, if ever there was one. He said he intended to stick around for the next season.

When Andrews returned, he had a different story. He was sick to the gullet of shell opening and weeks at sea. It was a tedious, mind-numbing existence. He spoke to Stanley Pigott and arranged for a release from his contract. He caught the next steamer south to Perth.

Over the next few weeks a forest of luggers slipped into channels dug in the mud. It had been a good year for the shellers. Although the prices bid for shell in London and New York had begun to weaken, they were still well above the levels of past years. Once again the lanes of Japtown throbbed with life. There was plenty of money in town, and the crews were back and ready for what the Asiatic Quarter could offer.

Hyland's circus opened under the big top for another season. Tom junior took charge of rehearsals and the trying task of organising the acts of his brothers and sisters. His sister Gertrude, the highwire performer, became the manager. In the absence of his father's horse-riding act, Tom was forced to allow the children to present conjuring routines, and Irish ditties and dancing, but these turned out to be the most popular of all. Night after night the circus was a sell-out.

Then fever broke out in the town. The first casualty was a 35-year-old man named Charles Bernard Norton who died in Dr Suzuki's hospital. Several more were rushed into the government hospital. There was a common thread, muttered the town – every one of the men infected had been a frequent visitor to the Asiatic Quarter. There was great uncertainty about what kind of fever it was and all sorts of names were bandied around: gaol fever, typhoid, septic fever, plague, typhus – all first cousins to each other and highly dangerous, and whatever the name, the cause was obvious. People remembered how the late Dr Blick had warned the town's medical board that the Asiatic Quarter could easily infect the rest of the town. Everyone knew that the boarding-house proprietors threw their night water into the bay and that the crews lodging in the foreshore camps were using the mangrove swamps as latrines. The citizens held that the council was equally to blame because it had never done anything about it.

Then another theory gained currency – that during the recent heavy rains, disease had leached through the sand from the Asiatic Quarter and infected the bore water the white people had to drink. The medical officer thought this theory a bit unlikely since the bore was sunk deep into sandstone beds, but to quell an excitable population he sent a sample to Perth for analysis and while the town awaited the results, he advised that all bore water should be boiled or dosed with potassium permanganate. The resulting telegraph from Perth said that apart from the fact that the water smelt horrible (which was no news) and had high percentages of salt, iron oxide and sulphate, it was perfectly safe to drink. It was suggested that in order to get rid of the smell and the unusual colour, the water should be drained through drums filled with shell grit.

At the December council meeting, the medical officer reported that although he had not yet been able to get to the bottom of the fever, whatever it was, only one more case had been notified. But he warned the council that if cholera, plague or smallpox ever took hold in the Asiatic Quarter, it would probably wipe out the whole community.

ON THE Wednesday night before Christmas 1912, a body was found about fifteen yards from the tent of Hyland's circus. The deceased was identified as Amid Bin Kadir, a young Malayan indentured worker on one of Robison & Norman's boats. There seemed to be no shortage of witnesses to the death of Kadir. Even Corporal Lamb's two young sons were there. With dismay, Corporal Lamb realised that it was his duty to charge with murder Tom Hyland junior, the blind jockey. From what Corporal Lamb was told, it seemed a rather simple case. Kadir was one of a group of Malays taking turns to watch the performance through a hole in the tent. Tom Hyland shouted at them to go away. When Tom felt from the rippling of the canvas that a face had reappeared, he punched as hard as he could. The head disappeared. And that was that.

Mrs Hyland, now without her husband and her eldest son, rallied the family – for the show must go on. A sell-out audience turned up to demonstrate their support for Tom in his time of trouble. To tremendous applause, an emotional crowd watched Miss Agnes Hyland ride bareback on her dancing horses with young Percy balanced on her shoulders, the blind Maudie Hyland performing acrobatics with Rose, and Darcy and Stanley, the blind songbirds, delighting with songs of Erin. Afterwards several of the gentlemen of the town took Mrs Hyland aside and told her not to worry – surely she could rely on a Broome jury to do the right thing.

The inquest into Amid Bin Kadir's death commenced before Mr Russell JP and a jury of three in the second week of January 1913. Hall appeared for Tom Hyland, while Coleman appeared for the Crown. Tom Hyland sat in the dock and listened as a series of witnesses swore they had seen nothing to link him with the murder. Corporal Lamb's children, Thomas aged thirteen and Roy aged eleven, said they saw the Malay looking through a hole in the tent and heard the sound of a blow, but Tom wasn't in the tent at the time.

Jack Leston, the circus clown, said that Tom was with him dressing for the jockey act. Harry Harris, a patron of the circus, said he saw a man on the ground whom he thought had had a fit. Another patron, Mr Roe, said he heard young Percy Hyland say, 'Come and have a look at the man Tom has knocked out.' Percy, Tom's seven-year-old brother, was careful to deny this – all he saw was a drunk man lying on the grass. Tom Hyland took the stand to say he did not leave the dressing room that night. The first he heard of the death was when the circus was over.[5]

The jury did not want to hear any more and brought in a verdict that the deceased had died by a blow to the mouth, but it was not possible to say who had struck the blow or how it was struck. Tom was released. It was a popular decision, at least among the white community. Said the *Echo* on 11 January 1913:

> To-night will witness the last appearance for the season of Hyland's well-known circus. Tom Hyland, for whom the whole

town genuinely sympathises in his troubles, had been put to heavy expenses, and a full house tonight would no doubt be the best manner in which the public could demonstrate their sympathy.

17 The Last of His Tribe

Came up on deck like a dead man, paralysed body and brain;
Suffered, while blood was returning, infinite tortures of pain.

'The Pearl Diver' by A.B. 'Banjo' Patterson

THE WEATHER WAS SETTLED for the beginning of the 1913 season and the fleet was able to take early to the seas. The master pearlers hoped it would be a good year. No one knew how many seasons they had left before the Labor government crippled them entirely.

Reid sailed out on one of Richardson's luggers for another year of indolent adventure as a shell opener. Sanders put to sea in charge of one of Alexander's boats and prepared to do the diving himself. Years later Alexander gave evidence to the Royal Commission about Sanders, saying how disappointed he was with the amount of shell Sanders brought up compared to a good Malay diver. Over several weeks Sanders became paralysed twice, recovered each time and returned to diving. He was nothing if not persistent. Sanders was then paralysed a third time and was disabled, so Alexander had to dismiss him. Alexander gave no information to the commission about the nature and extent of Sander's paralysis.

Beasily and his crew sailed out aboard the *Edgar Norman*. Beasily took her north, beyond Lacepede Islands, the Aboriginal settlements at Beagle Bay and Lombadina, and past Sunday Island where Syd Hadley conducted his mission. At the end of the third day's sailing, the *Edgar Norman* arrived in Cygnet Bay within King Sound. Cygnet Bay was where William Dampier, landing over two hundred years earlier, had decided that this was a land to be despised. King Sound had long had the reputation as a place where much shell could be found and where many deaths occurred. Steep red cliffs descend into waters which have no bottom, and tides of tremendous force become caught in a swirling pattern as they pass through the islands at the entrance to the Sound, causing whirlpools the size of a lugger in width. At times the tide is so strong that it can easily knock a diver off his feet and foul his lines. Because of its notoriety, one of the bays just within the entrance of the Sound is called the Graveyard, and even the Japanese divers shied clear of it.

Beasily ordered the sails reefed and the anchor dropped. He stood on the deck and looked westward where he could see birds spiralling through streaky clouds underlit by a red sunset. Waves rippled in a golden light and splashed against the cliffs. It was still hot and he took off his shirt. His skin had turned deep brown after days in the sun. He had let his hair grow long. He sat on the roof of the cabin and smoked his pipe while the cook prepared the evening meal. He decided he liked being skipper of a pearling lugger. Behind him his Malay tender tinkered with an air compressor bolted to the deck. It was brand new, from Heinke, in a fine oak cabinet with two brass gauges enclosed in shiny glass.

Several of the crew launched the dinghy and fished for the next day's breakfast. Beasily turned his face into the warmth of the sun and wiped the stubble on his chin. Now they were at sea he intended to shave only once a week. The tender closed the lid on the compressor and laid out the diver's outfit for the next day – a pair of silk pyjamas with Japanese prayers of good fortune embroidered across the front, two neck-to-knee drawers, and two rollneck jumpers. The tender pulled a long green bag from the cabin, untied the leather straps and spread Beasily's diving suit, whitened by the sea, on the deck. On hands and knees he began to check its strength. The cook, a smiling man with a face the texture of a crumpled brown paper bag, handed Beasily a bowl of noodles, chillies and strips of meat in a red soup. After the meal Beasily undressed, then dragged a bucket of sea water aboard. He soaped his body all over before upending the bucket over his head. Then he retired to his cabin and sat reading under a kerosene lamp.

Beasily worked within the bay for the next few days. Each evening he reflected with pleasure on the amount of shell he was collecting. He began to feel that he was capable of matching any coloured diver.

When Beasily awoke on 18 February, he saw the rigging glistening with moisture. He sat on the roof of the cabin and looked around. The air was still, yet so strong was the tide that the anchor rope trembled. Mist rose from the water, tumbling towards him in waves, and when he took a breath, it seemed to cloy his lungs. He stood up and looked over the side. The water slapping against the hull appeared dirty. He looked skyward. Although the sun was lost, there was a soft yellow to the clouds, lighting up the deck of the lugger. He ran his hand across his forehead and decided it would be pointless diving until the sun provided some light on the floor.

By mid morning the mist began to lift. The weather was extremely hot and humid. Even when he was still, beads of perspiration gathered on his brow. He took a cup of tea then, motioning to his tender to assist, began to prepare for the dive. Already he had lost several hours and the tide was beginning to turn.

Beasily dropped into a chasm of 20 fathoms. As he descended he was aware of the rip of the tide pushing him away from the lugger. As soon as he touched the bottom, he dragged his boots along the floor to slow himself down. At the first dive, he found shell. In the space of half an hour he had placed ten pairs in his net. He came to the surface and immediately descended again, this time taking two netted bags with him. It was to be the last dive he ever made.

This nasty little item, complete with misspellings of Beasily's name and the location of his death, appeared in the *Nor'-West Echo* of 1 March 1913:

> Report reached Broome on Wednesday that diver Beesley, working on one of Robison & Norman's boats, and the last of the imported white divers, had died from paralysis at the Grave Yard, Sygnet Bay, and was buried there. It will be remembered that Beesley resolved, in an endeavour to make a success of his search for shell, to abandon the scientific methods in diving, take a coloured tender, and dive for shell in a similar manner to that adopted by Asiatic divers. Ah! Lack!

The crew on the *Edgar Norman*, now without a diver, sailed to Beagle Bay to report Beasily's death to Father Walter at the Catholic mission.

How Beasily died remains unclear. Captain Ancell Gregory told the Royal Commission in 1916 that the cause of death 'was reck-lessness in rapid ascent. Besley [*sic*] was put overboard . . . for recompression but would not stay down and blew himself out of the water by closing the gas escape valve in the helmet'.[1] It was an explanation strikingly similar to the one given for Webber's death and if true, suggests that in the quest for shell safe diving practices were ignored by the Englishmen. Some of the divers now working in Perth (almost certainly Hockliss, Elphick and Rolland) were quoted in the Melbourne *Argus* as saying that Beasily was hauled out of the water dead, and there was nothing to show how he had lost his life.[2]

It was not uncommon for a diver to be dragged up dead for no apparent reason. In his book *Diver's Luck*, relating his experiences as a pearl diver in the 1920s, Clarence Benham wrote that:

Death caused by paralysis in deep water is absolutely painless; there can be nothing much better. Unlike an anaesthetic, it does not involve a lingering, beastly, stinking wait before passing out to nothingness. With no warning, or only the slightest, consciousness ceases; just a quiet, painless going out into the infinite darkness like the flame of a lamp.[3]

Benham survived to tell the story because his suit was inflated enough for him to float to the surface, where he was rescued by the crew. Beasily was not so lucky. The incredible pressures of the depths of King Sound may well have caused blood vessels in his brain to rupture, perhaps causing him to black out and die within minutes.

Captain Talboys told the press that the experiment of working pearl luggers with white divers was a failure and that all the imported divers were either paralysed or dead. Hockliss, Elphick and Rolland contacted the press to say that they were not paralysed and were very much alive and now working in Fremantle. An article in the *Argus* says that the three men:

> quoted figures to show that the white diver was every bit as successful a pearler as the coloured man, and for confirmation of their assertion they referred to Mr Stanley Pigott, a Broome master pearler, and one who has employed white men from the outset. The late Diver Beesley [Beasily], the last of the white divers to remain in Broome, secured 12 cwt. of shell in one month. He raised 2 cwt. on the day preceding his death, and also 2 cwt. on the day he died. This was equally as good as, and better in many cases, than the record of coloured divers, especially as the shell was raised during what was termed an off season.[4]

Stanley Pigott, furious that his name had been brought into the debate on the side of the white divers, wrote an angry rebuttal, expressing his surprise that he had been referred to as 'a master pearler who could confirm the assertion that the white divers were every bit as successful as the coloured men'. He went on:

> How much I wish it was true! Relying upon memory I cannot recall one diver of the nine who did not, on some occasion, become paralysed, though it is possible that one or two may have had the good fortune to escape from this prevalent accident . . . Suffice to say, so far as I am concerned, an offer of a Government bonus of £100 per ton on shell raised by white labour would not tempt me to again try the experiment of working a lugger by white divers. The statement that 2½ tons of shell was won in 14 weeks work by the two white divers employed by me on the Mollie is untrue; the men between them did not aggregate 1 ton 6 cwt. for the whole nine months they were on that vessel.[5]

The year 1913 did not prove prosperous for the pearl-shelling industry. The price of shell at the London and New York auctions tumbled. No one knew why. There was no recovery and by mid year it was rock bottom at £225 a ton. On average this was over £100 a ton less than bids a year earlier.

By August 1913 John Noury was living in Melbourne, and when the Royal Commission convened there, he was called to give evidence. He told the commissioners that the English divers were directed to places where there was little possibility of getting shell. The pearlers did that 'to baulk the attempt to introduce white labour'. He disputed the claim that the English divers were not as good as the Asiatics. He said that he conducted a test with one of the Malay divers and at the end of three days he had 26 shells and the Malay had only twenty. 'If I owned a lugger,' said Noury, 'I would take the responsibility of paying white divers and crew.'[6]

Noury also raised with the commission the circumstances of Beasily's death. There had been no inquiry into it. 'It was stated that this man had been brought up from below dead, but it was possible that he might have been killed, as the crew with whom he had been working consisted wholly of black men.[7]

In the same week that Noury gave evidence to the Royal Commission in Melbourne, Sanders began searching for work. It had taken him months to recover from the paralysis he had contracted while working on Alexander's boats, but slowly, week by week, he had regained full movement of his limbs. The hotels of Broome acted like a labour exchange and it was the lot of the white unemployed to wait, ever-available, in the gloom of the town's bars, hoping for an employer's call. Sanders waited and nothing happened, so from time to time he buttonholed a few of the master pearlers. He was an experienced diver, he told them, and given another chance he was sure he would be able to match the coloureds. He would even be prepared to work as a shell opener if that was available. Unfortunately, no one wanted to take him on. Someone suggested he speak to Alex Chamberlain, who was getting ready to sail to the pearling grounds off Cape Latouche.

Sanders found Chamberlain on board the *Coolgardie* at her mooring in Dampier Creek. Like the others, he had no work for him. Sanders asked for passage out to the fleet. If he could get himself out there, he could ask around for work as a shell opener, or as a diver. Chamberlain agreed, just so long as Sanders understood he was a passenger and not being engaged. Chamberlain already had a Malay diver and he opened the shell himself.

On 12 August 1913 the *Coolgardie* left Broome and arrived at Latouche the next day. Chamberlain took his lugger to the back of the fleet and began to drift for shell in water of 14 fathoms. Whenever a lugger or a floating station came near, Sanders rowed across to ask if there was any work for him to do. There didn't seem to be, but the men aboard agreed to spread the word that Sanders was there on the *Coolgardie*, ready and waiting.

A week passed and Sanders remained unemployed, but then he unexpectedly got his chance, on Chamberlain's boat. The Malay diver came up shaking with fever and retired to his bunk. Sanders argued with Chamberlain that he would lose nothing by giving him a trial. Reluctantly he agreed, and Sanders clambered into the suit recently vacated by the ill man. He was using a tender with whom he had never worked before, in 15 fathoms. Sanders dived for Chamberlain the next day, and the next. The amount of shell he collected was disappointing, but he claimed he was getting better. Perhaps he was, but it was never enough to cause Chamberlain to cease wishing his regular diver would recover.

On 23 August, Sanders clambered aboard the *Coolgardie* at 3.50 in the afternoon. He had completed the last dive of the day. He felt tired, so after the tender had taken his helmet off, he found some shade next to the cabin and sat on a wooden box, breathing deeply. From just after sunrise that morning he had been drifting across a floor of rocks and sand, trying his very best to find shell for Chamberlain. It was hard, distressing work and Sanders wondered if he could continue much longer. He lit his pipe and looked seaward across ruffled water. He could just make out another sail in the far distance, the size of a painter's touch on a canvas. The tender wanted to wash out the suit, so he asked Sanders to stand so he could undress him. Wearily Sanders got to his feet, then, without a word, fell forward into his tender's arms. The tender called for help and he and Chamberlain laid Sanders slowly out on the deck. He was dead.

Twelve pounds, fourteen shillings and some personal papers were found under Sanders' pillow, which Chamberlain handed to the clerk of courts.

Hunt read of Sanders' death in the Melbourne papers. So that was it. It was over. There were no more English divers left in Broome to die. Only one of the twelve remained and that was the tender Reid, now working as a shell opener. Hunt sent a telegram to the sub-collector of customs in Broome, asking for details of Sanders' death. A few weeks later he received a bare-boned report, stating times and places, and a newspaper cutting taken from the *Nor'-West Echo*:

The last of his tribe

Saunders [*sic*], the last of the nine white divers imported from
England, died last week from divers' paralysis. It appears that
Saunders, who was unemployed, went out to the grounds on a
schooner, and while there, although not on the articles, volunteered to do some diving for P. Chamberlain. One day, after
ascending from his final dip, he was seized with paralysis and
shortly afterwards died. The body was brought into Broome,
and, after a post mortem by Dr Goldstein, interred in the local
grave yard, where hundreds of other divers have found a last
resting place.

... Three out of 9 is a big average ... compared with the
12 per cent of coloured divers. But, if the deaths among
coloured divers are as frequent to the end of the season as they
have been during the past few months, this year's average will
be nearer 20 per cent than 12 per cent. Up to August 26 five
deaths from divers' paralysis were reported for the month.

News comes from the Beach, that during the 10 days pre-
ceding Aug. 29, some 22 divers were more or less affected by
paralysis.[8]

On 11 September 1913, the Minister of External Affairs,
announced that he had agreed to extend the deadline for ridding the
industry of coloured divers and tenders to the end of 1916. Coloured
divers and tenders were free to work on the boats until then. The reason given for the extension was that the Royal Commission had not
yet presented its report.

The absolute failure of the white experiment was received with
bewilderment by the Australian public. How was it possible that
white men had lost out to Asiatics? One explanation never likely to
be accepted was that the Asian man was more adept at shell collection than the white. Instead the evidence of John Noury was
remembered. His claim that the shellers had sabotaged the English

divers was given wide publicity. The executive of the Fremantle Trades Hall, suspecting conspiracy, set up a committee in 1913 to investigate the scandal of the failure of the white experiment. The committee found 'there was no desire on the part of the members of the Pearlers' Association to encourage the introduction of white labour'. The report concluded that 'many obstacles were placed in the way of the white divers, as they were given unsuitable boots and gear, and were not allowed the same freedom of choice as the Japanese divers, nor were they properly "tendered" . . . '. The Trades Hall called on the Labor Party to:

> put a stop to further encroachment of the alien, whose practical domination of the northwest is a grave damage to the industrial welfare and moral well being of that portion of the State . . . British and Australian workers will prove in the pearling industry, as they have done everywhere, their superiority over every class of alien that may be pitted against them.[9]

This was by no means a unanimous view. Some thought that pearl-shelling was a nasty little industry carried on at the end of the earth by yellow peasants and white rogues, so why did the government bother? Others argued that deep-sea shell diving was clearly deadly and it would be a shame if white men had to do it. It was pointed out by some commentators that in no other country was pearling done by whites. The common trochus of Malaya, the Japanese ear shell, the black-lipped shell of the South Pacific, and the pearl shell from Ceylon and the Persian Gulf were all picked by coloured men. In their view there was work which naturally fell for the white man and there was work which naturally fell for the coloureds, and there was no doubt on which side of the line mother-of-pearl collection fell.

IN OCTOBER 1913 the Bamford Royal Commission released its progress report. Although evidence had only been taken in Queensland, the commissioners were firmly of the view that this was an industry which should be made entirely white and that 'no reasonable expense should be spared in an endeavour to end a system so unanimously condemned and, from an Australian viewpoint, so negative in its results'.[10] Thankfully for those in Broome, the commission had held back from commenting on the situation in Western Australia. This, the commission said, would be dealt with in the final report, after evidence had been taken in the northwest. Not that there was any doubt about what the commission had in mind:

> The evidence has satisfied your Commissioners that the industry is at the present time unquestionably in the hands of the Japanese, who are masters of the situation . . .
>
> The shellers quite freely admitted that their business is to obtain shell, and that the locality or depth whence it is procured is left to the discretion of the diver. No instructions are given to divers (who have absolute control of the boats) as to where they should or should not fish, consequently the divers select the locality where, in their opinion, the take of shell will be greatest, irrespective of the risks taken . . .
>
> Although Malays and other coloured aliens are employed, undoubtedly the whole industry is, as has already [been] shown, dominated by the Japanese. This is admitted by the shellers themselves, who seem to have a wholesome fear of in any way provoking or offending their divers.

The commission suggested that suitable white labour could be obtained from 'the herring fisheries of Scotland', 'the sponge fisheries of Southern Europe' and from among the 'youths from the Queensland reformatories'. If its recommendations were followed, the commission believed that it would be 'practicable to eliminate coloured aliens from the industry . . . in five years' and supplant the coloured residents of Thursday Island with a wholy white population.

The progress report was in many ways a shameful document, driven by the rankest of racism. It made no mention of the fact that the master pearlers had no interest in doing anything about the alarming death rate of workers in the industry. The report recommended that diving in waters exceeding 25 fathoms be prohibited, otherwise it did not address, in the slightest way, the issue of why, if white divers entered the industry, they should not progressively die. Nothing was said about the absence of compensation for crippled workers or for their families. The plight of the Aborigines and Torres Strait Islanders was not discussed. Issues such as prostitution, the peddling of alcohol and opium, and the failure to pay wages to the Indigenous people were ignored.

The commission did not discuss the economic effects of paying white wages. Instead the commissioners made fanciful suggestions about recruiting white families from Scotland and Greece. These impractical solutions involved proposals of breathtaking injustice: that people who had made their homes on Thursday Island, who were given citizenship rights by the Queensland Government and had worked to build up their businesses, should be expelled to make way for white families. It was a report of rigid adherence to the White Australia Policy, written by a group of politicians who, having made up their minds before accepting their commissions, found it unnecessary to take in any of the evidence.

POSTSCRIPT

Just now the effects of the war fall heavily upon small propri-
etorships, many of which have had to suspend pearling
operations.

West Australian Pearlers' Association Annual Report, 1915

IN MAY 1914 DR SUZUKI said farewell to Broome in order to
pursue further studies in Japan. The news of his departure was
greeted with real sadness by all sections of the community. In four
years of service to the town, particularly during the illness of Dr
Blick, he had completely won over the white population and there
was not the slightest objection by the municipal council, or anyone
else, when his replacement at the Japanese hospital, Dr Yakuo
Harada, was granted a permit to enter the country.

When Europe plunged into war in August 1914, the Japanese
Emperor declared on the side of the British Empire. Suddenly the
Japanese were no longer aliens; they were allies. In Broome, as in
every city, town and hamlet across Australia, the declaration of war

was an occasion for great celebration. The mayor made speeches and young men and storekeepers paraded up and down the main street waving banners. In Broome, the whites and the Japanese got drunk together and slapped each other's backs as they discovered the surprising news that the hated enemy was now the Hun.

With Australia recruiting for a European war, many of the men who had acted as shell openers on the luggers were swept up to fill the trenches in France. Few of the boats now carried a white shell opener. At last, the pearls belonged to the Japanese.

IN APRIL 1916, after a number of false starts, the Bamford Royal Commission finally came to Broome. War economies meant that the number of commissioners had been reduced to five and there were no amanuenses to record the evidence. At a welcoming ceremony held at the Literary Institute, the mayor observed that Broome had sent 170 of its young men to the front and the town trusted that the commission would leave something of the pearl-shelling industry for the soldiers to come back to.

The mayor need not have worried. The war had brought changes. Mr Bamford made no inquiries about whether the Japanese flag was flown on boats. No longer were the Japanese taking over the industry. No one asked what happened to the pearls. The issue of displacing the Japanese by Malays was not raised. The Japanese were no longer a moral danger to the white community. Instead, a succession of witnesses blackened the names of the twelve English divers and tenders. The master pearlers told the commission that the English divers might have known all about wreck and salvage diving, but they knew nothing about the pearling business and couldn't recognise shell under their feet. Stanley Pigott denied entirely that the naval divers were imported for the purpose of discrediting the employment of white divers. He said that the English divers could not locate the shell, probably because their civilised upbringing rendered them less keen observers than the Asiatics. He produced certificates from Harvey and Elphick stating that they had worked well with a Darnley pump and it was very satisfactory to them.[1]

After nine days in Broome, including a day out at sea inspecting diving operations and an afternoon being entertained at the Japanese Club, the commissioners caught the steamer to the south. In the final report, published in September 1916, Bamford and his commissioners recanted on almost every conclusion of their 1913 report.

> Since presenting the progress report, the opinion of your Commissioners has undergone a change of considerable importance, particularly in regard to the labour question. Having carefully weighed the evidence, and having no reason to doubt the credibility of those who were examined on this point, and further, having visited the principal centres of the pearl-shelling industry in Australia and noted the conditions under which it is conducted, your Commissioners have decided that diving for shell is not an occupation which our workers should be encouraged to undertake. The life is not a desirable one, and the risks are great, as proved by the abnormal death rate amongst divers and try divers. The work is arduous, the hours long, and the remuneration quite inadequate. Living space is cramped, the food wholly preserved of its different kinds, and the life incompatible with that a European worker is entitled to live. Social life is impossible and enjoyment is out of the question.[2]

In November 1916, Hunt wrote a note to his minister that 'the commissioners have come to the conclusion that it would be neither desirable nor profitable to attempt, by any drastic method, to transfer the industry from Asiatic to European Labour'. He recommended that the bans on coloured divers and tenders be lifted. The minister stamped the memo 'Approved'.[3] For Stanley Pigott it must have been the sweetest of victories. He had been fighting this battle for over a decade, against the might of a hostile government, an unsympathetic press and the weight of public opinion. Somehow, against all those forces, he had succeeded.

Yet it was to prove a victory devoid of harvest, for war has no call for inlaid cigarette cases, piano keys which shimmer and pearl-handles for pistols. The ships to Europe were crowded with soldiers and armaments, and there was no longer a place for boxes of mother-of-pearl. Buttons were now made of tin, wood or bone. One by one the dealers in Vienna, then Paris and St Petersburg closed their doors. Huge piles of the shell were stored along the back walls of the packing sheds on Roebuck Bay. The price of shell plummeted to £120 a ton; never could it support white wages, even if white men were to be had – but they were wanted for purposes of killing, far, far away.

As the war dragged on the Japanese began to leave, Dr Harada departed and the Japanese hospital closed down. By 1916 there was no doctor at the government hospital either. Broome was empty of its young men and as the casualty list grew, people wondered how many would return. By 1918, the price of mother-of-pearl was so low that there seemed little point in sending the luggers out to sea. Stanley Pigott, along with the others who were too old to volunteer for the war, hoarded shell, waiting for a time when the world would turn its attention back to things of beauty. But it was a stockpile no one ever wanted. Even after the war the market for mother-of-pearl remained depressed. Fashions had changed and pearl-shelling was an industry about to be killed off by the plastic button.

THE DEPRESSION was harsh on Broome. Only a handful of luggers went to sea and so poverty stricken was the industry that most of the luggers could not afford the fuel and reverted to hand-turned pumps. The bungalows of the master pearlers were left empty and the Asiatic Quarter began to fall down.

Stanley Pigott sold his luggers and became a pearl buyer. He remained in Broome with his wife until 1942, hoping that the former glory days would return. He died in Claremont in 1955. His brother remained in Europe during World War I, and never returned to live in Broome.

There was no passing of the Aboriginal people. They remained resilient. Their numbers increased. When they returned to wander the streets of the town during the 1914–18 war, there was no one left to hunt them out. After the war, new laws armed the Protector of Natives with powers over the most intimate details of their lives. But the Protector's office was so underfunded and understaffed that his regime was alternately neglectful and then, in bursts of activity, irrationally interfering. Restrictions could be placed on where Aborigines could be employed and by whom. They could be mandatorily confined to reserves. Marriage with Asiatics was forbidden. Schooling for children, apart from at the missions, remained a dream. Many were employed, unpaid apart from keep, as station hands and servants. Leprosy among Aborigines continued to be a killer and was ignored by the authorities. The policy of exclusion from the towns continued.

When he had the inclination, the Protector seized half-caste children ('creamies', they were called) from screaming, crying mothers and placed them in orphanages, or adopted the pretty ones out into white families, while tea-coloured children from Asiatic liaisons were left behind. The last time police neck-chained gangs of Aborigines was during a strike of station hands in 1946.

As Australia became enmeshed in the grinding stalemate of World War I, far more epic events captured the interest of the country than the failure of the white experiment. In the northwest, inasmuch as it was discussed, it became folklore that the master pearlers had conspired to ensure the failure of the English divers, and, it was hinted darkly, had manipulated events to cause the deaths of several of them.

There is no doubt that it suited the purpose of the master pearlers for the English divers to fail. And as they began to fail, the master pearlers did nothing to alter that outcome. Of course, that is a long way from suggesting that the shellers planned the whole debacle from the outset or conspired to murder. It would have been an unnecessary conspiracy. This was an industry that claimed lives simply as a given of working in it.

The most likely sequence of events is that the executive of the Pearlers' Association felt it was tactically obliged to demonstrate to the government and the Royal Commission that it had at least tried to get white divers into the industry. Reluctantly, four shellers agreed to take an allocation of English divers. They may have hoped that with the new pumps taking the English divers deeper, they would at least be able to cover costs, and perhaps even show a profit. When the English divers were unable to collect shell from the deeps (or anywhere else, it seemed), the relationships soured. The employers resented the fact that they were saddled with a highly paid and loss-making workforce. It must have been obvious to the English, particularly when Sanders was imprisoned in an outrageous show of hometown justice, that the pearlers were more interested in gathering evidence of failure than in making the venture succeed. The callous reaction to the death of Webber must have dismayed them even more, particularly when the pearlers spread the story (barely plausible and grossly hypocritical) that it was Webber's fault because he was negligent in following the Admiralty tables and refused to decompress.

By the 1940s Broome had become a nondescript town on a lonely coast, falling into apathy and sun-bleached of its colour and rapidly losing traces of its past. The oceans washed across the pearling grounds as if none of this story had ever happened. It was a full circle, as history often is: nothing has changed, but everything is about to change as the circle moves to revolve again. Eco-tourism, camel rides and adventure holidays beckoned.

ENDNOTES

A Note about Terminology

1. H. Taunton, *Australind: Wanderings in Western Australia and the Malay East*, E. Arnold, London, 1903, p. 211.

Prologue

1. A.E. Boycott and G.C.C. Damant, 'Experiments on the Influence of Fatness on Susceptibility to Caisson Disease', *Journal of Hygiene*, vol. 8, no. 4, 1908, p. 455. *See also* A.E. Boycott, G.C.C. Damant and J.S. Haldane, 'The Prevention of Compressed-Air Illness', *Journal of Hygiene*, vol. 8, no. 3, 1908, p. 342. *The British Medical Journal* published a series of articles on the medical effects of exposure to compressed air in its journals of 18, 25 April and 27 June 1908, and 25 December 1909.

1 Whitewashing the Ocean

1. *Argus*, 2 February 1912, p. 6.

2 In Bare Pelt

1. *Inquirer*, 28 April 1875, quoted in Mike McCarthy, 'Before Broome', *Journal of the Australian Association for Maritime History*, vol. 16, no. 2, p. 81.
2. William Dampier, *Dampier's Voyages*, E. Grant Richards, London, vol. 1, 1906, pp. 453–54.
3. Quoted in Jas. S. Battye (ed.), *The History of the North West of Australia*, V.K. Jones, Perth, 1915, p. 8.
4. Maitland Brown, *Journal of an Expedition in the Roebuck Bay District*, Perth, p. 10, reprinted from the *Perth Gazette* and *W.A. Times* of 19 and 26 May 1865.

5. Brown, p. 21.
6. Nancy E. Withnell Taylor, *Yeera-Muk-A-Doo: a Saga of the North West*, Hesperian Press, Perth, 1987, pp. 115–16.
7. Quoted in Neville Green, 'Aborigines and White Settlers in the Nineteenth Century', in C.T. Stannage (ed.), *A New History of Western Australia*, University of Western Australia Press, Perth, 1981, p. 119.
8. Edwin W. Streeter, *Pearls and Pearling Life*, George Bell & Sons, London, 1886, p. 177.
9. A.C. Angelo, 'Kimberleys and North West Goldfields', *W.A. Historical Society Journal and Proceedings*, vol. 10, 1948.
10. H. Taunton, *Australind: Wanderings in Western Australia and the Malay East*, E. Arnold, London, 1903, pp. 237–38.
11. Taunton, pp. 233–34.
12. R. Thatcher, 'Visit to the North-West', *Herald* (W.A.), 23 October 1869, p. 3f, quoted in Mary Albertus Bain, *Full Fathom Five*, Artlook Books, Perth, 1982, p. 17.
13. Bain, p. 21.
14. Quoted in Brian W. Shepherd, 'A History of the Pearling Industry of the North-West Coast of Australia from its Origins until 1916', MA thesis, University of Western Australia, 1975, p. 106.

3 Boodungarry

1. Minutes of evidence, Walter E. Roth, Royal Commission on the Condition of the Natives, Western Australia Parliamentary Papers, Perth, 1905, p. 104.
2. Quotations in this chapter are from Walter E. Roth, Report and Minutes of Evidence, Royal Commission on the Condition of the Natives, Western Australia Parliamentary Papers, Perth, 1905.
3. Roth, Minutes of Evidence, Questions 1397 to 1402, 1405 to 1408.
4. Roth, Minutes of Evidence, Questions 1564 to 1570.
5. Jas. S. Battye (ed.), *The History of the North West of Australia*, V.K. Jones, Perth, 1915, p. 35.
6. *Broome Chronicle*, 19 June 1909.
7. University of Western Australia, *University Studies in Western Australian History*, vol. III, no. 1, 1957, p. 76.

4 A White Australia

1. Commonwealth Parliamentary Papers, no. 2, 1901–2, Melbourne, p. 855.
2. NSW Hansard, 1st series, 1879, 80/099–100.
3. *Adelaide Advertiser*, 4 July 1914.
4. Quoted in Raymond Evans, 'Keeping Australia Clean White', in Verity Burgmann and Jenny Lee (eds), *A Most Valuable Acquisition*, McPhee Gribble/Penguin, Victoria, 1988, p. 173.
5. Commonwealth Parliamentary Papers, no. 2, 1901–2, Melbourne, p. 855.
6. Quoted in Myra Willard, *History of the White Australia Policy*, Melbourne University Press, Melbourne, 1923, p. 126.
7. Quoted in the Annual Report of the West Australian Pearlers' Association, 1913.

8. Quoted in the Annual Report of the West Australian Pearlers' Association, 1913.
9. Staniforth Smith, *The West Australian Pearl-Shelling Industry*, V.K. Jones & Co., Perth, 1903, n.p.
10. Quoted in D.C.S. Sissons, 'Karayuki-San: Japanese Prostitutes in Australia 1887–1916', *Historical Studies*, University of Melbourne, vol. 17, p. 480.
11. *Broome Chronicle*, 28 August 1909.
12. *Nor'-West Echo*, 7 September 1912.

5 The Port of Pearling Luggers

1. Staniforth Smith, *The West Australian Pearl-Shelling Industry*, V.K. Jones & Co., Perth, 1903, n.p.
2. *Nor'-West Echo*, 27 December 1913.
3. *Broome Chronicle*, 26 November 1910; *Argus*, 25 November 1910, p. 7.
4. *Nor'-West Echo*, 27 December 1913.
5. *Broome Chronicle*, 17 July 1909.
6. *Broome Chronicle*, 23 January 1909.
7. *Broome Chronicle*, 1 October 1910.
8. *Broome Chronicle*, 6 November 1909.
9. *Nor'-West Echo*, 1 March 1913.
10. *Broome Chronicle*, 1 May 1909.
11. *Broome Chronicle*, 24 September 1910.
12. *Nor'-West Echo*, 19 October 1912.
13. *Broome Chronicle*, 1 April 1911.
14. Staniforth Smith, *The West Australian Pearl-Shelling Industry*, V.K. Jones & Co., Perth, 1903, n.p.

6 A Fine Stamp of Men

1. Elizabeth Salter, *Daisy Bates*, Angus & Robertson, Sydney, 1971, p. 91.
2. *Herald* (Melb.), 25 January 1912.
3. *Broome Chronicle*, 24 February 1912.
4. Evidence was given to the Royal Commission on the Pearl-Shelling Industry by Mr Herbert Sewell (*see* report of evidence in the *West Australian*, 28 April 1916) that Reid was Webber's nephew. The grandchildren of William Webber have written to the author saying family records do not reveal such a relationship.

7 The Master Pearlers

1. Australia, Senate, *Debates*, 2 November 1905, p. 4459.
2. Australia, Senate, *Debates*, 2 November 1905, p. 4462, quoting from Walter E. Roth, Royal Commission on the Condition of the Natives, Western Australia Parliamentary Papers, Perth, 1905, p. 11.
3. Australia, Senate, *Debates*, 2 November 1905, p. 4463.
4. Australia, Senate, *Debates*, 2 November 1905, p. 4463.
5. *Broome Chronicle*, 13 March 1909, quoting from *Truth* (Perth), 20 February 1909.
6. Australian Archives, Canberra, file A 1914/12612.

7. Australian Archives, Canberra, file A1 1910/3785.
8. Percy Fong, transcript, Oral History Programme of the J.S. Battye Library of West Australia, 1981, p. 14.
9. Australian Archives, Canberra, file A1 1911/1816.
10. Australian Archives, Canberra, file A1 1914/2487.
11. Australian Archives, Canberra, file A1 1914/2487.
12. *Broome Chronicle*, 14 January 1911.
13. *Broome Chronicle*, 21 January 1911.
14. *Argus*, 24 February 1911; *Broome Chronicle*, 25 February 1911.
15. Australia, House of Representatives, *Debates*, 26 October 1911, p. 1878.
16. *Royal Commission on the Pearl-Shelling Industry*, Australian Parliamentary Papers, vol. 3, 1913, p. 579.

8 The Deep

1. Quoted in John Bevan, *The Infernal Diver*, Submex, London, 1996, p. 192.
2. Papers of Mr Orr, Battye Library, Perth, cat. PR 6026.
3. N. Howard Mummery, 'Diving and Caisson Disease', *The British Medical Journal*, 27 June 1908, p. 1566.
4. *Nor'-West Echo*, 8 February 1913.
5. *Broome Chronicle*, 9 March 1912.
6. Mary Albertus Bain, *Full Fathom Five*, Artlook Books, Perth, 1982, p. 305.

9 The *Koombana*

1. Edwin W. Streeter, *Pearls and Pearling Life*, George Bell & Sons, London, 1886, p. 155.
2. *Broome Chronicle*, 6 April 1912.
3. *Broome Chronicle*, 30 March 1912.

10 Sail-out

1. D.C.S. Sissons, 'The Japanese in the Australian Pearling Industry', *Queensland Heritage*, vol. 3, no. 10, p. 18.
2. *West Australian*, 27 April 1916, p. 8.
3. Papers of Mr H.L. Richardson, Battye Library, Perth, cat. 1935 A/23, MN377.
4. James Taylor, *Spoils from the Sea*, Australasian Publishing Company, Sydney, pp. 28, 29.
5. Australian Archives, Canberra, file A1 1911/1816.
6. *Nor'-West Echo*, 27 December 1913.

11 White Men are Not Suitable

1. *Argus*, 8 August 1913.
2. Papers of the Broome Police Court, Battye Library, Perth, cat. A 352.
3. *Broome Chronicle*, 13 August 1910.
4. *Broome Chronicle*, 6 February 1909.
5. *Broome Chronicle*, 22 August 1908.
6. *Broome Chronicle*, 13 November 1909.

7. *Broome Chronicle*, 28 August 1909.
8. *Broome Chronicle*, 11 May 1912; Papers of the Broome police court, Battye Library, Perth, cat. A 352.
9. Minutes of evidence of the Royal Commission on the Pearl-Shelling Industry, Australian Parliamentary Papers, vol. 3, 1913, p. 58.
10. Royal Commission, p. 110.
11. Royal Commission, p. 183.
12. Royal Commission, p. 73.
13. Royal Commission, p. 81.
14. Royal Commission, p. 11.
15. Royal Commission, p. 11.
16. Progress Report on the Royal Commission on the Pearl-Shelling Industry, Australian Parliamentary Papers, vol. 3, 1913, p. xiii.
17. Progress Report, p. xiii.
18. Royal Commission, p. 117.

12 The Fleet

1. M.S. Warton, *Pearl-Shelling Industry Australia*, Australian Parliamentary Papers, 1901–2, p. 10.
2. *Broome Chronicle*, 13 March 1909, quoting from *Truth* (Perth), 20 February 1909.
3. *Broome Chronicle*, 25 May 1912.
4. *Nor'-West Echo*, 6 July 1912.
5. *Nor'-West Echo*, 6 July 1912.
6. *Broome Chronicle*, 25 May 1912.
7. *Nor'-West Echo*, 9 November 1912.
8. Minutes of evidence of the Royal Commission on the Pearl-Shelling Industry, Australian Parliamentary Papers, vol. 3, 1913, pp. 143, 145.

13 Webber

1. Minutes of evidence of the Royal Commission on the Pearl-Shelling Industry, Australian Parliamentary Papers, vol. 3, 1913, p. 74.
2. Australian Archives, Canberra, file A1 1913/15429.
3. Papers of Mr H.L. Richardson, Battye Library, Perth, cat. 1935 A/23, MN377.
4. Richardson.
5. Australian Archives, Canberra, file A1 1913/15429.
6. *Broome Chronicle*, 13 August 1910.
7. Western Australian House of Assembly, *Debates*, 7 August 1912, pp. 907–8.
8. Western Australian House of Assembly, *Debates*, 7 August 1912, pp. 906–7.
9. *Nor'-West Echo*, 29 June 1912.

14 Noury

1. Staniforth Smith, *The West Australian Pearl-Shelling Industry*, V.K. Jones & Co., Perth, 1903, n.p.
2. Graham Blick, 'Notes on Diver's Paralysis', *The British Medical Journal*, 25 December 1909, p. 1797.

3. *Nor'-West Echo*, 2 May 1914.
4. Immigration and Tourist Department, *The Handbook of Western Australia*, Perth, 1912, p. 208.
5. *Nor'-West Echo*, 30 August 1913.
6. Australian Archives, Canberra, file A1 1911/1816.
7. Ernest Freight, evidence to the Royal Commission, *West Australian*, 13 May 1916, p. 7.
8. Blick, p. 1797.
9. Blick, p. 1797.
10. Royal Commission, p. 154.

15 Barker, Leprosy and Rape

1. Minutes of evidence of the Royal Commission on the Pearl-Shelling Industry, Australian Parliamentary Papers, vol. 3, 1913, p. 149.
2. Minutes of evidence of the Royal Commission on the Pearl-Shelling Industry, Australian Parliamentary Papers, vol. 3, 1913, p. 140.
3. *Nor'-West Echo*, 2 May 1914.
4. *Nor'-West Echo*, 22 June 1912.
5. *Nor'-West Echo*, 24 August 1912.
6. *Nor'-West Echo*, 7 September 1912.
7. *Nor'-West Echo*, 5 October 1912.
8. *Nor'-West Echo*, 12 October 1912.
9. *Nor'-West Echo*, 19 October 1912.
10. *Nor'-West Echo*, 22 February 1913.
11. Quoted in David Horton (ed.), *The Encyclopaedia of Aboriginal Australia*, vol. 1, Aboriginal Studies Press, Canberra, 1994, p. 120.
12. Quoted in Kevin Lawton, 'Leprosy in Broome', in *Tales from Broome: Centennial Edition, 1883–1983*, Roundhead Enterprises, Perth, 1983.
13. *Nor'-West Echo*, 5 October 1912.
14. *Nor'-West Echo*, 5 October 1912.
15. *Nor'-West Echo*, 19 October 1912.

16 The Blind Rider

1. *Broome Chronicle*, 13 March 1909, quoting from *Truth* (Perth), 20 February 1909.
2. *Nor'-West Echo*, 12 October 1912: the unnamed diver could only be Noury.
3. *Nor'-West Echo*, 9 November 1912.
4. *Nor'-West Echo*, 27 December 1913.
5. *Nor'-West Echo*, 11 January 1913.

17 The Last of His Tribe

1. *West Australian*, 3 May 1916, p. 7.
2. *Argus*, 10 May 1913, p. 20.
3. Clarence Benham, *Diver's Luck*, Angus & Robertson, Sydney, 1949, p. 61.
4. *Argus*, 10 May 1913, p. 20.
5. *Nor'-West Echo*, 17 May 1913.

6. *Argus*, 9 August 1913, p. 19.
7. *Argus*, 9 August 1913, p. 19.
8. Australian Archives, Canberra, file A1 1913/15429 which contains a copy of the article on Sanders' death in the *Nor'-West Echo*, 30 August 1913.
9. *Westralian Worker*, 5 December 1912.
10. Progress Report of the Royal Commission on the Pearl-Shelling Industry, Australian Parliamentary Papers, vol. 3, 1913, p. x. The quotations in the rest of this chapter may be found on pp. vi, vii, x and xv.

Postscript

1. *West Australian*, 1 May 1916, p. 6.
2. Report of the Royal Commission on the Pearl-Shelling Industry, Australian Parliamentary Papers 1914–17, vol. 5, p. 836.
3. Australian Archives, Canberra, file A433 46/2/5457.

JOHN BAILEY has been a barrister in Melbourne, a public servant in Papua New Guinea, and a teacher in England. He presently lives close to the Queensland border in northern New South Wales.